Vocabulary improvement Program

for English Language Learners and Their Classmates

4th Grade

Vocabulary improvement Program

for English Language Learners and Their Classmates

4th Grade

by

Teresa Lively
University of California,
Santa Cruz

Diane August
Center for Applied Linguistics
Washington, D.C.

María Carlo
University of Miami
Coral Gables, Florida

Catherine Snow
Harvard Graduate School of Education
Cambridge, Massachusetts

·P A U L·H·
BROOKES
PUBLISHING C°.®

Baltimore • London • Sydney

Paul H. Brookes Publishing Co.
Post Office Box 10624
Baltimore, MD 21285-0624

www.brookespublishing.com

Typeset by Barton Matheson Willse & Worthington, Baltimore, Maryland.
Manufactured in the United States of America by
Versa Press, Inc., East Peoria, Illinois.

The development of the Vocabulary Improvement Program was supported by the Institute for Educational Sciences
Award No. R306F6077-97, from the National Institute on the Education of At Risk Students. However, no official
endorsement by the federal government should be inferred.

Library of Congress Cataloging-in-Publication Data

Vocabulary Improvement Program for English language learners and their classmates. 4th grade/by Teresa Lively...[et al.].
        p.   cm.
    Includes bibliographical references.
    ISBN 1-55766-631-8
    1. Vocabulary—Problems, exercises, etc.   2. English language—Textbooks for foreign speakers.   I. Lively, Teresa.
    PE1449.V63 2003
    428.1—dc21   2002043688

British Library Cataloguing in Publication data are available from the British Library.

Contents

About the Authors. vii
Acknowledgments. ix
Before You Begin xi
Introduction. xiii

Pretest for Lessons 1–4 1
    Teacher Answer Keys 3
    Reproducible Materials 9

Lesson 1: The Hen and the Apple Tree 15
    Teacher Answer Keys 33
    Reproducible Materials 41

Lesson 2: The Baboon's Umbrella. 59
    Teacher Answer Keys 73
    Reproducib e Materials 83

Lesson 3: The Poor Old Dog 101
    Teacher Answer Keys 115
    Reproducible Materials 123

Lesson 4: The Ostrich in Love 139
    Teacher Answer Keys 157
    Reproducible Materials 165

Lesson 5: Review Week 185
    Reproducible Materials 193

Pretest for Lessons 6–9 199
    Teacher Answer Keys 201
    Reproducible Materials 207

Lesson 6: Madame Rhinoceros and Her Dress 213
    Teacher Answer Keys 229
    Reproducible Materials 239

Lesson 7: The Pig at the Candy Store 257
    Teacher Answer Keys 271
    Reproducible Materials 279

Lesson 8: The Hippopotamus at Dinner. 295
    Teacher Answer Keys 311
    Reproducible Materials 319

Contents

Lesson 9: The Mouse at the Seashore 335
    Teacher Answer Keys 349
    Reproducible Materials 355

Lesson 10: Review Week 373
    Reproducible Materials 383

References 391
Student Word Book 393

About the Authors

Teresa Lively, M.S., Pacific Graduate School of Psychology, 940 East Meadow Drive, Palo Alto, California 94303

Ms. Lively has had a lifelong appreciation for the power and magic of words. This regard for words extended into her love of the Spanish language that developed during the 2 years she resided in Mexico as a child and again as a teenager. She can recall her struggles when first confronted with a new language and how these difficulties precluded communication with peers and completion of her schoolwork. She remembers equally well the satisfaction she experienced as her ability to understand and communicate increased. As part of this natural progression, during a 14-year bilingual teaching career, Ms. Lively realized that children's academic success is greatly influenced by the breadth and depth of their vocabulary knowledge. Therefore, in her classroom she emphasized learning the meanings of new words while encouraging both native English speakers and English language learners to develop a curiosity and appreciation for vocabulary.

Ms. Lively resides on the California coast. She enjoys spending time with her husband, who supports her passions and keeps her laughing, two wonderful grown children, and loyal friends who encourage her life journey. She is currently completing a doctoral program in clinical psychology.

Diane August, Ph.D., Senior Research Scientist, Center for Applied Linguistics, 4646 40th Street, NW, Washington, D.C. 20016

Dr. August is an independent consultant as well as a senior research scientist at the Center for Applied Linguistics in Washington, D.C. At the Center for Applied Linguistics, she directs a large, federally funded study investigating the development of literacy in English language learners. She is also the Staff Director for the National Literacy Panel on Language Minority Children and Youth. As an educational consultant, Dr. August has worked in the areas of literacy, program improvement, evaluation and testing, and federal and state education policy. She has been a senior program officer at the National Academy of Sciences and Study Director for the Committee on Developing a Research Agenda on the Education of Limited English Proficient and Bilingual Students.

Dr. August worked for 10 years as a public school teacher and school administrator in California. Subsequently, she served as Legislative Assistant in the area of education for a United States Congressman from California, worked as a grants officer for the Carnegie Corporation of New York, and served as Director of Education for the Children's Defense Fund. In 1981, she received her doctorate in education from Stanford University, and in 1982, she completed a postdoctoral fellowship in psychology, also at Stanford.

María Carlo, Ph.D., Assistant Professor, Teaching and Learning Program, School of Education, University of Miami, 1551 Brescia Avenue, Coral Gables, Florida 33146

Dr. Carlo is a psychologist studying bilingualism in children and adults. Her research focuses on the cognitive processes that underlie reading in a second language and on understanding the differences in the reading processes of bilinguals and monolinguals. She is Co-principal Investigator on a National Institute of Child Health and Human Development (NICHD)–funded project that investigates the transfer of reading skills from Spanish to English among primary school children. This research seeks to understand the role played by the native language in the development of second-language literacy. Dr. Carlo has written articles and book chapters on the role of mother-tongue literacy in second-language literacy, and on the literacy assessment of bilingual learners. She received her doctorate from the University of Massachusetts, Amherst.

Catherine Snow, Ph.D., Henry Lee Shattuck Professor of Education, Harvard Graduate School of Education, Larsen 313, Cambridge, Massachusetts 02138

Dr. Snow is the Henry Lee Shattuck Professor of Education at the Harvard Graduate School of Education. She received her doctorate in psychology from McGill University and worked for several years in the linguistics department of the University of Amsterdam. Her research interests include children's language development as influenced by interaction with adults in home and preschool settings, literacy development as related to language skills and as influenced by home and school factors, and issues related to the acquisition of English oral and literacy skills by language minority children. She has co-authored books on language development (e.g., *Pragmatic Development: Essays in Developmental Science,* co-authored with Anat Ninio [Westview Press, 1996]) and on literacy development (e.g., *Unfulfilled Expectations: Home and School Influences on Literacy,* co-authored with Wendy S. Barnes, Lowry Hemphill, Jean Chandler, and Irene F. Goodman [iUniverse.com, 2000]) and has published widely on these topics in refereed journals and edited volumes.

Dr. Snow's contributions to the field include serving on several journal editorial boards, as co-director of the Child Language Data Exchange System for several years, and as editor of *Applied Psycholinguistics.* She served as a board member at the Center for Applied Linguistics and was a member of the National Research Council Committee on Establishing a Research Agenda on Schooling for Language Minority Children. She also chaired the National Research Council (NRC) Committee on Preventing Reading Difficulties in Young Children, which produced a report that has been widely adopted as a basis for reform of reading instruction and professional development. She currently serves on the NRC's Council for the Behavioral and Social Sciences and Education and is President of the American Educational Research Association.

A member of the National Academy of Education, Dr. Snow has held visiting appointments at the University of Cambridge, England, Universidad Autónoma in Madrid, and The Institute of Advanced Studies at Hebrew University in Jerusalem, and has guest taught at Universidad Central de Caracas in Venezuela, El Colegio de Mexico, Odense University in Denmark, and several institutions in The Netherlands.

Acknowledgments

I would like to acknowledge Barry McLaughlin for his creative and thoughtful leadership throughout the development of the Vocabulary Improvement Program; David Lippman for completing numerous and varied tasks with quiet grace; and Sharon Maxwell, who creatively envisioned the organization and layout of the materials. I would also like to acknowledge the teachers at DeLaveaga, Bayview, and Branciforte Elementary Schools in Santa Cruz, California, who enthusiastically contributed to the development of the VIP.—T.L.

I would like to acknowledge the teachers at Bailey's Elementary School for the Arts and Sciences in Falls Church, Virginia, for helping us to develop the vocabulary materials. I would also like to acknowledge Barry McLaughlin, whose idea it was to undertake research in vocabulary and who led us in our efforts to develop, implement, and research the materials that appear in these books.—D.A.

Before You Begin

Welcome to the Vocabulary Improvement Program! Following are a few notes to guide you through the curriculum.

1. The curriculum consists of two units with five lessons each. The fifth lesson of each unit uses new activities to review all of the target words learned in the previous four lessons.

2. Each unit begins with a pretest and culminates with a posttest so that you are able to measure your students' vocabulary growth.

3. Each lesson in this manual contains three sections:
   - Instructions for the daily activities
   - Teacher Answer Keys
   - Reproducible Materials

4. The text and target word definitions for each lesson are included at the back of this manual to facilitate construction of a Student Word Book for each student. The Student Word Book is intended to include
   - Front cover
   - Text for Lessons 1–4 and 6–9
   - Target word definitions for Lessons 1–4 and 6–9
   - Hints for Solving Mystery Words to be printed on the inside of the back cover

5. You will need sticky notes, index cards, or other paper for students to record sentences for Word Wizard.

6. Lessons 1–4 and 6–9 are from *Fables* by Arnold Lobel (HarperCollins, 1980). Although the text and color pictures for the lessons are included in this manual, you may want to have a copy of the book from which to read aloud and further enrich your curriculum.

Recommendations for the other materials:

- Photocopy or write the Classroom Word Lists on colored card stock, and tape them together to make a continuous list. The students will continue to refer to them if you leave them posted.

- Print the game cards on card stock, and laminate them to preserve for future use.

- Print the two pages of the assessment back-to-back.

Have fun as you see your students learn!

Introduction

WHAT IS THE VOCABULARY IMPROVEMENT PROGRAM?

The Vocabulary Improvement Program (VIP) is a research-based program designed to enrich the vocabulary of fourth-, fifth-, and sixth-grade students by utilizing a combination of strategies aimed at various aspects of vocabulary knowledge—word definitions, recognizing words in context, awareness of the multiple meanings of words, word associations, and cognates for native Spanish speakers.

The VIP was initially designed for classroom teachers working with heterogeneous groups of children, consisting of English-only students and Spanish-speaking English language learners; however, the program would be equally effective in English-only, Spanish-only, and English as a second language classrooms as well as for an extended age range.

In accordance with research indicating words are best learned from rich semantic contexts, the target vocabulary words are embedded in brief, engaging reading passages. Each lesson of the curriculum focuses on a relatively small number of vocabulary items (12–14 per lesson) that students at each level are likely to encounter repeatedly across texts in different domains, including literature, science, social science, and written material outside of the classroom. Although the focus is on only a few words each week, the curriculum's activities help children make semantic links to other words and concepts and thus attain a deeper and richer understanding of each target word's meaning as well as learn other words and concepts related to the target word. Thus, the curriculum is designed to increase students' breadth and depth of word knowledge. In keeping with research-based best practice, the lessons also teach students to infer meanings from context and to use roots, affixes, cognates, morphological relationships, and comprehension monitoring as tools to determine the meaning of unfamiliar words wherever they are encountered.

Throughout the lessons are features that research has found to effectively build children's vocabulary. First, teachers are encouraged to use the vocabulary-building strategies learned during the VIP lessons in subject-matter instruction throughout the day. The curriculum includes mini-lessons (Teacher Tips) for teachers to help them accomplish this. Mini-lessons include, for example, how to help students do the following: infer meaning from text; attain richer, deeper understandings of word meanings; use cognates; understand multiple word meanings; and use roots and affixes.

Second, most of the activities combine teacher-directed instruction and cooperative group learning, a format that works well with heterogeneous groups of students. The activity begins with teacher explanation and modeling of the activity, followed by whole group practice, and then cooperative group work. At the conclusion of each activity, or concurrently with the group work, the teacher pulls the students together to report on their work, with teacher feedback and help when necessary.

Third, the program uses Spanish-speaking English language learners' first language in a few lessons to bolster students' vocabulary knowledge and text comprehension. One of the homework assignments in the fifth-grade curriculum entails students asking their parents about family immigration experiences. These conversations take place in the home language.

Fourth, almost all of the lessons involve collaborative and cooperative learning between English language learners and English-only students. For example, in activities that require students to use contextual clues to select the correct target word to complete a sentence, heterogeneous groups of students work together to arrive at the correct answer. The cooperative group work on cognates depends on the expertise of the Spanish-speaking English language learners. One of the strongest features of the intervention is that it provides opportunities for English language learners to converse in English with fluent English speakers in a meaningful way.

Fifth, homework assignments reinforce class learning. For example, in Word Wizard, students record the use of target words encountered outside of class (at home, on the television, with friends), present the "found" sentences to their classmates, and may post the sentences in a class book. As homework assignments, students also generate new sentences, complete crossword puzzles, and work on contexting activities that use the target words.

Sixth, teachers assess students at the end of each lesson to monitor students' instructional progress. Finally, every fifth lesson is a review so students have an opportunity to consolidate what they have learned.

WHAT ARE THE COMPONENTS OF THE CURRICULUM?

The target words are drawn from and embedded in a variety of literary genres. The words for the fourth-grade curriculum are drawn from Arnold Lobel's *Fables*. The words for the fifth-grade curriculum are drawn from *A Journey to the New World: The Diary of Remember Patience Whipple* by Katheryn Lasky (from the *Dear America* series) and *Immigrant Kids* by Russell Freedman. The words for the sixth-grade curriculum are drawn from *New Kids in Town: Oral Histories of Immigrant Teens* by Janet Bode and *The New York Times* "Here and There" series on immigration, which has been modified for sixth-grade students. These texts were chosen both for their appeal and their ability to expose students to a variety of literary genres.

At each grade level, the curriculum consists of 10 lessons. Each lesson is composed of eight days, with the exception of two review lessons that are composed of five days each. The review lessons use new activities to review all of the words learned in the previous four lessons.

Each lesson follows a similar format. During the first day of each lesson, the teacher introduces a story and helps students predict the story line and connect the story to their background knowledge. During the second day, through teacher-directed classroom discussion, students learn the definitions for the target words and how to infer word meaning from text for a subset of these words.

The third day is devoted to building depth of word meaning through engaging activities that encourage students to process new word meanings. For example, in one "deep-processing" activity from the fifth-grade curriculum, students interview each other using questions that contain the target words (e.g., What has caused the most *torment* in your life? Name three things that commonly *arouse* a teacher's anger?) The fourth and sixth days provide students with tools that can be used in any setting to decipher the meanings of unfamiliar vocabulary. For example, children work on cognates and morphological relationships and learn to use affixes, roots, cognates, and comprehension monitoring.

During the fifth day of the lesson, students work in heterogeneous cooperative groups on word contexting activities to build depth of word meaning. They are given sentences with a missing word and are directed to select the correct target word based on the sentence context and then to explain why they have selected that particular word.

During the seventh day, students share sentences they have recorded for Word Wizard, an activity that encourages students to listen and look for vocabulary outside the context of the classroom. During the eighth day, students complete an assessment of the lesson's target words so teachers can monitor the students' progress.

IN-DEPTH LOOK AT FOUR KEY COMPONENTS OF THE CURRICULUM

Contexting Activities

According to Stahl (1999), because most words are learned from context, good vocabulary instruction should simulate learning from context. Toward this end, each lesson begins with an exercise in which students infer the meaning of specific words from the text for that week. Words are deliberately selected to ensure there are enough clues for students to determine the meaning.

On the fifth day of the lesson, students further develop their inferencing skills by working in small, heterogeneous groups on contexting activities. Each group is challenged to figure out the correct target words for sentences that support the words' meaning and then to explain why the answer makes sense. Note that students have already learned the definitions of the target words. This activity is intended to give students practice inferring meaning from text and building depth of word meaning. Two examples follow (target words to be located by the students are italicized):

1. "I think my teacher symbolizes Colombia. She *represents* the country, language, and the country's traditions."
2. "When the new boy was asked a question in English, he felt foolish and embarrassed. The teacher *humiliated* the boy accidentally because he didn't know the boy had recently come from the Dominican Republic."

Teachers also help children use strategies outside of the specific vocabulary lessons. Because some passages don't have enough clues to help figure out what a word means, students are taught to

1. Note context clues (if any)
2. Determine if there are enough context clues to figure out a target word's meaning and, if so, provide a plausible meaning and explanation for why the meaning is plausible

3. Ask a friend or use a dictionary if the context does not support the word's meaning. Ideally, teachers model this process throughout the day on a variety of sentences with different levels of supporting context.

Deep Processing

One of the most difficult tasks in vocabulary instruction is to encourage students to process new words at a deep level. By this, we mean providing opportunities for students to make semantic links to other words and concepts and thus attain a deeper and richer understanding of a word's meaning. Beck and colleagues (1982, 1987) have suggested that one way to have students make these connections and process words more deeply is through answering questions about target words to indicate that they have a clear understanding of their meaning and then to write a sentence that uses the word in a related way. The curriculum modifies this strategy by selecting the target words from the curriculum text, teaching students the word meanings prior to the activity, and engaging students in activities to use the words in novel ways.

The curriculum also adapts well-known games in order to build depth of word meaning. For example, in Charades, students have to act out a target word's meaning for their team. In Word Bee, team members work together to define a target word given and then present the definition to classmates for approval. In Word Substitution, team members replace a target word presented in a sentence with another word or phrase that means the same thing. In Word Guess, the teams of students attempt to guess a target word with the fewest clues possible.

To help students process words more deeply outside the vocabulary activities, teachers are trained to use similar strategies in a less structured way throughout the day. For example, if teachers encounter the target word *degree* in science, they may ask for the definition of the word in its scientific context as well as what the word may mean in other contexts (math, literature, or geography). They may then ask students to think up new sentences on the spot using various definitions of the target word.

Using Cognates (for Spanish-Speaking English Language Learners)

Cognates are a rich source of information for many English language learners, especially those whose first language is Spanish. Research has found that among English language learners with equal English vocabulary knowledge, Spanish vocabulary knowledge and ability to recognize cognates predicted English reading comprehension, indicating students were making use of cognate relationships in English reading (Nagy, Garcia, Durgunoglu, & Hancin-Bhatt, 1993).

In one activity that helps students learn more about cognates, the class is divided into four heterogeneous groups. Each group is given four or five Spanish words and a passage from *Fables*. Students must locate the corresponding English cognates for the Spanish words. In each group, English-only students receive help from their Spanish-speaking classmates. Utilizing the Spanish-speaking students' knowledge of Spanish, the group verifies that the English word means the same thing as the cognate.

Structural Analysis

Some reading researchers (Dale & O'Rourke, 1986; Nagy & Anderson, 1984; Stahl, 1999) have argued that one of the best ways to expand a child's vocabulary is through "structural analysis" or helping children recognize the parts of words and what these parts mean. For example, the word *unfruitful* has the prefix *un-*, the root *fruit*, and the suffix *-ful*. Other words, such as *snowman*, are compounds of two words. Because children enjoy word play and games with words, the curriculum includes a number of games to teach roots and affixes.

In teaching structural analysis, the curriculum keeps several issues in mind. It avoids "phantom" prefixes, such as *re-* in *reality*, so that students will not look for "little words in big words" (leading to such mistakes as finding *moth* in *mother* and *fat* in *father*). In developing the exercises, we recognized that some suffixes are relatively easy to teach, such as *-ness* and *-ity*. Others, such as *-tion*, have meanings that are more abstract and are difficult to convey. Finally, where possible, we begin with words that are already familiar to the students.

WHY USE THE VOCABULARY IMPROVEMENT PROGRAM?

There is no better predictor of school success than reading comprehension. Nor is there a better predictor of reading comprehension than vocabulary knowledge. Vocabulary development is a lifetime project in which we are constantly expanding and deepening our understanding of words. Children need to learn the definitions of words but also need to learn strategies to decipher meaning when they encounter unknown words. Therefore, in this program the students learn a relatively small number of vocabulary items (12–14 per lesson) while the focus is on strategies that will generalize to contact with other words. Through the course of this program, students learn strategies such as structural analysis (root words and affixes), multiple meanings, cognates, and inferring meaning from context. Teachers and students who participated in the project expressed their appreciation enthusiastically.

The ideas for the vocabulary improvement activities were initially drawn from the literature on vocabulary acquisition and from classroom teacher suggestions. They were further developed through pilot testing and extensive teacher–researcher collaboration. The curriculum was implemented in fourth- and fifth-grade classrooms for more than 2 years, rigorously tested, and found to be highly effective. More specifically, a multivariate analysis of variance was performed on the dependent measures for which scores were available in both the fall and spring of each year to test the effects of predictor variables—school in which the program was implemented, language status (English-only or English language learner), and treatment.[1] VIP was found to improve children's performance in three areas: knowledge of the words taught, knowledge of word analysis, and comprehension of texts including challenging words. Furthermore, the curriculum was effective with children who speak English as a second language as well as with English-only children. Finally, 2 years of exposure to the vocabulary intervention had a greater effect on outcome measures than 1 year.

---

[1] The data analyses and complete results are fully reported in McLaughlin and colleagues (2001).

REFERENCES

Beck, I., McKeown, M.G., & Omanson, R.C. (1987). The effects and uses of diverse vocabulary instructional techniques. In M.G. McKeown & M.E. Curtis (Eds.), *The nature of vocabulary acquisition* (pp. 147–163). Mahwah, NJ: Lawrence Erlbaum Associates.

Beck, I.L., Perfetti, C.A., & McKeown, M.G. (1982). Effects of long-term vocabulary instruction on lexical access and reading comprehension. *Journal of Educational Psychology, 74,* 506–521.

Bode, J. (1989). *New kids in town.* New York: Scholastic.

Dale, E., & O'Rourke, J. (1986). *Vocabulary building.* Columbus, OH: Zaner-Bloser.

Freedman, R. (1995). *Immigrant kids.* New York: Penguin Putnam Books for Young Readers.

Lasky, K. (1996). *A Journey to the New World: The Diary of Remember Patience Whipple.* New York: Scholastic.

Lobel, A. (1980). *Fables.* New York: HarperCollins Publishers.

McLaughlin, B., August, D., Snow, C.E., Carlo, M.S., Dressler, C., White, C., Lively, T., & Lippman, D. (2001). *Closing the Gap: Addressing the needs of English language learners in bilingual and mainstream classrooms.* Paper prepared for publication, Harvard Graduate School of Education, Cambridge, MA.

Nagy, W.E., & Anderson R.C. (1984). How many words are there in printed school English? *Reading Research Quarterly, 19,* 304–330.

Nagy, W.E., Garcia, G.E., Durgunoglu, A., & Hancin, B. (1993). Spanish-English bilingual children's use and recognition of cognates in English reading. *Journal of Reading Behavior, 25*(3), 241–259.

Stahl, S.A. (1999). *Vocabulary development.* Cambridge, MA: Brookline Press.

▼ **Prepare for activity**

- Make two copies of each of the three Lessons 1–4 assessment forms for each student. Save one copy for the posttest.

- Separate students so that they will work individually.

▼ **Introduce the activity**

Say: *In this lesson, you will complete three worksheets to find out which of the words we will study in the coming weeks you might already know and which are new to you. You have probably done activities like these before. I will show you examples of each of the three different activities before you begin.*

1.   Write the following example on the board.

fun	big	happy

I am _____ when the sun is shining.

Say: *The first worksheet has a box at the top with words in it. Sentences below the box have a line in them to show that a word is missing. First, you will read a sentence. Then, you will look in the box for a word that makes sense if you write it in the space.*

Who can read the sentence on the board? Good, now what word makes the most sense if we put it in the space? That's right, so I am going to write **happy** *in the space.*

Note: Be sure that students know they are to **use each word only one time.**

2.   Again, please write the example on the board.

A toy that spins

sled	**top**	**puzzle**	**kite**

Say: *The second worksheet has definitions and four words from which to choose. Who can raise their hand to read the definition on the board? Good, now who can read the four words below the definition? Which word goes with the definition? That's right, so now I will draw a circle around the word* **top**.

3.   Say: *For the last worksheet, you are going to work with words that have more than one meaning. For example, let's think about the word top again. Who can think of one meaning of top? You can tell me either a definition or a sentence.*

Write responses on the board, eliciting examples of both definitions and meaningful sentences for the word *top*. For example:

1.   María stood on *top* of the table.

2. A *top* is a toy that spins around quickly.

3. José was the *top* student in his class.

4. Jenny wore a new *top*.

5. I save bottle *tops*.

Say: *In this activity, you will see four words that have more than one meaning. Think about the different meanings of each word. Write one sentence for each of the meanings that you know, or write the definition if that is easier for you. Write as many meanings as you can, but do not feel bad if you cannot think of all of the meanings.*

• Distribute the activity.

• Leave the examples on the board as a reference for the students.

• Monitor the students as they work to be certain they understand the activity.

Teacher answer keys

VOCABULARY ASSESSMENT I

tattered	courage	solution	gibbon	reward
cozy	surely	quickly	stuck	whirled
fluttered	delicious	delightful	furry	annoyed
odd				

- Find the word that **best** fits in the sentence.
- Use each word only **one** time.

1. We knew how much ____**courage**____ Melissa had when she saved the kitten from the burning building.

2. Our school's ping-pong team has never lost a game, so they will ____**surely**____ win the finals.

3. Efren ____**whirled**____ about the dance floor so quickly that he became dizzy.

4. The stamp is ____**stuck**____ to the envelope.

5. The sweet and juicy apple was the most ____**delicious**____ I had ever tasted.

6. We always eat cereal for breakfast, so it was very ____**odd**____ when Mom offered us cake.

7. I had an absolutely ____**delightful**____ time when I went to the amusement park with my best friend.

8. The ____**solution**____ to the puzzle was printed in the back of the book.

9. It feels ____**cozy**____ to sit by the fire on a rainy day.

10. My favorite pants became ____**tattered**____ after I wore them many times to go rock-climbing.

11. My dad was _____**annoyed**_____ when I spilled juice on the clean floor.

12. I would love to go to a zoo so that I could see a _____**gibbon**_____ swing through the trees.

13. Anna wanted to play, so she finished her homework _____**quickly**_____.

14. Sara offered a five dollar _____**reward**_____ to anyone who found her kitten.

15. I like to pet the _____**furry**_____ little dog.

16. The butterfly _____**fluttered**_____ its wings as it began to fly.

VOCABULARY ASSESSMENT 2

• Circle the word that matches the definition.

1. Proved to be true

    unreal   odd   predicament   (certain)

2. To defeat by being a quick thinker

    (outsmart)   quiver   ordinary   wealthy

3. A suggestion about what someone should do

    rumor   (advice)   shade   reward

4. Under or below

    above   sideways   (underneath)   tattered

5. To make something appear larger by shaking or brushing

    smooth   erupt   (fluff)   create

6. Attractive in appearance

    unpleasing   jolly   lovable   (handsome)

7. Not controlled; unruly

    (wild)   content   dreamy   comfortable

8. An awkward or difficult situation

    pavement   (predicament)   waltz   overjoyed

9. To swell or curve outward

    forgive   blame   shrink   (bulge)

10. Having a large amount of money or property

    proper   (wealthy)   single   overjoyed

11. Uncooperative; bad tempered

    ill   (disagreeable)   weak   disappointed

12. To shake or move with a slight tremble; to vibrate

    quick   outsmart   annoy   (quiver)

13. Plentiful or more than enough

    (profuse)　　　　popular　　　　poor　　　　profound

14. Wild, uncontrollable anger

    shade　　　　solution　　　　reward　　　　(rage)

15. Old, torn, and worn out

    timid　　　　(ragged)　　　　shy　　　　tangled

16. Extremely happy

    ragged　　　　gathered　　　　(overjoyed)　　　　delicious

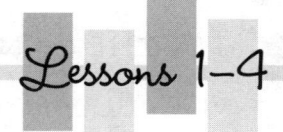

VOCABULARY ASSESSMENT 3

- In this activity, you will see four different words that have more than one meaning.
- Think about the different meanings of each word.
- Write one sentence for each of the meanings that you know, or write the definitions.

1. trunk

1) the main stem of a tree; 2) a large case used for storage or for carrying clothing on a long journey; 3) the long nose of an elephant; 4) enclosed part of a car where luggage and a spare tire can be stored

2. shade

1) area sheltered from light; 2) something that provides shelter from light; 3) to shelter from light; 4) the degree of darkness of a color; 5) to make part of a drawing darker than the rest; 6) a small amount or difference

3. compose

1) to write music or poetry; 2) to make calm and quiet; 3) to be formed from (composed of)

4. shy

1) uncomfortable or nervous around people; 2) lacking or falling short; 3) to draw back suddenly, as from fear or caution

Reproducible materials

VOCABULARY ASSESSMENT 1

tattered	courage	solution	gibbon	reward
cozy	surely	quickly	stuck	whirled
fluttered	delicious	delightful	furry	annoyed
odd				

- Find the word that **best** fits in the sentence.

- Use each word only **one** time.

1. We knew how much _____ Melissa had when she saved the kitten from the burning building.

2. Our school's ping-pong team has never lost a game, so they will _____ win the finals.

3. Efren _____ about the dance floor so quickly that he became dizzy.

4. The stamp is _____ to the envelope.

5. The sweet and juicy apple was the most _____ I had ever tasted.

6. We always eat cereal for breakfast, so it was very _____ when Mom offered us cake.

7. I had an absolutely _____ time when I went to the amusement park with my best friend.

8. The _____ to the puzzle was printed in the back of the book.

9. It feels _____ to sit by the fire on a rainy day.

10. My favorite pants became _____ after I wore them many times to go rock-climbing.

Vocabulary Improvement Program for English Language Learners and Their Classmates, 4th Grade, by Teresa Lively, Diane August, María Carlo, and Catherine Snow © 2003 Paul H. Brookes Publishing Co., Inc. All rights reserved.

VOCABULARY ASSESSMENT 1 *(continued)*

11. My dad was _____ when I spilled juice on the clean floor.

12. I would love to go to a zoo so that I could see a _____ swing through the trees.

13. Anna wanted to play, so she finished her homework _____.

14. Sara offered a five dollar _____ to anyone who found her kitten.

15. I like to pet the _____ little dog.

16. The butterfly _____ its wings as it began to fly.

VOCABULARY ASSESSMENT 2

• Circle the word that matches the definition.

1. Proved to be true

    unreal   odd   predicament   certain

2. To defeat by being a quick thinker

    outsmart   quiver   ordinary   wealthy

3. A suggestion about what someone should do

    rumor   advice   shade   reward

4. Under or below

    above   sideways   underneath   tattered

5. To make something appear larger by shaking or brushing

    smooth   erupt   fluff   create

6. Attractive in appearance

    unpleasing   jolly   lovable   handsome

7. Not controlled; unruly

    wild   content   dreamy   comfortable

8. An awkward or difficult situation

    pavement   predicament   waltz   overjoyed

9. To swell or curve outward

    forgive   blame   shrink   bulge

10. Having a large amount of money or property

    proper   wealthy   single   overjoyed

11. Uncooperative; bad tempered

    ill   disagreeable   weak   disappointed

12. To shake or move with a slight tremble; to vibrate

    quick   outsmart   annoy   quiver

Name: _____

VOCABULARY ASSESSMENT 2 *(continued)*

13. Plentiful or more than enough

   profuse   popular   poor   profound

14. Wild, uncontrollable anger

   shade   solution   reward   rage

15. Old, torn, and worn out

   timid   ragged   shy   tangled

16. Extremely happy

   ragged   gathered   overjoyed   delicious

Vocabulary Improvement Program for English Language Learners and Their Classmates, 4th Grade, by Teresa Lively, Diane August, María Carlo, and Catherine Snow © 2003 Paul H. Brockes Publishing Co., Inc. All rights reserved.

Name: _____

VOCABULARY ASSESSMENT 3

- In this activity, you will see four different words that have more than one meaning.
- Think about the different meanings of each word.
- Write one sentence for each of the meanings that you know, or write the definitions.

1. trunk

_____

_____

2. shade

_____

_____

3. compose

_____

_____

4. shy

_____

_____

THE HEN AND THE APPLE TREE

One October day, a Hen looked out her window. She saw an apple tree growing in her backyard.

"Now that is odd," said the Hen. "I am certain that there was no tree standing in that spot yesterday."

"There are some of us that grow fast," said the tree.

The Hen looked at the bottom of the tree.

"I have never seen a tree," she said, "that has ten furry toes."

"There are some of us that do," said the tree. "Hen, come outside and enjoy the cool shade of my leafy branches."

The Hen looked at the top of the tree.

"I have never seen a tree," she said, "that has two long, pointed ears."

"There are some of us that have," said the tree. "Hen, come outside and eat one of my delicious apples."

"Come to think of it," said the Hen, "I have never heard a tree speak from a mouth that is full of sharp teeth."

"There are some of us that can," said the tree. "Hen, come outside and rest your back against the bark of my trunk."

"I have heard," said the Hen, "that some of you trees lose all of your leaves at this time of the year."

"Oh, yes," said the tree, "there are some of us that will." The tree began to quiver and shake. All of its leaves quickly dropped off.

The Hen was not surprised to see a large Wolf in the place where an apple tree had been standing just a moment before. She locked her shutters and slammed her window closed.

The Wolf knew that he had been outsmarted. He stormed away in a hungry rage.

It is always difficult to pose as something that one is not.

From *Fables* by Arnold Lobel. © 1980 by Arnold Lobel.
Reprinted by permission of HarperCollins Publishers.

THE BABOON'S UMBRELLA

The Baboon was taking his daily walk in the jungle. He met his friend, the Gibbon, on the path.

"My good friend," said the Gibbon, "how strange to find you holding an open umbrella over your head on such a sunshiny day as this."

"Yes," said the Baboon. "I am most annoyed. I cannot close this disagreeable umbrella. It is stuck. I would not think of walking without my umbrella in case it should rain. But, as you see, I am not able to enjoy the sunshine underneath this dark shadow. It is a sad predicament."

"There is a simple solution," said the Gibbon. "You need only to cut some holes in your umbrella. Then the sun will shine on you."

"What a good idea!" cried the Baboon. "I do thank you."

The Baboon ran home. With his scissors, he cut large holes in the top of his umbrella. When the Baboon returned to his walk, the warm sunshine came down through the holes.

"How delightful!" said the Baboon.

However, the sun disappeared behind some clouds. There were a few drops of rain. Then it began to pour. The rain fell through all of the holes in the umbrella. In just a short time, the unhappy Baboon was soaked to the skin.

Advice from friends is like the weather. Some of it is good; some of it is bad.

From *Fables* by Arnold Lobel. © 1980 by Arnold Lobel.
Reprinted by permission of HarperCollins Publishers.

THE POOR OLD DOG

There was an old Dog who was very poor. The only coat he had to wear was mostly holes held together by ragged threads. He could feel the pebbles on the pavement through the thin soles of his tattered shoes. He slept in the park because he had no home.

The Dog spent most of his time searching in garbage cans. He found bits of string and buttons. These he sold for pennies to passersby.

The Dog always walked with his nose close to the curb, looking for things to sell. That is how he came to find the gold ring that was lying in the gutter.

"My luck has changed," cried the Dog, "for I am sure that this is a magic ring!"

The Dog rubbed the ring and said, "I wish for a new coat. I wish for new shoes. I wish for a house to live in. I wish these wishes would come true right now!"

But nothing happened. The Dog felt the wind through the holes in his coat. He felt the pebbles under his thin shoes. That night he slept on his usual bench in the park.

Several days later, the Dog saw a note on a lamppost. The note said "Lost: gold ring. Large reward. Mr. Terrier. Ten Wealthy Lane."

The old Dog hurried to Wealthy Lane. Mr. Terrier was overjoyed to have his ring returned. He thanked the Dog profusely and gave him a bulging purse that was full of coins.

The Dog bought a warm fur coat. He bought a pair of good shoes with thick soles.

There was a large amount of money left over. The Dog used the rest of it as a down payment on a cozy little house. He moved right in and never had to sleep in the park again.

Wishes, on their way to coming true, will not be rushed.

THE OSTRICH IN LOVE

On Sunday the Ostrich saw a young lady walking in the park. He fell in love with her at once. He followed behind her at a distance, putting his feet in the very places where she had stepped.

On Monday the Ostrich gathered violets as a gift to his beloved. He was too shy to give them to her. He left them at her door and ran away, but there was a great joy in his heart.

On Tuesday the Ostrich composed a song for his beloved. He sang it over and over. He thought it was the most beautiful music he had ever heard.

On Wednesday the Ostrich watched his beloved dining in a restaurant. He forgot to order supper for himself. He was too happy to be hungry.

On Thursday the Ostrich wrote a poem to his beloved. It was the first poem he had ever written, but he did not have the courage to read it to her.

On Friday the Ostrich bought a new suit of clothes. He fluffed his feathers, feeling fine and handsome. He hoped that his beloved might notice.

On Saturday the Ostrich dreamed that he was waltzing with his beloved in a great ballroom. He held her tightly as they whirled around and around to the music. He awoke feeling wonderfully alive.

On Sunday the Ostrich returned to the park. When he saw the young lady walking there, his heart fluttered wildly, but he said to himself, "Alas, it seems that I am much too shy for love. Perhaps another time will come. Yet, surely, this has been a week well spent."

Love can be its own reward.

MADAME RHINOCEROS AND HER DRESS

Madame Rhinoceros saw a dress in the window of a shop. It was covered with polka dots and flowers. It was adorned with ribbons and lace. She admired it for a moment and then entered the shop.

"That dress in the window," said Madame Rhinoceros to a salesperson, "I would like to try it on."

Madame Rhinoceros put on the dress. She looked at herself in the mirror. "I do not think this dress is at all attractive on me," she said.

"But Madame," said the salesperson, "you are completely wrong. This dress makes you look glamorous and alluring."

"If only I were sure," said Madame Rhinoceros.

"Ah, Madame," said the salesperson, "everyone who sees you wearing this dress will be filled with admiration and envy."

"Do you really think so?" asked Madame Rhinoceros, turning around and around in front of the mirror.

"Absolutely," said the salesperson. "You have my word."

"Very well," said Madame Rhinoceros, "I will buy the dress, and I will wear it now."

Madame Rhinoceros left the shop. As she walked up the avenue, she saw that people were smiling and laughing at her.

"Admiration," thought Madame Rhinoceros.

She saw some people who were shaking their heads and frowning.

"Envy," thought Madame Rhinoceros.

She continued up the avenue. Everyone who saw her stopped and stared. Madame Rhinoceros felt more glamorous and alluring with every step.

Nothing is harder to resist than a bit of flattery.

THE PIG AT THE CANDY STORE

All night long, the sleeping Pig dreamed of candy. He sprouted wings of spun sugar. He flew up through marshmallow clouds to a glowing marzipan moon. The stars that twinkled in the sky were chocolate kisses wrapped in shiny foil.

The Pig woke up with his mouth watering.

"Candy!" he cried. "I must have some this minute!"

The Pig ran to the candy dish. It was empty. The box of chocolate creams in the cupboard contained nothing but paper wrappers.

"I will go to the candy store," said the Pig, as he put on his clothes and rushed out of his house.

"On second thought," said the Pig, "I must remember that candy is bad for me. It makes me fatter than I already am. It gives me gas and heartburn."

Then the Pig remembered his sweet dreams. He decided that since he was halfway to the candy store, he might as well finish the journey.

"Just a few peppermints will not hurt me," he said.

As the Pig came near the store, his mouth began to water again.

"Maybe I will buy a small bag of gumdrops as well," he said.

But the candy store was closed. A sign on the door said "On Vacation."

The Pig went back home.

"What wonderful willpower I have!" he cried happily. "I did not eat a single piece of candy!"

That night the Pig had a vegetable salad for supper. He drank a glass of cold, fresh milk. He felt thin and had neither gas nor heartburn.

A locked door is very likely to discourage temptation.

From *Fables* by Arnold Lobel. © 1980 by Arnold Lobel. Reprinted by permission of HarperCollins Publishers.

From *Fables* by Arnold Lobel. © 1980 by Arnold Lobel. Reprinted by permission of HarperCollins Publishers.

THE HIPPOPOTAMUS AT DINNER

The Hippopotamus went into a restaurant. He sat at his favorite table.

"Waiter!" called the Hippopotamus. "I will have the bean soup, the Brussels sprouts, and the mashed potatoes. Please hurry, I am enormously hungry tonight!"

In a short while, the waiter returned with the order. The Hippopotamus glared down at his plate.

"Waiter," he said, "do you call this a meal? These portions are much too small. They would not satisfy a bird. I want a *bathtub* of bean soup, a *bucket* of Brussels sprouts, and a *mountain* of mashed potatoes. I tell you I have an APPETITE!"

The waiter went back into the kitchen. He returned carrying enough bean soup to fill a bathtub, enough Brussels sprouts to fill a bucket, and a mountain of mashed potatoes. In no time, the Hippopotamus had eaten every last morsel.

"Delicious!" said the Hippopotamus, as he dabbed his mouth with a napkin and prepared to leave.

To his surprise, he could not move. His stomach, which had grown considerably larger, was caught between the table and the chair. He pulled and tugged, but it was no use. He could not budge.

The hour grew late. The other customers in the restaurant finished their dinners and left. The cooks took off their aprons and put away their pots. The waiters cleared the dishes and turned out the lights. They all went home.

The Hippopotamus remained there, sitting forlornly at the table.

"Perhaps I should not have eaten quite so many Brussels sprouts," he said, as he gazed into the gloom of the darkened restaurant. Occasionally, he burped.

Too much of anything often leaves one with a feeling of regret.

THE MOUSE AT THE SEASHORE

A Mouse told his mother and father that he was going on a trip to the seashore.

"We are very alarmed!" they cried. "The world is full of terrors. You must not go!"

"I have made my decision," said the Mouse firmly. "I have never seen the ocean, and it is high time that I did. Nothing can make me change my mind."

"Then we cannot stop you," said Mother and Father Mouse, "but do be careful!"

The next day, in the first light of dawn, the Mouse began his journey. Even before the morning had ended, the Mouse came to know trouble and fear.

A Cat jumped out from behind a tree.

"I will eat you for lunch," he said.

It was a narrow escape for the Mouse. He ran for his life, but he left a part of his tail in the mouth of the Cat.

By afternoon the Mouse had been attacked by birds and dogs. He had lost his way several times. He was bruised and bloodied. He was tired and frightened.

At evening the Mouse slowly climbed the last hill and saw the seashore spreading out before him. He watched the waves rolling onto the beach, one after another. All the colors of the sunset filled the sky.

"How beautiful!" cried the Mouse. "I wish that Mother and Father were here to see this with me."

The moon and the stars began to appear over the ocean. The Mouse sat silently on the top of the hill. He was overwhelmed by a feeling of deep peace and contentment.

All the miles of a hard road are worth a moment of true happiness.

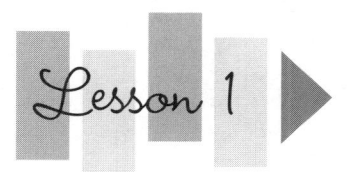

The Hen and the Apple Tree

OVERVIEW OF ACTIVITIES

Day 1	Day 2	Day 3	Day 4
TEXT INTRODUCTION • Predict storyline • Read fable • Discuss fable	**VOCABULARY INTRODUCTION** • Circle vocabulary • Extract definitions • Assign homework	**EXPAND MEANING** • Review homework • Related Words	**TOOLS TO DEVELOP VOCABULARY** • Multiple Meanings

Day 5	Day 6	Day 7	Day 8
USING WORDS IN CONTEXT • Contexting activity	**TOOLS TO DEVELOP VOCABULARY** • Idioms • Assign homework	**TOOLS TO DEVELOP VOCABULARY** • Review homework • Idioms	**ASSESSMENT**

WORD LIST

The word in bold is the base word, followed by its definition. If the word has more than one meaning, then we provide only the definition used in the text. *Please review the definitions prior to instruction.*

1. **bark:** the hard covering on the outside of a tree
2. **certain:** proved beyond all doubt to be true
3. **delicious:** very pleasing to taste or smell
4. **fur:** the soft, thick, hairy coat of an animal
5. **leaf:** the flat and usually green parts of a plant or tree that grow out from a stem, twig, or branch
6. **odd:** strange or unusual
7. **outsmart:** to defeat by being clever
8. **quick:** rapid; fast
9. **quiver:** to shake or move with a slight tremble; to vibrate
10. **rage:** wild, uncontrollable anger
11. **shade:** area sheltered from light
12. **trunk:** the main stem of a tree

IDIOMATIC EXPRESSIONS

- **come to think of it:** just realize
- **stormed away:** left angrily

OTHER WORDS WORTH DEFINING

- **shutters:** movable cover for the outside of a window
- **pose:** pretend to be someone else in order to deceive people

Day 1
TEXT INTRODUCTION

▼ **Prepare for activity**

Post Classroom Word List.

Materials: Student Word Books, *Fables*

▼ **Introduce Arnold Lobel and *Fables***

Say: *Does anyone know what a **fable** is?* Encourage responses. *That's right, a fable is a story that teaches a lesson. Fables are fun because the main characters are often animals that talk and act like people. Has anyone ever read or heard a fable? A famous book of fables was written by Arnold Lobel. Since the publication in 1962 of his first picture book, Mr. Lobel has become one of the most well-loved creators of children's books. He has written and/or illustrated more than 60 books for children and is perhaps best known for his **I Can Read** books about Frog and Toad. In 1981, **Fables** received the Caldecott Medal for most distinguished picture book of the year.*

This year we are going to learn new vocabulary while studying fables. Why would you want to learn new vocabulary words? Elicit benefits such as better understanding of books, newspapers, and magazines, as well as the ability for students to better express themselves when writing and speaking.

▼ **Predict storyline**

Show students the illustration for "The Hen and the Apple Tree" in the color insert or turn to page 10 of *Fables*

Say: *Today we are going to read the fable "The Hen and the Apple Tree." What do you think this fable will be about when you look at the illustration and hear the title?*

Encourage a student discussion.

▼ **Ask the students to listen as you read the fable aloud**

▼ **Discuss the fable and moral and relate it to the students' lives**

* *Who are the main characters in this fable?*
* *Have any of you ever heard a hen or apple tree talk? Of course not! Pretending that they can talk makes the story more interesting and fun.*
* *What time of year did this fable take place?*
* *What was the first clue Hen noticed that made her suspect that there was something strange about the apple tree?*
* *What were the other things that made Hen suspicious?*
* *Why do you think the wolf was trying to disguise himself as an apple tree?*

▼ **Reread the moral**

- *What do you think the moral means?*
- *Have any of you ever pretended to be something that you weren't? How did it work out?*
- *Do you think it is better to be who you are or pretend to be someone else? Why?*

The Hen and the Apple Tree

One October day, a Hen looked out her window. She saw an apple tree growing in her backyard.

"Now that is **odd**," said the Hen. "I am **certain** that there was no tree standing in that spot yesterday."

"There are some of us that grow fast," said the tree.

The Hen looked at the bottom of the tree.

"I have never seen a tree," she said, "that has ten **furry** toes."

"There are some of us that do," said the tree. "Hen, come outside and enjoy the cool **shade** of my **leafy** branches."

The Hen looked at the top of the tree.

"I have never seen a tree," she said, "that has two long, pointed ears."

"There are some of us that have," said the tree. "Hen, come outside and eat one of my **delicious** apples."

"Come to think of it," said the Hen," I have never heard a tree speak from a mouth that is full of sharp teeth."

"There are some of us that can," said the tree. "Hen, come outside and rest your back against the **bark** of my **trunk.**"

"I have heard," said the Hen, "that some of you trees lose all of your leaves at this tine of the year."

"Oh, yes," said the tree, "there are some of us that will." The tree began to **quiver** and shake. All of its leaves **quickly** dropped off.

The Hen was not surprised to see a large Wolf in the place where an apple tree had been standing just a moment before. She locked her shutters and slammed her window closed.

The Wolf knew he had been **outsmarted.** He stormed away in a hungry **rage.**

It is always difficult to pose as something that one is not.

From *Fables* by Arnold Lobel. © 1980 by Arnold Lobel. Reproduced by permission from HarperCollins Publishers.

▼ Read posted target words to students, or ask students to read them

▼ Quickly review the section titled "Other Words Worth Defining"

▼ Reread the fable to define words and infer meaning

- Before you reread the fable, say: *Follow along in your Student Word Book as I read the fable again. Circle each target word when I read it. If you think you know what the word means* **without reading the definition,** *then raise your hand, and I will call on you.* After students have suggested meanings, say: *Let's check the definition to see how close you were.*

  Note: The target words appear in the same order in the fable as on the word list. To help students find the words more easily, point out each target word on the list before looking for it in the text.

- Meaning can be inferred for **shade**, **quiver**, and **rage**. When you reach **shade**, say: *Sometimes you can figure out what a word means by skipping over it and finishing the sentence. Or, you can reread the sentence while thinking about what the word might mean. Let me show you how this works by reading the sentence with* **shade** *in it. "Hen, come outside and enjoy the* **cool** *shade of my leafy branches." Let's see, where there is shade it is cool. Shade also has something to do with leafy branches. So, I wonder if shade means that place under trees where it's dark and cool. Let's look up the definition to see if that's what it means.*

- When you reach **quiver** (related to **shake** and **all leaves falling off**) and **rage** (related to **storming away**), ask students to "think aloud" to explain how the clues in the fable can help them figure out what the words mean. You may need to continue modeling the strategy.

▼ Assign Vocabulary Review homework

Instruct students to write the correct vocabulary word in the space beside the definition.

TARGET WORD DEFINITIONS

- The base word is bold and is the word defined.
- If there is more than one meaning, then the bold definition is the one used in the fable.
- The Spanish translation is provided for the meaning used in the fable.

1. **bark**
   a) short, loud sound that an animal makes
   b) the hard covering on the outside of a tree
   c) to shout at someone gruffly
   • corteza; parte exterior y dura de un árbol

2. **certain**
   a) proved beyond all doubt to be true
   b) particular
   • saber; tener certeza: conocimiento seguro y claro de alguna cosa

3. **delicious**
   very pleasing to taste or smell
   • delicioso; placentero al olfato o paladar

4. **furry (fur)**
   the soft, thick, hairy coat of an animal
   • peludo; con mucho pelo

5. **leafy (leaf)**
   a) the flat and usually green parts of a plant or tree that grow out from a stem, twig, or branch
   b) removable parts of a table top
   c) to turn over pages
   • frondoso; abundante en hojas y ramas

6. **odd**
   a) strange or unusual
   b) not matching
   c) a number that cannot be divided evenly by two
   • extraño; raro o singular

7. **outsmarted (outsmart)**
   to defeat by being clever
   • ser más listo engañar

8. **quickly (quick)**
   a) rapid; fast
   b) fast in understanding or thinking
   • rápidamente; con ímpetu, rapidez o celeridad

9. **quiver**
   a) to shake or move with a slight tremble; to vibrate
   b) a case for carrying arrows
   • estremecerse; temblar repentinamente

10. **rage**
    a) wild, uncontrollable anger
    b) to be violent without control
    c) a very popular fashion
    • rabia; ira, enojo, cólera

11. **shade**
    a) area sheltered from light
    b) something that provides shelter from light
    c) to shelter from light
    d) the degree of darkness of a color
    e) to make part of a drawing darker than the rest
    f) a small amount or difference
    • sombra; área protegida de la luz

12. **trunk**
    a) the main stem of a tree
    b) a large case used for storage or for carrying clothes on a long journey
    c) the long nose of an elephant
    d) enclosed part of a car where luggage and a spare tire can be stored
    • tronco; tallo fuerte y macizo de los árboles y arbustos

EXPAND MEANING:
Related Words

▼ **Review Vocabulary Review homework**

1. Ask students for answers.

2. Direct students to correct their own answers if needed.

▼ **Prepare for activity**

1. Read "Teacher Tip: Rich Instruction" before teaching the lesson.

2. Divide students into heterogeneous language pairs.

Materials: Related Words worksheet for each student

▼ **Introduce the concept: Related Words**

Say: *New words will mean more to you when you can relate them to other words that you already know and to experiences you've had in your life. For example, think about the word* **odd**. *Raise your hand after you have thought of something you've seen that is* **odd?** Encourage discussion. *Do you see how the word means more when you've thought about it in relationship to* **your** *life? You are more apt to remember it.*

▼ **Introduce the activity**

Say: *Today you will work in pairs and pretend that one of you is someone famous and the other is a reporter for a magazine. The reporter's job is to ask the questions on the Related Words worksheet and write down the answers. After a few minutes, you will change roles so that everyone will have a turn to be both the famous person and the reporter.*

Circulate among the groups, providing guidance as needed. Allow the students to work together for 10–12 minutes before asking them to change roles.

Note: You may choose to have one of the pair answer questions 1–6 and have his or her partner answer questions 7–12.

▼ **Review the activity**

Say: *What was the most interesting thing you learned about your partner? Do you think differently about any of the words now? Do you understand them in a different way?*

Teacher Tip

RICH INSTRUCTION

One of the primary goals of the Vocabulary Improvement Program is for students to acquire word knowledge that is rich and proficient enough to facilitate reading comprehension. The various instructional activities we propose are targeted to this goal. It is important, however, for vocabulary learning to go on throughout the day, in all subjects.

Teachers can arrange instructional conditions to provide diverse opportunities for a maximum amount of processing of words. They need to require that students manipulate words in varied and rich ways. For example, new words can be related to other words and to familiar experiences in the lives of the children. Students need to use the new words in ways that foster strong relationships and associations with other words in their vocabularies.

When new words are encountered, several activities might be helpful in promoting deeper and richer relationships and associations.

1. *Ask students to provide superordinate and subordinate instances.* For example, "A *tyrant* is a type of what?" (superordinate category: ruler); "Can you give me examples of *tyrants?*" (subordinate categories: older brothers, Macbeth)

2. *If the word is a noun, then ask the students to provide three adjectives that fit with it.* For example, if the target word is *dictator,* then the students might provide adjectives such as *harsh, cruel,* or *military.* These answers show some understanding of the meaning of the term *dictator.* Other responses such as *old* or *good* can be used with most nouns but do not show much understanding of the meaning of the word *dictator.*

3. *if the word is a verb, then ask the students for three adverbs or phrases that fit with it.* For example, if the target word is *persevere,* the students might give answers such as *steadily, firmly,* or *with determination.*

4. *Ask the students for synonyms and antonyms of the target word.* "What is another word for *tyrant?*" "Can you tell me what the opposite of a *dictator* is?"

Research shows that words are learned best if they are encountered and used frequently by the child. A child might be able to define a *miser* as someone who saves money and lives as if he or she were poor. However, having a rich understanding involves being able to give examples of miserly behavior, knowing the consequences of acting like a miser, and being able to use the word beyond typical contexts—for example, by extending the concept to describe people who are stingy with other things besides money such as time or love.

A great deal of vocabulary learning goes on in social studies, science, and mathematics. Children will learn the words they need in these subjects if they encounter them repeatedly or in different contexts and if they use them in their own speech. In this way, words will become part of the children's lexical knowledge, and children will have a network of associations for these words. For example, children can learn to use the word *hypothesis* not only in science and mathematics but also in talking about different theories regarding a story's meaning.

Rich networks of word relationships and associations are likely to develop if children are exposed to a verbal environment in which unfamiliar vocabulary (not too far in advance of the child's abilities) is used in a reflective and playful manner. Such an environment helps children notice words they do not know and raises their consciousness about word learning.

Day 4
TOOLS TO DEVELOP VOCABULARY: Multiple Meanings

Lesson 1

▼ **Prepare for activity**

Divide students into heterogeneous language groups of four or five.
Materials: Multiple Meanings worksheet

▼ **Introduce the concept: Multiple Meanings**

Say: *Many words that you use have more than one meaning. Think about the word* **top**. *Who can tell me what* **top** *means? You may give either a definition or a sentence that shows the meaning. Now, who can give me another meaning?* Encourage students to think of the following meanings:

1. The highest point or part of something: I wrote my name at the *top* of the page.
2. A cover or lid: I collect bottle *tops*.
3. Highest rank or position: I am the *top* math student in the class.
4. A piece of clothing for the upper part of the body: Your new *top* looks comfortable.
5. A toy that spins and is shaped like a cone: I love to play with *tops*.

Say: *Look at all of the meanings you know for top! You may not have even been aware that you knew more than one meaning.*

▼ **Introduce the activity**

Say: *Today we are going to study some of the words from this week's text that have more than one meaning, or multiple meanings. Who can tell me one meaning for the word* **bark?** Correct and elaborate on students' definitions.

Continue with definitions for *leaf, odd,* and *trunk.*

1. **bark**
    a) short, loud sound that an animal makes
    b) the hard covering on the outside of a tree
    c) to shout at someone gruffly

2. **leaf**
    a) the flat and usually green parts of a plant or tree that grow out from a stem, twig, or branch
    b) removable parts of a table top
    c) to turn over pages

3. **odd**
   a) strange or unusual

   b) not matching

   c) a number that cannot be divided evenly by two

4. **trunk**
   a) the main stem of a tree

   b) a large case used for storage or for carrying clothes on a long journey

   c) the long nose of an elephant

   d) enclosed part of a car where luggage and a spare tire can be stored

▼ Multiple Meanings worksheet

Say: *Now, you will work in your groups on a worksheet. The definitions that we just talked about for **bark, leaf, odd,** and **trunk** are in the boxes. Below each box are sentences that use a word that has more than one meaning. The word with more than one meaning is underlined. Your job is to figure out which definition in the box best fits the way the word is used in each sentence. Write the letter for that definition in the space at the end of the sentence. The other words in the sentence—the context—will help you know which meaning fits.*

▼ Review the activity

Call on students to read the sentences aloud from the Multiple Meanings worksheet and provide the correct answers.

Day 5
USING WORDS IN CONTEXT

Using Words in Context is designed to develop students' ability to decipher the meaning of a word by using clues in the surrounding text.

▼ Prepare for activity

Place students in heterogeneous language groups, ideally four to five students per group.

Materials: Using Words in Context worksheet for each student.

If this activity is challenging for your students, then you may choose to complete it as a whole-group activity. It is helpful to make the worksheet into a transparency so that you can point out the context clues.

▼ Introduce the activity

Say: *Today's activity will help you practice using the target words in sentences. Your job is to figure out which word fits in the blank using the clues that are in the sentence. After you figure out the right word, think about **how** you figured it out; what were the clues in the rest of the sentence that helped you. When everyone in the group knows the correct word and **why it fits,** raise your hands. I'll call on one of the first groups ready. You will get a point if you get the correct answer* (you may choose not to use points). *Remember, everyone in your group must know the answer and why it is correct.*

Read the first sentence aloud to the class to illustrate the process.

▼ Review the activity

Ask one student at a table for the correct answer **and to explain how he or she figured it out**—which clues in the context helped. (The context clues are bold in sentences 1–10 to help students learn how to look for the clues in the text.) Explaining the thought process that led to the answer helps the students realize that they know how to use the clues in the text and will demonstrate the process to those students who have not yet developed the skill.

Continue until the lesson is completed, giving each group one point for the correct answer (you may choose not to use points).

TOOLS TO DEVELOP VOCABULARY: Idioms

Lesson 1

▼ **Prepare for activity**

1. Read "Teacher Tip: Sayings and Expressions" before teaching the lesson.

2. Divide students into heterogeneous language pairs.

3. Materials: Cut the Idioms List into strips so that each pair of students will have one idiom and definition. Provide 12-inch by 18-inch drawing paper for each pair of students.

▼ **Introduce the concept: Idioms**

Say: *Does anyone know what an* **idiom** *is? Idioms are commonly used expressions or phrases that mean something different than the words themselves. "It's raining cats and dogs" is an idiom. Who knows what it means? That's right, it means that it's raining* **really hard.**

In this week's fable, there are two idioms: **come to think of it** *and* **stormed away***. What would the words mean if they weren't idioms? What do you think the idiomatic meanings are?*

Encourage discussion and expand upon students' suggestions to arrive at the conventionally accepted meanings:

• **Come to think of it:** just realize

• **Stormed away:** left angrily

▼ **Introduce the activity**

Say: *Today I am going to give each pair of students an idiom. You will work together to draw a picture of the literal meaning of the idiom—or what the words really mean. Figure out how to explain to the class what the idiom has come to mean. Students may choose to illustrate the idiom's meaning by acting it out. Think of a sentence that uses the idiomatic meaning. Tomorrow you will share it with the class.*

Allow students sufficient time to complete the drawings and write the sentences.

▼ **Assign homework**

Give students the crossword puzzle; review the instructions and the due date.

SAYINGS AND EXPRESSIONS

Another way to engage children in language is to make them aware of all of the sayings that we have in English. Spanish-speaking children could be encouraged to think of similar expressions in their language. Some English sayings include

It's easy to be brave from a safe distance.
A bad worker blames his or her tools.
A bird in the hand is worth two in the bush.
Life is what happens to you while you are making plans.
The tree is known by its fruit.
Well begun is half done.
Human blood is all one color.
Birds of a feather flock together.
A squeaky wheel gets the grease.
A friend in need is a friend indeed.
The best things in life are free.
A little knowledge is a dangerous thing.
A rolling stone gathers no moss.
Might makes right.
Don't put off until tomorrow what you can do today.
Talk of the devil, and he's bound to appear.
The exception proves the rule.
Tit for tat.
Too many cooks spoil the broth.
A stitch in time saves nine.
Time is a great healer.

Ask your Spanish-speaking students to bring some similar expressions to class after talking to their parents and other relatives. Translate them literally into English, and ask the English-only students to guess what they mean. Some Spanish sayings include

Tener carta blanca: Have carte blanche
Quemarse las pestañas: Burn your eyelashes
Esto no tiene ni pies ni cabeza: This doesn't have either feet or head
Matar dos pájaros de un tiro: Kill two birds with one throw
No dar el brazo a torcer: Don't give your arm to be twisted
Esto cuesta un ojo de la cara: This costs an eye from your face
Meter las narices en todo: Put your nose into everything
Es un círculo vicioso: It's a vicious circle
Encontrarse entre la espada y la pared: Find yourself between a sword and the wall

¿Qué mosca le ha picado?: What fly has bitten you?

Romper el hielo: Break the ice

Consultarlo con la almohada: Consult with your pillow

Buscar una aguja en un pajar: Look for a needle in a haystack

Day 7
TOOLS TO DEVELOP
VOCABULARY: Idioms

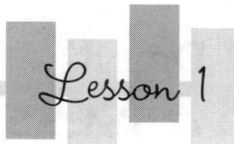

▼ **Review the crossword puzzle homework**

1. Ask students for answers.

2. Direct students to correct their own answers if needed.

▼ **Review Day 6: Idioms**

1. Direct each pair of students to read their idiom to the class and show the picture that demonstrates the literal meaning.

2. The students may then ask their classmates what they think the idiom has come to mean.

3. The students then explain or dramatize the idiomatic meaning for the class.

4. The students read the sentence they composed to the class.

5. Ask other students to create a sentence using the idiom.

6. If time allows, look up the origins of the sayings in the *Dictionary of Idioms* (Terban, 1996)—*very* interesting!

7. Continue until all idioms have been explained.

ASSESSMENT

▼ **Vocabulary assessment**

Part 1: Instruct the students to circle the word that corresponds to the definition on the Vocabulary Assessment worksheet.

Part 2: Instruct students to write sentences that demonstrate their knowledge of the word's meaning on the Vocabulary Assessment Sentences worksheet.

Hint: You may need to provide examples of sentences that demonstrate knowledge of the meaning. For example, if the vocabulary word were **ring**, then the sentence "I have a ring" does not demonstrate knowledge of the meaning. **Nose**, **car**, **friend**, **house**, or any number of other words could be substituted for **ring** in the sentence. The sentence "I wear a ring on my finger" demonstrates knowledge of the meaning.

Teacher answer keys

VOCABULARY REVIEW HOMEWORK

- Read the definitions.
- Find the word in the box that matches the definition.
- Write the correct word next to the definition.

bark	odd	rage	certain
fur	delicious	trunk	quiver
quick	leaf	outsmart	shade

1. __**odd**__ : strange or unusual

2. __**trunk**__ : the main stem of a tree

3. __**bark**__ : the hard covering on the outside of a tree

4. __**fur**__ : the soft, thick, hairy coat of an animal

5. __**quiver**__ : to shake or move with a slight tremble; to vibrate

6. __**shade**__ : area sheltered from light

7. __**certain**__ : proved beyond all doubt to be true

8. __**outsmart**__ : to defeat by being clever

9. __**rage**__ : wild, uncontrollable anger

10. __**delicious**__ : very pleasing to taste or smell

11. __**leaf**__ : flat and usually green parts of a plant or tree that grow out from a stem, twig, or branch

12. __**quick**__ : rapid; fast

Lesson 1

MULTIPLE MEANINGS WORKSHEET

- Read each sentence below.
- Choose the meaning for each bold word from the definitions in the box.
- Write the letter for that meaning in the space at the end of the sentence.
- The sentences contain clues that will help you figure out which meaning is used.

> A. Short, loud sound that an animal makes
>
> B. To shout at someone gruffly
>
> C. The hard covering on the outside of a tree
>
> D. Not matching
>
> E. Strange or unusual
>
> F. A number that cannot be divided evenly by two

1. I scraped my leg on the rough **bark**. __C__

2. The loud **bark** awakened me from a deep sleep. __A__

3. I feel scared when you **bark** at me. __B__

4. I lost one of my socks; now I have an **odd** sock. __D__

5. Thirty-five is an **odd** number. __F__

6. It was **odd** to see the teacher do a cartwheel when he first entered the classroom. __E__

MULTIPLE MEANINGS WORKSHEET *(continued)*

G. Enclosed part of a car where luggage and a spare tire can be stored

H. Removable parts of a table top

I. A large case used for storage or for carrying clothes on a long journey

J. The long nose of an elephant

K. To turn over pages

L. The main stem of a tree

M. The flat and usually green parts of a plant or tree that grow out from a stem, twig, or branch

7. When my cousins come over, we add a **leaf** to the table so that we can all sit together. __H__

8. When I read the encyclopedia, I often **leaf** through it to see what else interests me. __K__

9. The **leaf** floated down from the big maple tree. __M__

10. The tree **trunk** was so big that three men could barely reach around it. __L__

11. Dumbo used his **trunk** to pick up peanuts. __J__

12. When we go on a picnic, we put the ice chest in the **trunk** of the car. __G__

13. When my mother sailed to America, she brought her belongings in a **trunk**. __I__

USING WORDS IN CONTEXT WORKSHEET

bark	certain	furry	leafy	odd
outsmarted	quiver	rage	shady	trunk

1. The hen thought it was **strange** to see a tree next to her house.
   She said, "Now that is _____**odd**_____."

2. The hen was **sure** that the tree wasn't there yesterday.
   She was _____**certain**_____ that she hadn't seen that tree before.

3. The wolf **has fur** all over his body.
   Even his toes are _____**furry**_____.

4. The apple tree **has lots of leaves.**
   It is very _____**leafy**_____.

5. Under the big tree, it's **not sunny.**
   It's cool and _____**shady**_____.

6. The hen **tricked** the wolf.
   She _____**outsmarted**_____ him.

7. The wolf was **very angry** with the hen.
   He ran off in a _____**rage**_____.

8. A flower has a **stem,** and a tree has a _____**trunk**_____.

9. People have **skin,** and **trees** have _____**bark**_____.

10. Sometimes people's bodies **shake** when they feel angry.
    We can say that their bodies _____**quiver**_____ with rage.

USING WORDS IN CONTEXT WORKSHEET (continued)

| bark | certain | furry | leafy | odd |
| outsmart | shade | shades | trunks | |

11. Bears don't feel cold in the snow because they are so _____**furry**_____.

12. The cactus is not a _____**leafy**_____ plant.

13. Two, four, and six are even numbers, but one, three, and five are _____**odd**_____ numbers.

14. The sky is very dark and cloudy. It's _____**certain**_____ to rain.

15. In a lot of cartoons, the little mice _____**outsmart**_____ the big, bad cat.

16. At night in our house, we pull down all the window _____**shades**_____.

17. In my crayon box, there is a dark blue crayon and a light blue crayon. Which _____**shade**_____ of blue do you like better?

18. Here's a riddle: What do a tree and an elephant both have? They both have _____**trunks**_____.

19. Here's another riddle. What do trees have and dogs do? The answer is _____**bark**_____.

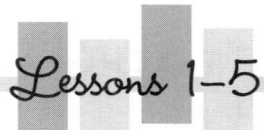

LESSON 1

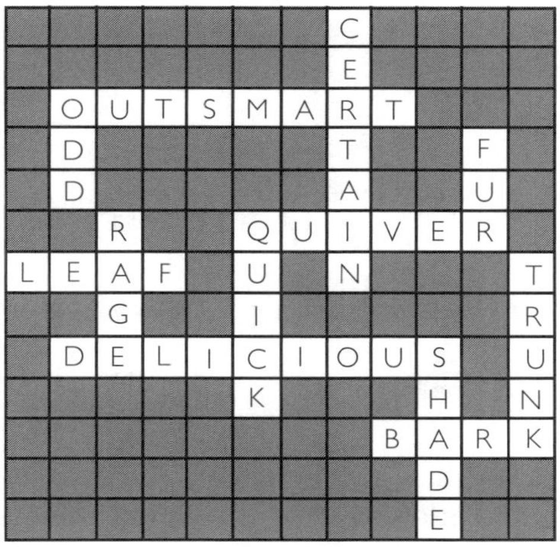
CERTAIN
OUTSMART
ODD
FUR
RAG
QUIVER
QUICK
LEAF
TRUNK
DELICIOUS
SHADE
BARK

LESSON 2

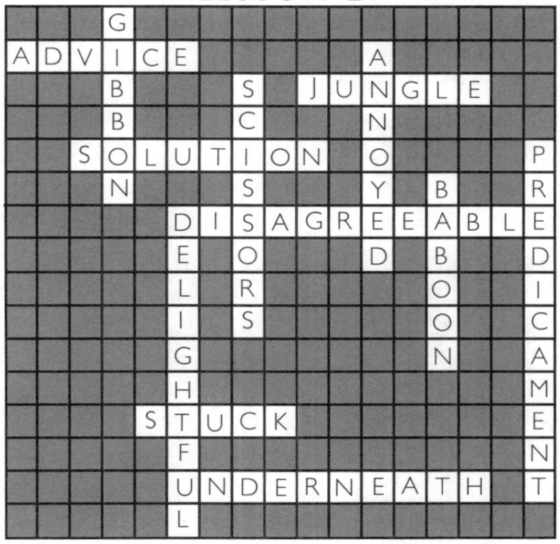
GIBBON
ADVICE
ANNOYED
SCISSORS
JUNGLE
SOLUTION
PREDICAMENT
BABOON
DISAGREEABLE
DELIGHTFUL
STUCK
UNDERNEATH

LESSON 3

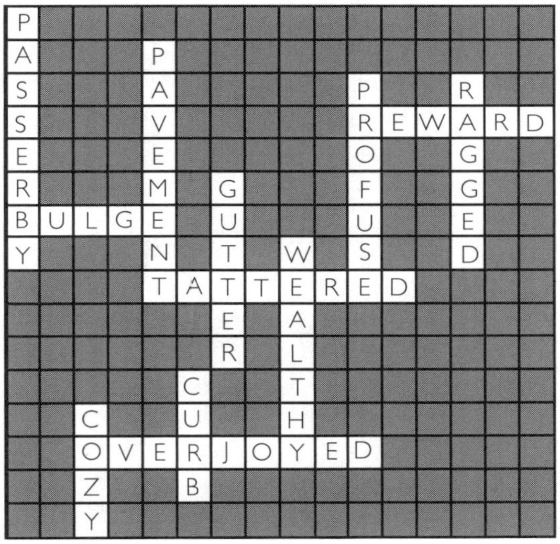
PASSERBY
PAVEMENT
PROFUSE
RAGGED
REWARD
GUTTER
BULGE
WEALTH
TATTERED
CUB
COZY
OVERJOYED

LESSON 4

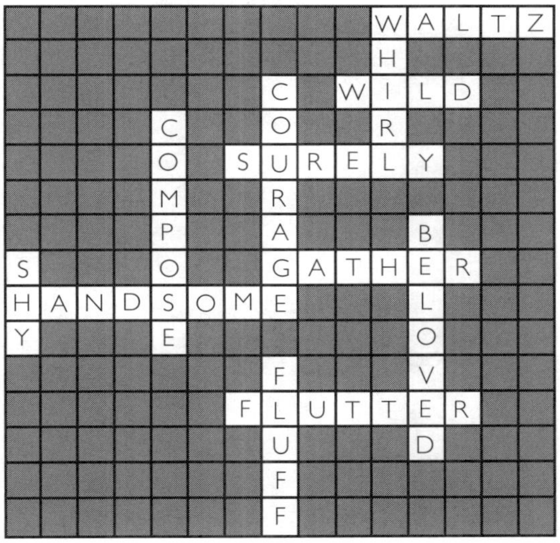
WALTZ
WHIRL
WILD
COURAGE
COMPOSE
SURELY
BELOVED
SHY
GATHER
HANDSOME
FLUFF
FLUTTER

LESSON 5

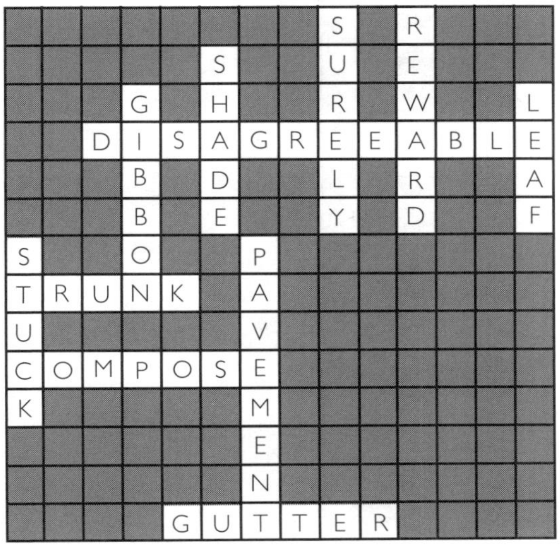
SURELY
REWARD
SHADE
GIBBON
LEAF
DISAGREEABLE
STUCK
PAVEMENT
TRUNK
COMPOSE
GUTTER

VOCABULARY ASSESSMENT WORKSHEET

- Circle the word that matches the definition.

1. The soft, thick, hairy coat of an animal

    odd   (fur)   quick   trunk

2. Flat and usually green parts of a plant or tree that grow out from a stem, twig, or branch

    quiver   certain   rage   (leaf)

3. Strange or unusual

    certain   fur   (odd)   leaf

4. Rapid; fast

    (quick)   rage   outsmart   odd

5. The main stem of a tree

    leaf   (trunk)   delicious   bark

6. Wild, uncontrollable anger

    (rage)   quiver   shade   certain

7. To shake or move with a slight tremble; to vibrate

    odd   trunk   outsmart   (quiver)

8. Proved beyond all doubt to be true

    fur   shade   delicious   (certain)

9. Area sheltered from light

    bark   outsmart   (shade)   leaf

10. Very pleasing to taste or smell

    rage   (delicious)   quick   odd

11. The hard covering on the outside of a tree

    quiver   certain   (bark)   leaf

12. To defeat by being clever

    (outsmart)   shade   certain   rage

Reproducible materials

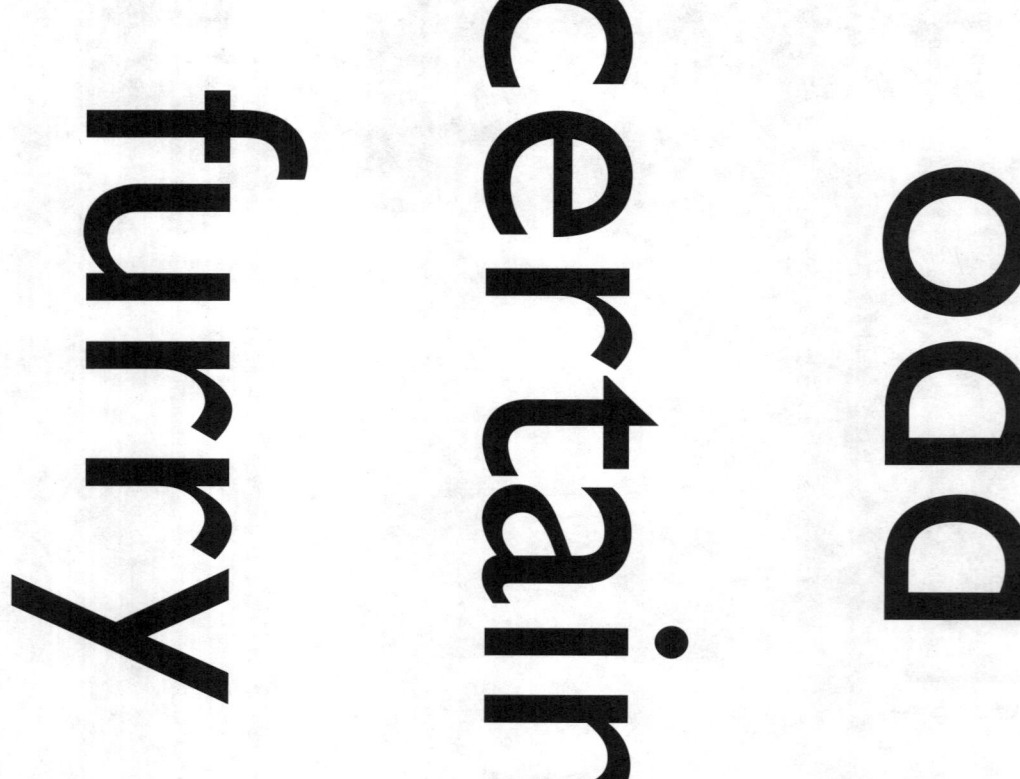

furry

certain

odd

Lesson 1

delicious

leafy

shade

quiver

trunk

bark

rage

outsmarted

quickly

Vocabulary Improvement Program for English Language Learners and Their Classmates, 4th Grade, by Teresa Lively, Diane August, María Carlo, and Catherine Snow © 2003 Paul H. Brookes Publishing Co., Inc. All rights reserved.

Name: _____

VOCABULARY REVIEW HOMEWORK

- Read the definitions.
- Find the word in the box that matches the definition.
- Write the correct word next to the definition.

bark	odd	rage	certain
fur	delicious	trunk	quiver
quick	leaf	outsmart	shade

1. _____: strange or unusual

2. _____: the main stem of a tree

3. _____: the hard covering on the outside of a tree

4. _____: the soft, thick, hairy coat of an animal

5. _____: to shake or move with a slight tremble; to vibrate

6. _____: area sheltered from light

7. _____: proved beyond all doubt to be true

8. _____: to defeat by being clever

9. _____: wild, uncontrollable anger

10. _____: very pleasing to taste or smell

11. _____: flat and usually green parts of a plant or tree that grow out from a stem, twig, or branch

12. _____: rapid; fast

Name: _____

Lesson 1

RELATED WORDS WORKSHEET

1. Name three things that you think are **odd**.

_____

_____

_____

2. What is one thing of which you are **certain**?

_____

_____

3. What are three things that you have done **quickly**?

_____

_____

_____

4. What are three **furry** things that you have seen?

_____

_____

_____

5. What are two words that could describe **shade**?

_____

_____

6. Describe the most **delicious** food that you have ever tasted.

_____

_____

7. What are two words that could describe **bark**?

_____

_____

8. What are two words that mean the same as (are synonyms for) **quiver**?

_____

_____

9. Have you ever **outsmarted** anyone? How?

_____

_____

10. What are two words that mean the opposite of (are antonyms for) **rage**?

_____

_____

11. What are three words that could describe a tree **trunk**?

_____

_____

_____

12. Describe the most **leafy** plant that you have ever seen.

_____

_____

MULTIPLE MEANINGS WORKSHEET

- Read each sentence below.
- Choose the meaning for each bold word from the definitions in the box.
- Write the letter for that meaning in the space at the end of the sentence.
- The sentences contain clues that will help you figure out which meaning is used.

A. Short, loud sound that an animal makes

B. To shout at someone gruffly

C. The hard covering on the outside of a tree

D. Not matching

E. Strange or unusual

F. A number that cannot be divided evenly by two

---

1. I scraped my leg on the rough **bark**. _____

2. The loud **bark** awakened me from a deep sleep. _____

3. I feel scared when you **bark** at me. _____

4. I lost one of my socks; now I have an **odd** sock. _____

5. Thirty-five is an **odd** number. _____

6. It was **odd** to see the teacher do a cartwheel when he first entered the classroom. _____

Name: _____

MULTIPLE MEANINGS WORKSHEET *(continued)*

G. Enclosed part of a car where luggage and a spare tire can be stored

H. Removable parts of a table top

I. A large case used for storage or for carrying clothes on a long journey

J. The long nose of an elephant

K. To turn over pages

L. The main stem of a tree

M. The flat and usually green parts of a plant or tree that grow out from a stem, twig, or branch

---

7. When my cousins come over, we add a **leaf** to the table so that we can all sit together. __

8. When I read the encyclopedia, I often **leaf** through it to see what else interests me. ____

9. The **leaf** floated down from the big maple tree. ____

10. The tree **trunk** was so big that three men could barely reach around it. ____

11. Dumbo used his **trunk** to pick up peanuts. ____

12. When we go on a picnic, we put the ice chest in the **trunk** of the car. ____

13. When my mother sailed to America, she brought her belongings in a **trunk**. ____

Name: _____

USING WORDS IN CONTEXT WORKSHEET

bark	certain	furry	leafy	odd
outsmarted	quiver	rage	shady	trunk

1. The hen thought it was **strange** to see a tree next to her house.
   She said, "Now that is _____."

2. The hen was **sure** that the tree wasn't there yesterday.
   She was _____ that she hadn't seen that tree before.

3. The wolf **has fur** all over his body.
   Even his toes are _____.

4. The apple tree **has lots of leaves.**
   It is very _____.

5. Under the big tree, it's **not sunny.**
   It's cool and _____.

6. The hen **tricked** the wolf.
   She _____ him.

7. The wolf was **very angry** with the hen.
   He ran off in a _____.

8. A flower has a **stem,** and a tree has a _____.

9. People have **skin,** and **trees** have _____.

10. Sometimes people's bodies **shake** when they feel angry.
    We can say that their bodies _____ with rage.

Name: _____

USING WORDS IN CONTEXT WORKSHEET *(continued)*

bark	certain	furry	leafy	odd
outsmart	shade	shades	trunks	

11. Bears don't feel cold in the snow because they are so _____.

12. The cactus is not a _____ plant.

13. Two, four, and six are even numbers, but one, three, and five are _____ numbers.

14. The sky is very dark and cloudy. It's _____ to rain.

15. In a lot of cartoons, the little mice _____ the big, bad cat.

16. At night in our house, we pull down all the window _____.

17. In my crayon box, there is a dark blue crayon and a light blue crayon. Which _____ of blue do you like better?

18. Here's a riddle: What do a tree and an elephant both have? They both have _____.

19. Here's another riddle. What do trees have and dogs do? The answer is _____.

Vocabulary Improvement Program for English Language Learners and Their Classmates, 4th Grade, by Teresa Lively, Diane August, María Carlo, and Catherine Snow © 2003 Paul H. Brookes Publishing Co., Inc. All rights reserved.

IDIOMS LIST

1. **High time:** the proper time for something

2. To be on a **high horse:** acting as if one is better than others; acting superior

3. **Change my mind:** form a new opinion

4. **You have my word:** I promise

5. **Hit the books:** study hard

6. **Keep a stiff upper lip:** to be brave and not show feelings in a time of trouble

7. **Keep** something **under your hat:** to keep something secret

8. **Kick the bucket:** to die

9. **Keep your fingers crossed:** to wish good luck and success for someone

10. **Let the cat out of the bag:** to give away a secret

11. **Lend an ear:** to listen and pay attention

12. **Long in the tooth:** aged; old

13. **Make** your **mouth water:** to look so good that you want to have it very much

14. **Make waves:** to cause trouble; to create a problem

15. **A needle in a haystack:** something hard or impossible to find

Vocabulary Improvement Program for English Language Learners and Their Classmates, 4th Grade, by Teresa Lively, Diane August, María Carlo, and Catherine Snow © 2003 Paul H. Brookes Publishing Co., Inc. All rights reserved.

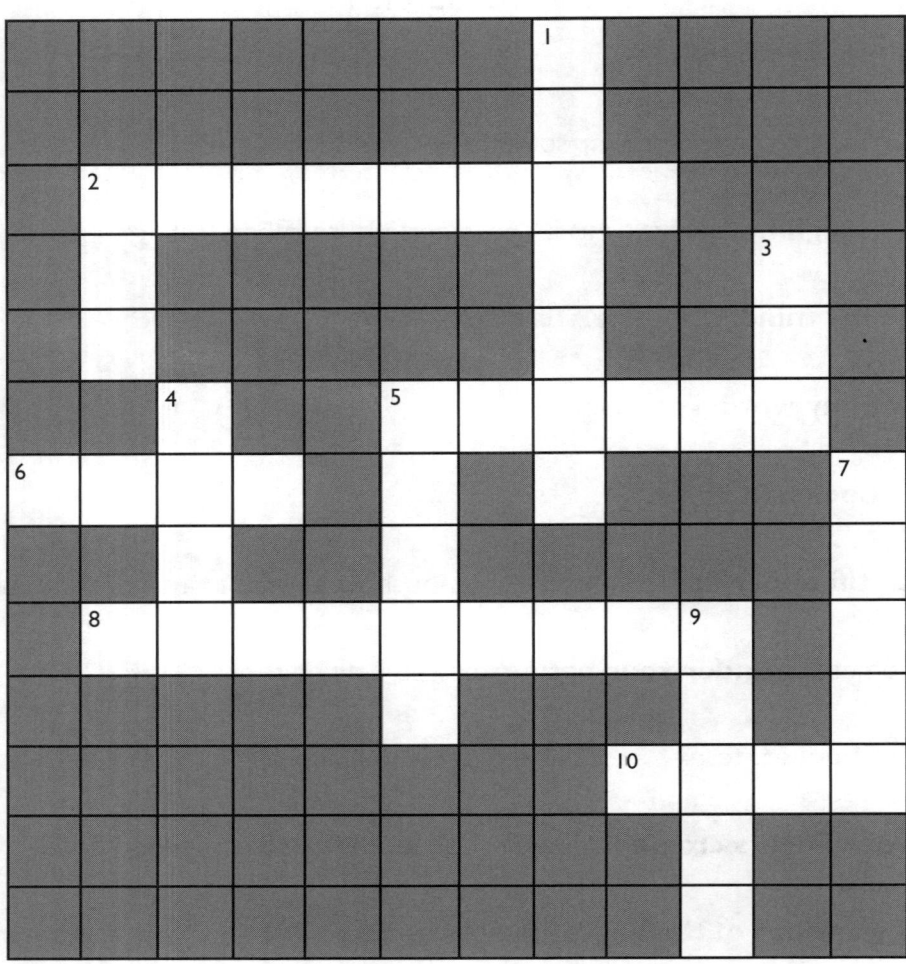

ACROSS

2. To defeat by being clever
5. To shake or move with a slight tremble; to vibrate
6. The flat and usually green parts of a plant or tree that grow out from a stem, twig, or branch
8. Very pleasing to taste or smell
10. The hard covering on the outside of a tree

DOWN

1. Proved beyond all doubt to be true
2. Strange or unusual
3. The soft, thick, hairy coat of an animal
4. Wild, uncontrollable anger
5. Rapid; fast
7. The main stem of a tree
9. Area sheltered from light

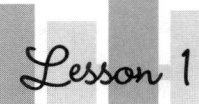

bark

certain

delicious

fur

leaf

odd

outsmart

quick

quiver

rage

shade

trunk

VOCABULARY ASSESSMENT WORKSHEET

• Circle the word that matches the definition.

1. The soft, thick, hairy coat of an animal
   odd   fur   quick   trunk

2. Flat and usually green parts of a plant or tree that grow out from a stem, twig, or branch
   quiver   certain   rage   leaf

3. Strange or unusual
   certain   fur   odd   leaf

4. Rapid; fast
   quick   rage   outsmart   odd

5. The main stem of a tree
   leaf   trunk   delicious   bark

6. Wild, uncontrollable anger
   rage   quiver   shade   certain

7. To shake or move with a slight tremble; to vibrate
   odd   trunk   outsmart   quiver

8. Proved beyond all doubt to be true
   fur   shade   delicious   certain

9. Area sheltered from light
   bark   outsmart   shade   leaf

10. Very pleasing to taste or smell
    rage   delicious   quick   odd

11. The hard covering on the outside of a tree
    quiver   certain   bark   leaf

12. To defeat by being clever
    outsmart   shade   certain   rage

Vocabulary Improvement Program for English Language Learners and Their Classmates, 4th Grade, by Teresa Lively, Diane August, María Carlo, and Catherine Snow © 2003 Paul H. Brookes Publishing Co., Inc. All rights reserved.

Name: _____

VOCABULARY ASSESSMENT
SENTENCES WORKSHEET

• Write a sentence with each of these four vocabulary words to show that you know what the word means.

<table>
<tr><td>bark</td><td>rage</td><td>outsmart</td><td>quiver</td></tr>
</table>

1. _____

   _____

2. _____

   _____

3. _____

   _____

4. _____

   _____

Vocabulary Improvement Program for English Language Learners and Their Classmates, 4th Grade, by Teresa Lively, Diane August, María Carlo, and Catherine Snow © 2003 Paul H. Brookes Publishing Co., Inc. All rights reserved.

The Baboon's Umbrella

OVERVIEW OF ACTIVITIES

Day 1	Day 2	Day 3	Day 4
TEXT INTRODUCTION	**VOCABULARY INTRODUCTION**	**EXPAND MEANING**	**WORD WIZARD INTRODUCTION**
• Predict storyline • Read fable • Discuss fable	• Circle vocabulary • Extract definitions • Assign homework	• Review homework • Related Words	• Introduce Word Wizard • Assign homework

Day 5	Day 6	Day 7	Day 8
TOOLS TO DEVELOP VOCABULARY	**USING WORDS IN CONTEXT**	**WORD WIZARD REVIEW**	**ASSESSMENT**
• Word Webs	• Contexting activity • Assign homework	• Review homework • Review Word Wizard	

WORD LIST

The word in bold is the base word, followed by its definition. If the word has more than one meaning, then we provide only the definition used in the text. *Please review the definitions prior to instruction.*

1. **advice:** a suggestion about what someone should do

2. **annoy:** to make someone lose patience or feel angry

3. **baboon:** a large monkey that lives in the jungle

4. **delightful:** giving great pleasure

5. **disagreeable:** uncooperative; bad tempered

6. **gibbon:** a small ape with long, slender arms and no tail

7. **jungle:** land in warm, tropical areas near the equator, covered with trees, vines, and bushes

8. **predicament:** an awkward or difficult situation

9. **scissors:** a sharp tool with two blades used for cutting paper or fabric

10. **solution:** the answer to a problem

11. **stuck:** fixed in a particular position

12. **underneath:** under or below

IDIOMATIC EXPRESSIONS

- **soaked to the skin:** thoroughly wet

OTHER WORDS WORTH DEFINING

- **pour:** rain that falls hard and steadily

Day 1
TEXT INTRODUCTION

▼ **Prepare for activity**

Post Classroom Word List.

Materials: Student Word Books, *Fables*

▼ **Predict storyline**

Show students the illustration for "The Baboon's Umbrella" in the color insert or turn to page 13 of *Fables*.

Say: *Today we are going to read the fable "The Baboon's Umbrella." What do you think this fable will be about when you look at the illustration and hear the title?*

Encourage a student discussion.

▼ **Ask the students to listen as you read the fable aloud**

▼ **Discuss the fable and moral; relate it to the students' lives**

- *Who are the main characters in this fable?*
- *Have any of you ever seen a baboon or gibbon?*
- *Have you ever heard them talk? Of course not! Pretending that they **can** talk makes the story more interesting and fun.*
- *What was Baboon's problem at the beginning of the fable?*
- *What was Baboon's problem at the end of the fable?*
- *What caused Baboon's problem at the end of the fable?*

▼ **Reread the moral**

- *What do you think the moral means?*
- *Is it always a good idea to follow a friend's advice? Why or why not?*

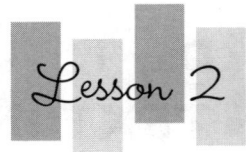

The Baboon's Umbrella

The **Baboon** was taking his daily walk in the **jungle.** He met his friend, the **Gibbon,** on the path.

"My good friend," said the Gibbon, "how strange to find you holding an open umbrella over your head on such a sunshiny day as this."

"Yes," said the Baboon. "I am most **annoyed.** I cannot close this **disagreeable** umbrella. It is **stuck.** I would not think of walking without my umbrella in case it should rain. But, as you see, I am not able to enjoy the sunshine **underneath** this dark shadow. It is a sad **predicament**."

"There is a simple **solution**," said the Gibbon, "You need only to cut some holes in your umbrella. Then the sun will shine on you."

"What a good idea!" cried the Baboon. "I do thank you."

The Baboon ran home. With his **scissors,** he cut large holes in the top of his umbrella. When the Baboon returned to his walk, the warm sunshine came down through the holes.

"How **delightful**," said the Baboon.

However, the sun disappeared behind some clouds. There were a few drops of rain. Then it began to pour. The rain fell through all of the holes in the umbrella. In just a short time, the unhappy Baboon was soaked to the skin.

Advice from friends is like the weather. Some of it is good; some of it is bad.

From *Fables* by Arnold Lobel. © 1980 by Arnold Lobel. Reproduced by permission from HarperCollins Publishers.

Day 2
VOCABULARY INTRODUCTION

Lesson 2

▼ Review the sections titled "Idiomatic Expressions" and "Other Words Worth Defining"

▼ Read posted target words to students, or ask students to read them

- Before you reread the fable, say: *Follow along in your Student Word Book as I read the fable again. Circle each target word when I read it. If you think you know what the word means **without reading the definition,** then raise your hand, and I will call on you.* After students have suggested meanings, say: *Let's check the definition to see how close you were.*

    Note: The target words appear in the same order in the fable as on the word list. To help students find the words more easily, point out each target word on the list before looking for it in the text.

- Meaning can be inferred for **scissors** and **stuck.** When you reach **scissors,** say: *Sometimes you can figure out what a word means by skipping over it and finishing the sentence. Or, you can reread the sentence while thinking about what the word might mean. Let me show you how this works by reading the sentence with **scissors** in it. "With his scissors he **cut** large holes in the top of his umbrella." I see that scissors can cut because it says that Baboon cut holes in his umbrella with them. Let's look up the definition to see if that's what it means.*

- When you reach **stuck** (related to **cannot close**), ask students to "think aloud" to explain how the clues in the fable can help them figure out what the word means. You may need to continue modeling the strategy.

▼ Assign Vocabulary Review homework

Instruct students to write the correct vocabulary word in the space beside the definition.

TARGET WORD DEFINITIONS

- The base word is bold and is the word defined.
- If there is more than one meaning, then the bold definition is the one used in the fable.
- The Spanish translation is provided for the meaning used in the fable.

1. **advice**
   a suggestion about what someone should do
   - consejo; sugerencia, parecer, o dictamen que se da o toma con respecto a algo

2. annoyed (**annoy**)
   to make someone lose patience or feel angry
   - enfadado; irritado, enojado, disgustado

3. **baboon**
   a large monkey that lives in the jungle
   - mandril; mono de gran tamaño que vive en la jungla (selva)

4. **delightful**
   giving great pleasure
   - que deleita; que produce placer

5. **disagreeable**
   a) describing something or someone that causes discomfort
   b) uncooperative; bad tempered
   - desagradable; de mal genio

6. **gibbon**
   a small ape with long, slender arms and no tail
   - mono pequeño de brazos largos y delgados, sin rabo

7. **jungle**
   land in warm, tropical areas near the equator covered with trees, vines, and bushes
   - jungla; terreno de vegetación muy espesa (selva)

8. **predicament**
   an awkward or difficult situation
   - apuro o predicamento; aprieto, conflicto, dificultad

9. **scissors**
   a sharp tool with two blades used for cutting paper or fabric
   - tijeras; instrumento compuesto de dos cuchillos de un sólo filo que se usa para cortar

10. **solution**
    a) the answer to a problem
    b) a liquid mixture
    - solución; respuesta a una duda o dificultad

11. **stuck**
    fixed in a particular position
    - atorado; atascado

12. **underneath**
    under or below
    - debajo

Day 3

EXPAND MEANING:
Related Words

▼ **Review Vocabulary Review homework**

1. Ask students for answers.

2. Ask students to correct their own answers if needed.

▼ **Prepare for activity**

1. Place students in heterogeneous language groups of three to four students.

2. Write the following example on the board:

happy is to sad

as

cold is to _____

Materials: Related Words worksheet for each student

▼ **Introduce the concept: Related Words**

Say: *Words can be related to each other in many ways. They can be antonyms, synonyms, or related in another way.*

Review the following concepts with the students:

• Synonyms are words that have the same or similar meanings (happy and joyful).

• Antonyms are words that have opposite meanings (happy and sad).

• Related words are words that are associated in another way (happy and smile).

▼ **Introduce the activity**

Say: *In this activity, your job is to find relationships between pairs of words. For example, the first part of the sentence gives a pair of words that are antonyms, synonyms, or related in another way.*

Point to the example on the board. *For example, happy is to sad—happy is **the opposite of** sad. In the second part of the sentence there is another word and a space to be filled in with a vocabulary word. The words are related in the same way as the words in the first part of the sentence. Happy **is the opposite of** sad, and cold **is the opposite of** _____?*

You will work in your groups to figure out which vocabulary word fits in the space on the Related Words worksheet.

Day 3: EXPAND MEANING

▼ **Review the activity**

Ask students to state the relationship between the word pairs: Are they synonyms, antonyms, or related in another way?

▼ **Prepare for activity**

Word Wizard is an ongoing activity designed to enhance student involvement with the target vocabulary by looking for target words in students' everyday activities, both at school and at home. You will need to do the following before starting this lesson:

1. Arrange bulletin board space or poster for posting each group's sentences.
2. Give students index cards or sticky notes.
3. Make copies of the Word Wizard List for each student.
4. Divide students into heterogeneous language groups.

▼ **Introduce Word Wizard**

Say: *One of the games we will be playing this week is called Word Wizard. Who knows what a wizard is?* (Students suggest meanings.)

*Yes, you're right! The term **wizard** could be used to refer to someone who is a magician or sorcerer. But, we also use the term wizard to refer to someone who is very clever or skillful. For example, a math wizard is someone who is very clever at math. So, what do you think a word wizard is?* (Students suggest meanings.)

Yes! A word wizard is someone who is very smart and clever about words. In this game, we are all going to be word wizards. Wizards are always trying to show their wizardry, so we need to always be on the lookout for opportunities to use and demonstrate our wizardry.

Now I want you to demonstrate your wizardry in the following ways: Each time you read or hear one of the words on this list used in a sentence at home, on television, in a book, or here at school, I want you to write the sentence on an index card or sticky note. Next week, each group will read their sentences to the class and put them on the wall!

If you use the vocabulary words in other lessons, then it will help the students learn to listen for the words. You may need to emphasize the words the first few times until the students have become accustomed to listening for the words out of context.

You may choose to encourage participation by introducing the element of competition.

▼ **Assign homework**

1. Send home the Word Wizard List and two index cards (or sticky notes) with each student.
2. Make additional cards available to students to keep in their desks.

TOOLS TO DEVELOP VOCABULARY: Word Webs

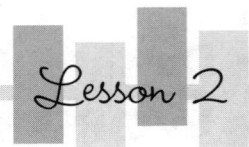

Lesson 2

▼ **Prepare for activity**

Divide students into heterogeneous language groups of four to five students.

Materials: three blank Word Web worksheets for each group, dictionaries, Student Word Books

You may choose to make the Word Webs into transparencies and complete the activity as a whole group.

▼ **Introduce the concept**

The objective of this lesson is for students to study word meanings, usage, and relationships by completing a Word Web.

Say: *Today you will complete an activity that will help you think carefully about words in order to understand them better. Each group will study one vocabulary word from this week's lesson and see if they can find synonyms, antonyms, other forms of the word, and other meanings and write a new sentence with the word.*

You will analyze three words from the text: **annoy, delightful,** and **disagreeable.**

1. Begin by writing the target word in the center box.
2. Locate the target word in the text in the Student Word Book.
3. Record the sentence containing the target word in the corresponding box (i.e., "Sentence from fable").
4. Write the definition in the appropriate box (i.e., 'Definition"); students may refer to their Student Word Book if needed.
5. Complete the remaining information boxes on the Word Web using dictionaries as needed.

▼ **Review the activity**

Ask each group to share their completed Word Webs.

Day 6
USING WORDS IN CONTEXT

Lesson 2

Using Words in Context is designed to develop students' ability to decipher the meaning of a word by using clues in the surrounding text.

▼ **Prepare for activity**

Place students in heterogeneous language groups, ideally four to five students.

Materials: Using Words in Context worksheet for each student

   If this activity is challenging for your students, then you may choose to complete it as a whole-group activity. It is helpful to make the worksheet into a transparency so that you can point out the context clues.

▼ **Introduce the activity**

Say: *Today's activity will help you practice using the vocabulary words in sentences. Your job is to figure out which word fits in the blank using the clues that are in the sentence. After you figure out the right word, think about* **how** *you figured it out; what were the clues in the rest of the sentence that helped you. When everyone in the group knows the correct word and* **why it fits,** *raise your hands.* The context clues are bold in some sentences to help students learn how to look for the clues in the text. *I'll call on one of the first groups who are ready. You will get a point if you get the correct answer* (you may choose not to use points). *Remember, everyone in your group must know the answer and why it is correct.*

   Read the first sentence aloud to the class to illustrate the process.

▼ **Review the activity**

Ask one student at a table for the correct answer **and to explain how he or she figured it out**—which clues in the context helped. Explaining the thought process that led to the answer helps the students realize that they know how to use the clues in the text and will demonstrate the process to those students who have not yet developed the skill.

   Continue until the lesson is completed, giving each group one point for the correct answer (you may choose not to use points).

▼ **Assign homework**

Give students the crossword puzzle; review the instructions and the due date.

Day 7

WORD WIZARD REVIEW

Lesson 2

▼ **Review the crossword puzzle homework**

1. Ask students for answers.

2. Direct students to correct their own answers if needed.

3. The crossword puzzle answer key for Lessons 1–5 can be found in the Teacher Answer Keys for Lesson 1.

▼ **Prepare for activity**

Instruct students to divide into their Word Wizard groups, taking the sentences they have collected throughout the week.

▼ **Review Word Wizard**

• Allow students a few minutes to share sentences within their group and tell where they heard or read the word.

• Ask each group to share a few sentences with the class.

  Hint: The more enthusiasm you demonstrate and motivation you provide for this activity, the more the students will participate. Once the students are "hooked," it is rewarding to observe their enthusiasm and to know that they have incorporated the vocabulary activities into other areas of their lives. In the beginning, you may want to bring in a few examples of your own for extra motivation.

• Allow students to post their sentences on the Word Wizard Wall.

  You may choose to give the teams points to encourage participation.

▼ **Vocabulary assessment**

Part 1: Instruct the students to circle the word that corresponds to the definition on the Vocabulary Assessment worksheet.

Part 2: Instruct students to write sentences that demonstrate their knowledge of the word's meaning on the Vocabulary Assessment Sentences worksheet.

Hint: You may need to provide examples of sentences that demonstrate knowledge of the meaning. For example, if the vocabulary word were **ring,** then the sentence "I have a ring" does not demonstrate knowledge of the meaning. **Nose, car, friend, house**, or any number of other words could be substituted for **ring** in the sentence. The sentence "I wear a ring on my finger" demonstrates knowledge of the meaning.

Teacher answer keys

VOCABULARY REVIEW HOMEWORK

- Read the definitions.
- Find the word in the box that matches the definition.
- Write the correct word next to the definition.

annoy	baboon	scissors	stuck
underneath	gibbon	delightful	jungle
predicament	solution	advice	disagreeable

1. __**advice**__ : a suggestion about what someone should do

2. __**scissors**__ : a sharp tool with two blades used for cutting paper or fabric

3. __**annoy**__ : to make someone lose patience or feel angry

4. __**predicament**__ : an awkward or difficult situation

5. __**solution**__ : the answer to a problem

6. __**baboon**__ : a large monkey that lives in the jungle

7. __**jungle**__ : land in warm, tropical areas near the equator covered with trees, vines, and bushes

8. __**stuck**__ : fixed in a particular position

9. __**underneath**__ : under or below

10. __**delightful**__ : giving great pleasure

11. __**gibbon**__ : a small ape with long, slender arms and no tail

12. __**disagreeable**__ : uncooperative; bad tempered

RELATED WORDS WORKSHEET

1. Arctic is to polar bear as jungle is to   __**baboon or gibbon**__ .
     The Arctic is where polar bears live.
     The jungle is where baboons and gibbons live.

2. Bread is to knife as paper is to __**scissors**__ .
     Bread is cut by a knife.
     Paper is cut by scissors.

3. Question is to answer as problem is to __**solution**__ .
     Antonyms

4. Dog is to collie as ape is to __**gibbon**__ .
     One type of dog is a collie.
     One type of ape is a gibbon.

5. Ice is to cold as glue is to __**stuck**__ .
     Ice causes things to become cold.
     Glue causes things to become stuck.

6. Top is to bottom as above is to __**underneath**__ .
     Antonyms

7. Unpleasant is to disagreeable as pleasant is to __**delightful**__ .
     Synonyms

8. Good is to bad as please is to __**annoy**__ .
     Antonyms

9. Dry is to desert as humid is to __**jungle**__ .
     It is dry in the desert.
     It is humid in the jungle.

10. Difficult is to hard as problem is to __**predicament**__ .
     Synonyms

11. "What" is to question as "You should..." is to __**advice**__ .
     Questions often begin with "what."
     Advice often begins with "you should."

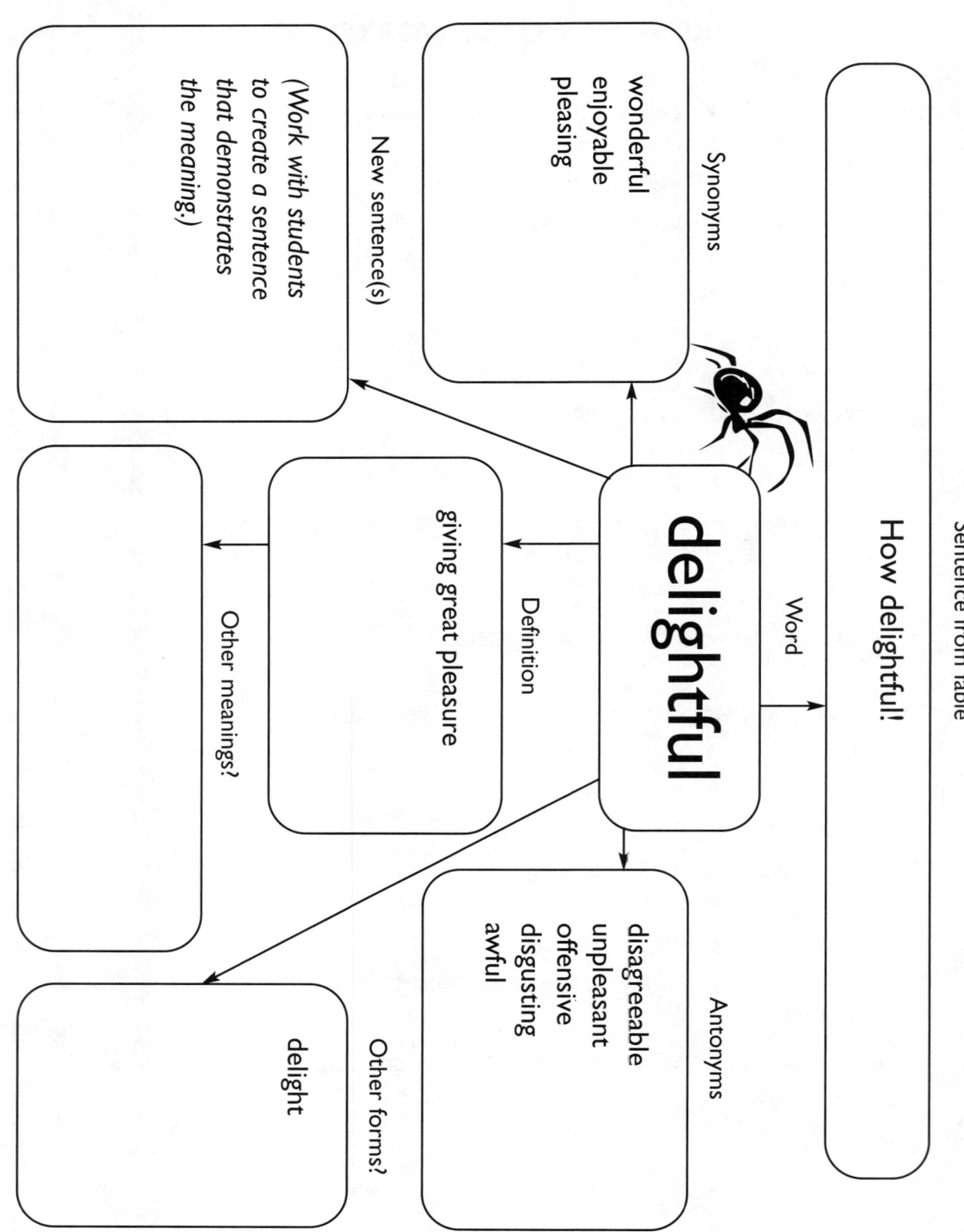

Synonyms

wonderful
enjoyable
pleasing

New sentence(s)

(Work with students
to create a sentence
that demonstrates
the meaning.)

Sentence from fable

How delightful!

Word

delightful

Definition

giving great pleasure

Other meanings?

Antonyms

disagreeable
unpleasant
offensive
disgusting
awful

Other forms?

delight

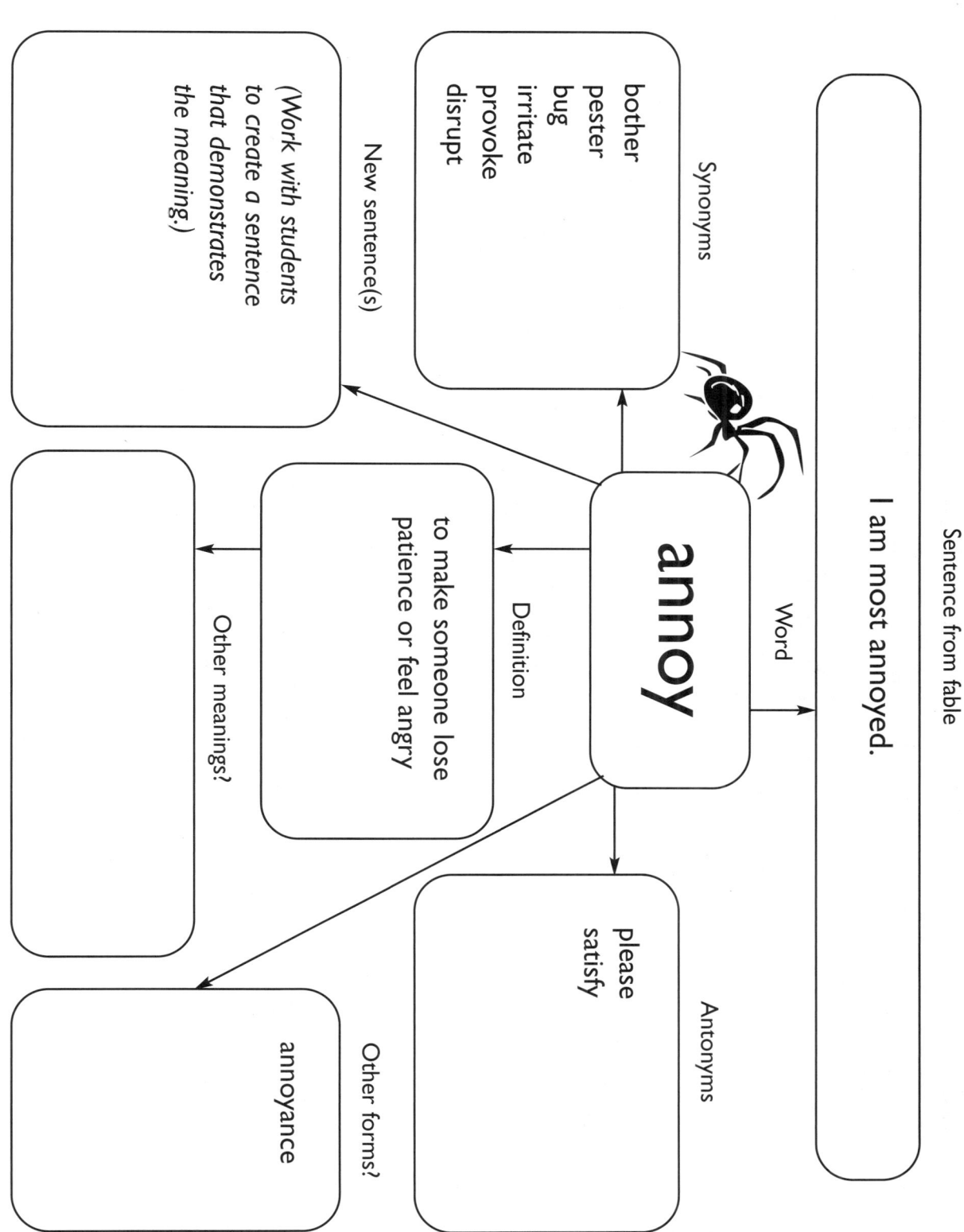

Sentence from fable

I am most annoyed.

Word

annoy

Synonyms

bother
pester
bug
irritate
provoke
disrupt

New sentence(s)

(Work with students to create a sentence that demonstrates the meaning.)

Definition

to make someone lose patience or feel angry

Other meanings?

Antonyms

please
satisfy

Other forms?

annoyance

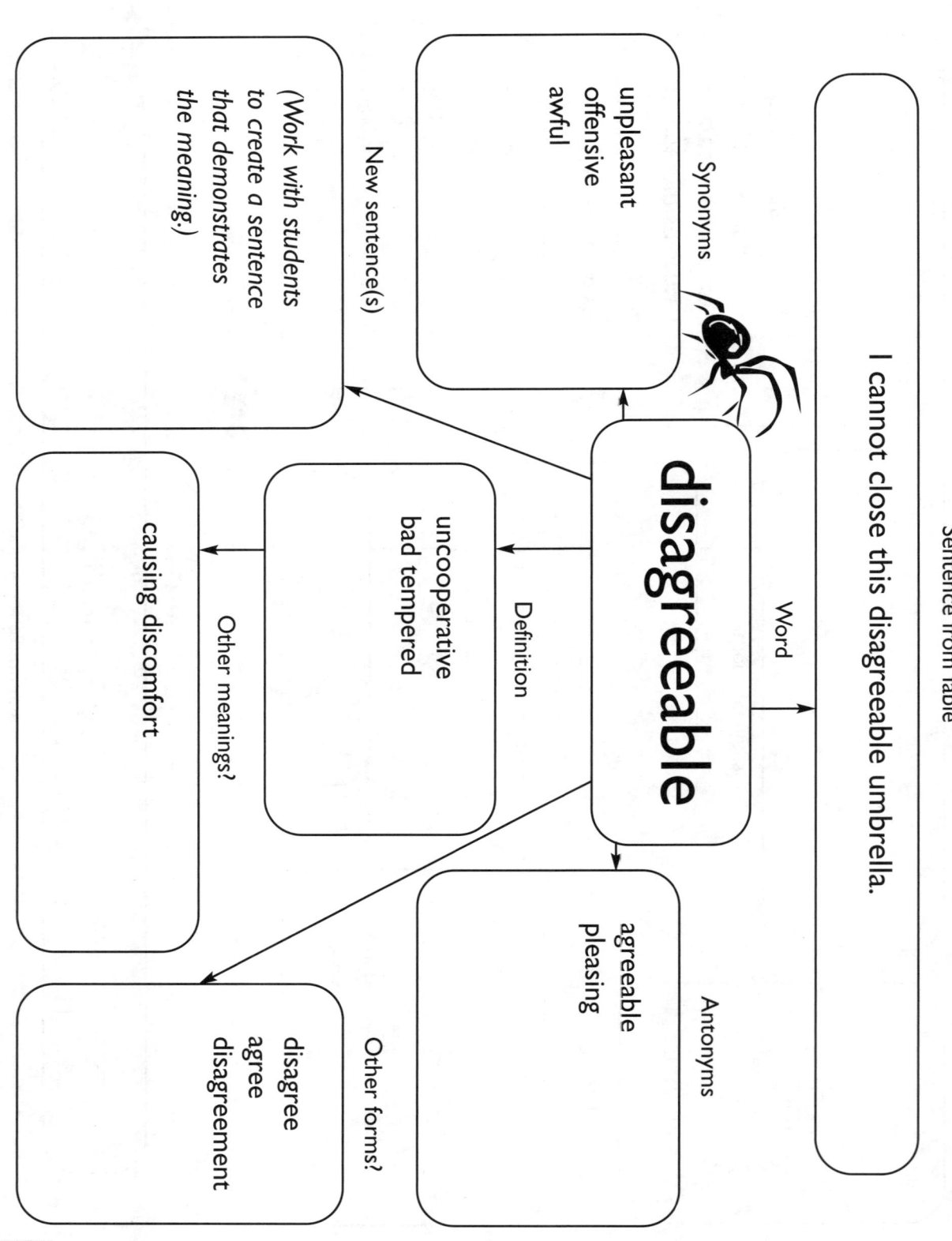

Synonyms

unpleasant
offensive
awful

New sentence(s)

(Work with students
to create a sentence
that demonstrates
the meaning.)

disagreeable

Word

I cannot close this disagreeable umbrella.

Sentence from fable

Definition

uncooperative
bad tempered

Other meanings?

causing discomfort

Antonyms

agreeable
pleasing

Other forms?

disagree
agree
disagreement

USING WORDS IN CONTEXT WORKSHEET

delightful	annoyed	baboon	stuck	disagreeable
gibbon	predicament	solution	advice	underneath

1. The animals in this fable are both **monkeys**.
   One is a ___**baboon**___, and the other is a ___**gibbon**___.

2. In this fable, Baboon was a **little angry** that his umbrella didn't open.
   He wasn't in a rage, but he was ___**annoyed**___.

3. Winnie the Pooh got his head ___**stuck**___ in a honey jar.

4. It's shady ___**underneath**___ the trees.

5. The woman thinks her **lovely** garden is ___**delightful**___.

6. The man is **not nice** to his neighbors.
   He is very ___**disagreeable**___.

7. I have a **problem**. My dog ate my homework.
   That's my ___**predicament**___.

8. My teacher **told** me **what to do**.
   She said, "Don't let your dog near your homework; that's my ___**advice**___."

9. I started putting my homework on a high shelf.
   That was the ___**solution**___ to my problem.

| advice | annoy | disagreeable | predicament |
| solution | solution | underneath | jungle |

10. Monkeys, such as the baboon and the gibbon, don't live in the city or in the desert, their habitat is the _____**jungle**_____.

11. The **top** of the desk was clean, but there was a lot of chewing gum stuck _____**underneath**_____.

12. If two friends invite you to birthday parties on the same day, then you have a _____**predicament**_____.

13. My brother didn't know what college to choose, so he asked my uncle for _____**advice**_____.

14. If you can't **solve** that crossword puzzle, look in the back of the book. The _____**solution**_____ to the puzzle is on page 99.

15. My mother cleans her contact lenses with **water and salt mixed** together. The salt **dissolves** in the water. This **liquid** is called "saline _____**solution**_____."

16. Sometimes when I'm watching television, my brother just comes in and changes the channel. I think he does it to _____**annoy**_____ me.

17. In the movie, *101 Dalmatians,* Cruella De Vil is **not nice or agreeable**. She is a most _____**disagreeable**_____ character.

VOCABULARY ASSESSMENT WORKSHEET

• Circle the word that matches the definition.

1. A suggestion about what someone should do

   jungle   predicament   (advice)   scissors

2. Uncooperative; bad tempered

   annoy   (disagreeable)   underneath   gibbon

3. An awkward or difficult situation

   stuck   delightful   baboon   (predicament)

4. Land in warm, tropical areas near the equator covered with trees, vines, and bushes

   (jungle)   advice   delightful   stuck

5. A sharp tool with two blades used for cutting paper or fabric

   gibbon   disagreeable   annoy   (scissors)

6. Under or below

   (underneath)   advice   scissors   predicament

7. Giving great pleasure

   solution   (delightful)   advice   jungle

8. A small ape with long, slender arms and no tail

   annoy   scissors   jungle   (gibbon)

9. Fixed in a particular position

   solution   disagreeable   (stuck)   baboon

10. The answer to a problem

    advice   (solution)   disagreeable   annoy

11. A large monkey that lives in the jungle

    scissors   underneath   (baboon)   delightful

12. To make someone lose patience or feel angry

    (annoy)   disagreeable   jungle   solution

Reproducible materials

The Baboon's Umbrella

CLASSROOM WORD LIST

gibbon

jungle

baboon

annoyed

disagreeable

stuck

underneath

predicament

solution

advice

delightful

scissors

VOCABULARY REVIEW HOMEWORK

- Read the definitions.
- Find the word in the box that matches the definition.
- Write the correct word next to the definition.

annoy	baboon	scissors	stuck
underneath	gibbon	delightful	jungle
predicament	solution	advice	disagreeable

1. _____ : a suggestion about what someone should do

2. _____ : a sharp tool with two blades used for cutting paper or fabric

3. _____ : to make someone lose patience or feel angry

4. _____ : an awkward or difficult situation

5. _____ : the answer to a problem

6. _____ : a large monkey that lives in the jungle

7. _____ : land in warm, tropical areas near the equator covered with trees, vines, and bushes

8. _____ : fixed in a particular position

9. _____ : under or below

10. _____ : giving great pleasure

11. _____ : a small ape with long, slender arms and no tail

12. _____ : uncooperative; bad tempered

Vocabulary Improvement Program for English Language Learners and Their Classmates, 4th Grade, by Teresa Lively, Diane August, María Carlo, and Catherine Snow © 2003 Paul H. Brookes Publishing Co., Inc. All rights reserved.

Name: _____

RELATED WORDS WORKSHEET

1. Arctic is to polar bear   **as**   jungle is to _____

2. Bread is to knife   **as**   paper is to _____

3. Question is to answer   **as**   problem is to _____

4. Dog is to collie   **as**   ape is to _____

5. Ice is to cold   **as**   glue is to _____

6. Top is to bottom   **as**   above is to _____

7. Unpleasant is to disagreeable   **as**   pleasant is to _____

8. Good is to bad   **as**   please is to _____

9. Dry is to desert   **as**   humid is to _____

10. Difficult is to hard   **as**   problem is to _____

11. "What" is to question   **as**   "You should…" is to _____

Vocabulary Improvement Program for English Language Learners and Their Classmates, 4th Grade, by Teresa Lively, Diane August, María Carlo, and Catherine Snow © 2003 Paul H. Brockes Publishing Co., Inc. All rights reserved.

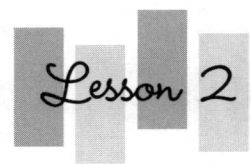

WORD WIZARD LIST

• Each time you hear or read one of these words used in a sentence at home, at school, on television, or on the radio, write the sentence on an index card or sticky note.

advice: a suggestion about what someone should do

annoyed (annoy): to make someone lose patience or feel angry

baboon: a large monkey that lives in the jungle

delightful: giving great pleasure

disagreeable: uncooperative; bad tempered

gibbon: a small ape with long, slender arms and no tail

jungle: land in warm, tropical areas near the equator covered with trees, vines, and bushes

predicament: an awkward or difficult situation

scissors: a sharp tool with two blades used for cutting paper or fabric

solution: the answer to a problem

stuck: fixed in a particular position

underneath: under or below

WORD WEB

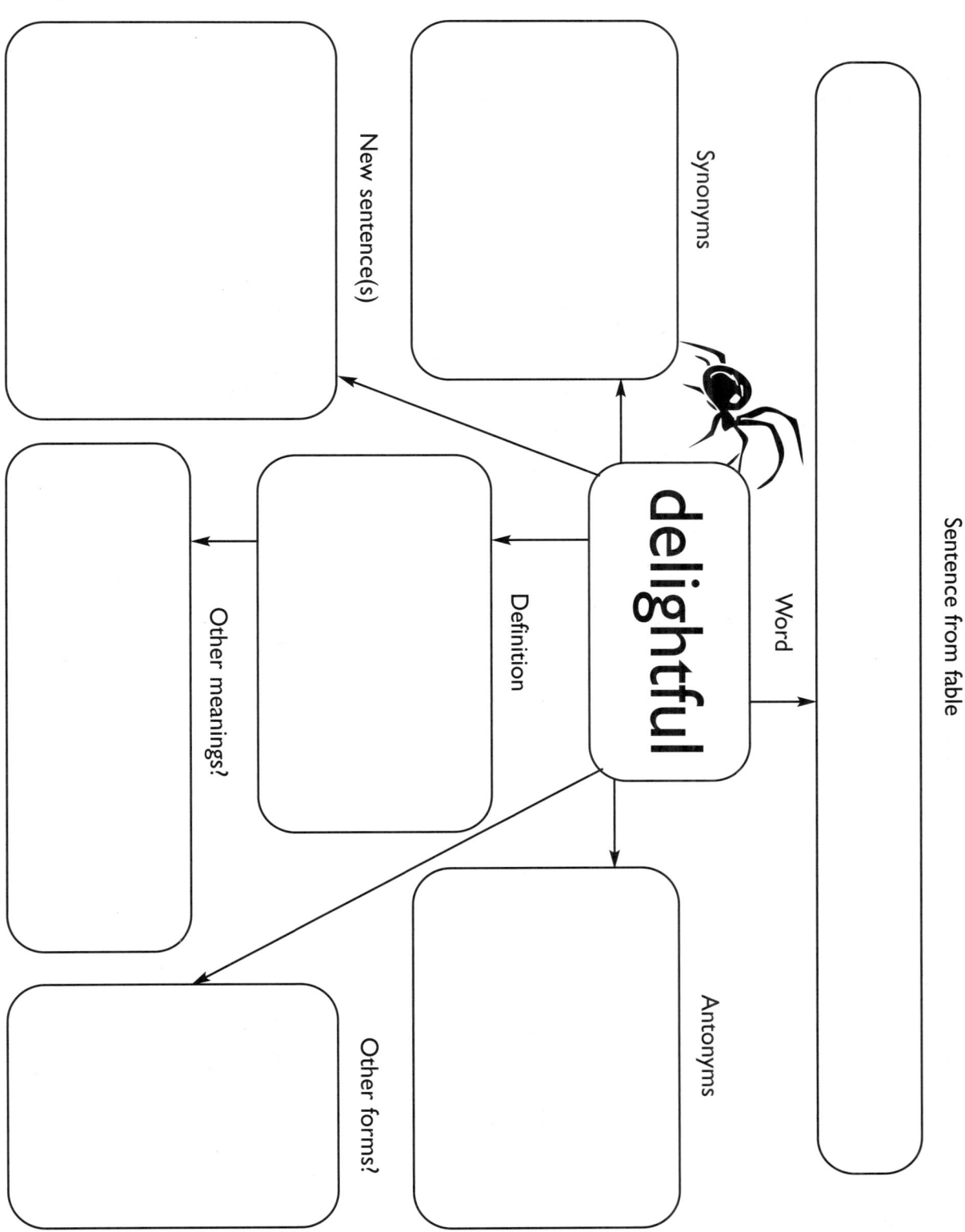

New sentence(s)

Synonyms

Sentence from fable

Other meanings?

Definition

delightful

Word

Other forms?

Antonyms

WORD WEB

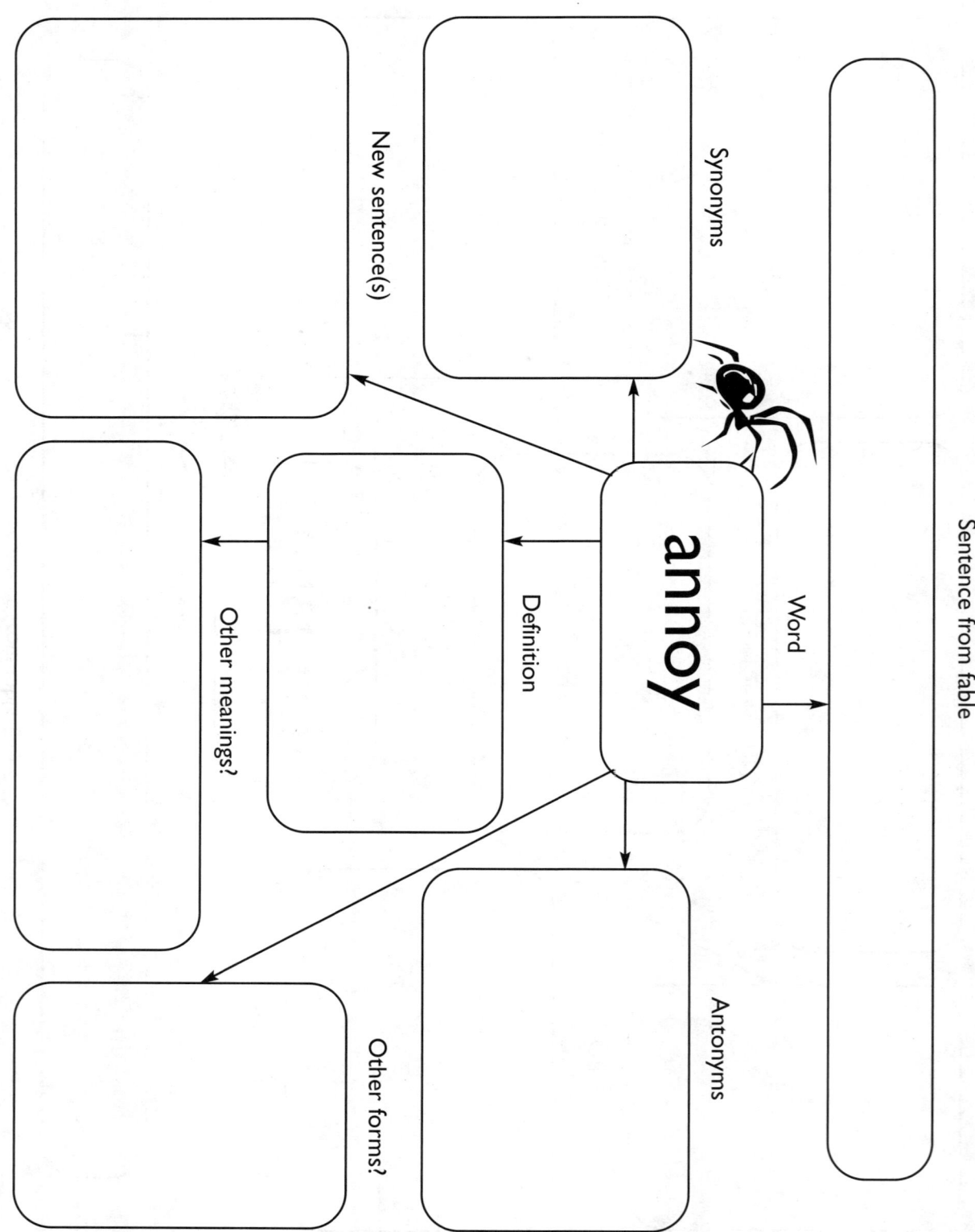

New sentence(s)

Synonyms

Other meanings?

Definition

annoy

Word

Sentence from fable

Other forms?

Antonyms

WORD WEB

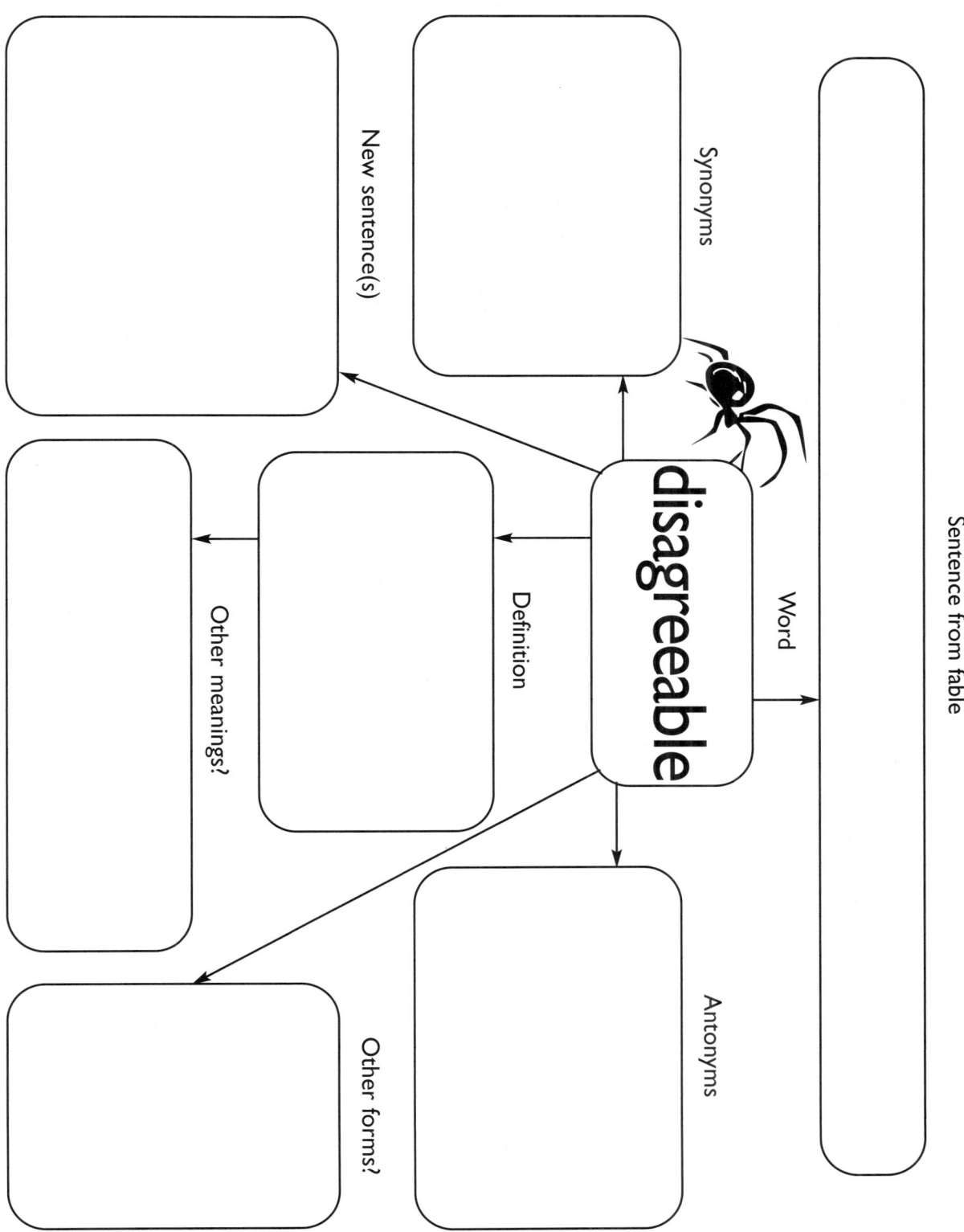

New sentence(s)

Synonyms

Other meanings?

Definition

disagreeable

Word

Sentence from fable

Other forms?

Antonyms

USING WORDS IN CONTEXT WORKSHEET

| delightful | annoyed | baboon | stuck | disagreeable |
| gibbon | predicament | solution | advice | underneath |

1. The animals in this fable are both **monkeys**.
   One is a _____, and the other is a _____.

2. In this fable, Baboon was a **little angry** that his umbrella didn't open.
   He wasn't in a rage, but he was _____.

3. Winnie the Pooh got his head _____ in a honey jar.

4. It's shady _____ the trees.

5. The woman thinks her **lovely** garden is _____.

6. The man is **not nice** to his neighbors.
   He is very _____.

7. I have a **problem**. My dog ate my homework.
   That's my _____.

8. My teacher **told** me **what to do**.
   She said, "Don't let your dog near your homework; that's my _____."

9. I started putting my homework on a high shelf.
   That was the _____ to my problem.

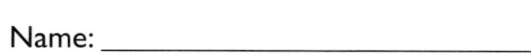

Name: _____

USING WORDS IN CONTEXT WORKSHEET *(continued)*

advice	annoy	disagreeable	predicament
solution	solution	underneath	jungle

10. Monkeys, such as the baboon and the gibbon, don't live in the city or in the desert, their habitat is the _____.

11. The **top** of the desk was clean, but there was a lot of chewing gum stuck

    _____.

12. If two friends invite you to birthday parties on the same day, then you have a

    _____.

13. My brother didn't know what college to choose, so he asked my uncle for

    _____.

14. If you can't **solve** that crossword puzzle, look in the back of the book. The _____ to the puzzle is on page 99.

15. My mother cleans her contact lenses with **water and salt mixed** together. The salt **dissolves** in the water. This **liquid** is called "saline _____."

16. Sometimes when I'm watching television, my brother just comes in and changes the channel. I think he does it to _____ me.

17. In the movie, *101 Dalmatians,* Cruella De Vil is **not nice or agreeable**. She is a most _____ character.

Name: _____

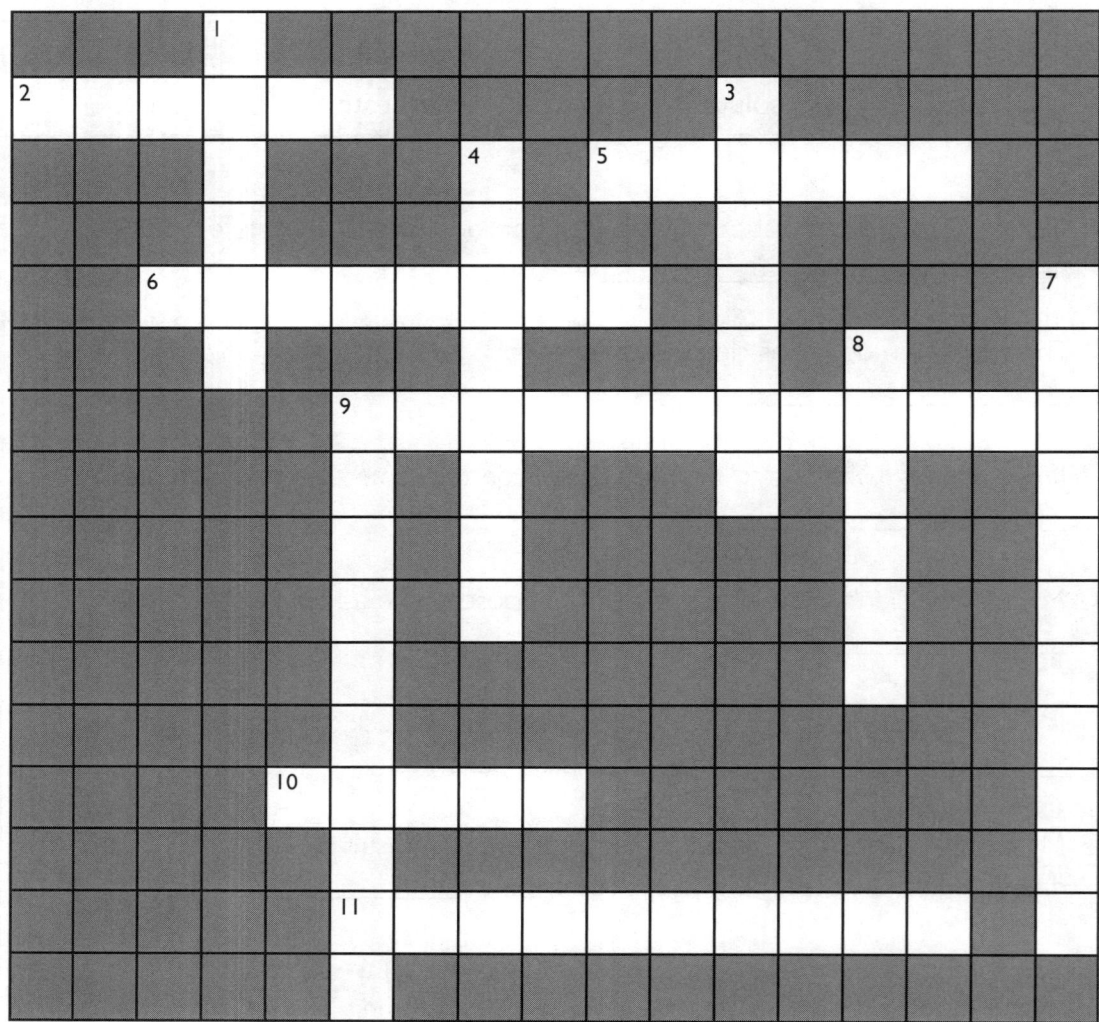

ACROSS

2. A suggestion about what someone should do
5. Land in warm, tropical areas near the equator covered with trees, vines, and bushes
6. The answer to a problem
9. Uncooperative; bad tempered
10. Fixed in a particular position
11. Under or below

DOWN

1. A small ape with long, slender arms and no tail
3. To make someone lose patience or feel angry
4. A sharp tool with two blades used for cutting paper or fabric
7. An awkward or difficult situation
8. A large monkey that lives in the jungle
9. Giving great pleasure

advice

annoyed

baboon

delightful

disagreeable

gibbon

jungle

predicament

scissors

solution

stuck

underneath

Vocabulary Improvement Program for English Language Learners and Their Classmates, 4th Grade, by Teresa Lively, Diane August, María Carlo, and Catherine Snow © 2003 Paul H. Brookes Publishing Co., Inc. All rights reserved.

Name: _____

Lesson 2

VOCABULARY ASSESSMENT WORKSHEET

• Circle the word that matches the definition.

1. A suggestion about what someone should do

    jungle   predicament   advice   scissors

2. Uncooperative; bad tempered

    annoy   disagreeable   underneath   gibbon

3. An awkward or difficult situation

    stuck   delightful   baboon   predicament

4. Land in warm, tropical areas near the equator covered with trees, vines, and bushes

    jungle   advice   delightful   stuck

5. A sharp tool with two blades used for cutting paper or fabric

    gibbon   disagreeable   annoy   scissors

6. Under or below

    underneath   advice   scissors   predicament

7. Giving great pleasure

    solution   delightful   advice   jungle

8. A small ape with long, slender arms and no tail

    annoy   scissors   jungle   gibbon

9. Fixed in a particular position

    solution   disagreeable   stuck   baboon

10. The answer to a problem

    advice   solution   disagreeable   annoy

11. A large monkey that lives in the jungle

    scissors   underneath   baboon   delightful

12. To make someone lose patience or feel angry

    annoy   disagreeable   jungle   solution

Lesson 2

VOCABULARY ASSESSMENT
SENTENCES WORKSHEET

Write a sentence with each of the four vocabulary words to show that you know what the word means.

advice   predicament   stuck   underneath

1. _____

_____

2. _____

_____

3. _____

_____

4. _____

_____

The Poor Old Dog

▼ OVERVIEW OF ACTIVITIES

Day 1	Day 2	Day 3	Day 4
TEXT INTRODUCTION	**VOCABULARY INTRODUCTION**	**EXPAND MEANING**	**TOOLS TO DEVELOP VOCABULARY**
• Predict storyline • Read fable • Discuss fable	• Circle vocabulary • Extract definitions • Assign homework	• Review homework • Word associations • Assign homework	• Cognates

Day 5	Day 6	Day 7	Day 8
USING WORDS IN CONTEXT	**TOOLS TO DEVELOP VOCABULARY**	**WORD WIZARD REVIEW**	**ASSESSMENT**
• Contexting activity	• Prefixes • Assign homework	• Review homework • Word Wizard review	

▼ WORD LIST

The word in bold is the base word, followed by its definition. If the word has more than one meaning, then we provide only the definition used in the text. *Please review the definitions prior to instruction.*

1. **bulge:** to swell or curve outward
2. **cozy:** comfortable or snug
3. **curb:** a raised border along the edge of a paved street
4. **gutter:** a channel or length of tubing through which rain is drained away from a road or from the roof of a building
5. **overjoyed:** extremely happy
6. **passerby:** someone who happens to be going past
7. **pavement:** a hard material, such as concrete or asphalt, that is used to cover roads or sidewalks
8. **profuse:** plentiful or more than enough
9. **ragged:** old, torn, and worn out
10. **reward:** something that is received for doing something good or useful
11. **tattered:** old and torn
12. **wealthy:** having a large amount of money or property

IDIOMATIC EXPRESSIONS

- none this week

OTHER WORDS WORTH DEFINING

- **soles:** bottoms of shoes, boots, or socks
- **pebbles:** small, round stones
- **lamppost:** a tall support for a lamp that lights a public area

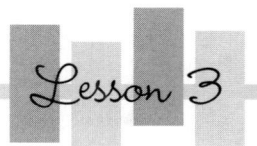

TEXT INTRODUCTION

▼ **Prepare for activity**

Post Classroom Word List.

Materials: Student Word Books, *Fables*

▼ **Predict storyline**

Show students the illustration for "The Poor Old Dog," in the color insert or turn to page 24 of *Fables*.

Say: *Today we are going to read the fable "The Poor Old Dog." What do you think this fable will be about when you look at the illustration and hear the title?*

Encourage a student discussion.

▼ **Ask the students to listen as you read the fable aloud**

▼ **Discuss the fable and moral; relate it to the students' lives**

- *Who are the main characters in this fable?*
- *Have you ever seen a poor, old dog?*
- *How would you know that a dog was poor and old?*
- *What did old Dog spend most of his time doing at the beginning of the fable?*
- *What happened to old Dog that changed his life?*
- *Have you ever found anything special?*
- *How did old Dog's life change?*

▼ **Reread the moral**

- *What do you think the moral means?*
- *Have you ever had to wait a long time for something you wanted very much?*

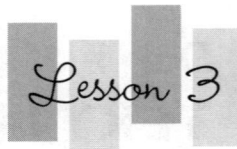

The Poor
Old Dog

There was an old Dog who was very poor. The only coat he had to wear was mostly holes held together by **ragged** threads. He could feel the pebbles on the **pavement** through the thin soles of his **tattered** shoes. He slept in the park because he had no home.

The Dog spent most of his time searching in garbage cans. He found bits of string and buttons. These he sold for pennies to **passersby.**

The Dog always walked with his nose close to the **curb,** looking for things to sell. That is how he came to find the gold ring that was lying in the **gutter.**

"My luck has changed," cried the Dog, "for I am sure that this is a magic ring!"

The Dog rubbed the ring and said, "I wish for a new coat. I wish for new shoes. I wish for a house to live in. I wish these things would come true right now!"

But nothing happened. The Dog felt the wind through the holes in his coat. He felt the pebbles under his thin shoes. That night he slept in his usual bench in the park.

Several days later, the Dog saw a note on a lamppost. The note said "Lost: gold ring. Large **reward.** Mr. Terrier. Ten **Wealthy** Lane."

The old Dog hurried to Wealthy Lane. Mr. Terrier was **overjoyed** to have his ring returned. He thanked the Dog **profusely** and gave him a **bulging** purse full of coins.

The Dog bought a warm fur coat. He bought a pair of good shoes with thick soles.

There was a large amount of money left over. The Dog used the rest of it as a down payment on a **cozy** little house. He moved right in and never had to sleep in the park again.

Wishes, on their way to coming true, will not be rushed.

▼ Review the section titled "Other Words Worth Defining"

▼ Read posted target words to students, or ask students to read them

- Before you reread the fable, say: *Follow along in your Student Word Book as I read the fable again. Circle each target word as I read it. If you think you know what the word means **without reading the definition,** then raise your hand, and I will call on you.* After students have suggested meanings, say: *Let's check the definition to see how close you were.*

    Note: The target words appear in the same order in the fable as on the word list. To help students find the words more easily, point out each target word on the list before looking for it in the text.

- Meaning can be inferred for **tattered** and **bulging**. When you reach **tattered,** say: *Sometimes you can figure out what a word means by skipping over it and finishing the sentence. Or, you can reread the sentence while thinking about what the word might mean. Let me show you how this works by reading the sentence with **tattered** in it. "He could **feel the pebbles** on the pavement through the **thin** soles of his tattered shoes." Let's see, he could feel the pebbles through the soles of his shoes. It also says that the soles of his shoes are thin. So, do you think his shoes are new? I wonder if **tattered** has something to do with being old and worn out. Let's look up the definition to see if that's what it means.*

- When you reach **bulging** (related to **full of coins**), ask students to "think aloud" to explain how the clues in the fable can help them figure out what the word means. You may need to continue modeling the strategy.

- When you reach **stuck** (related to **cannot close**), ask students to "think aloud" to explain how the clues in the fable can help them figure out what the word means. You may need to continue modeling the strategy.

▼ Assign Vocabulary Review homework

Instruct students to write the correct vocabulary word in the space beside the definition.

TARGET WORD DEFINITIONS

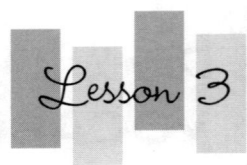

- The base word is bold and is the word defined.
- If there is more than one meaning, then the bold definition is the one used in the fable.
- The Spanish translation is provided for the meaning used in the fable.

1. bulging (**bulge**)
   to swell or curve outward
   - protuberante; que sobresale

2. **cozy**
   comfortable or snug
   - cómodo

3. **curb**
   a) **a raised border along the edge of a paved street**
   b) to control or hold something back
   - orilla de la acera

4. **gutter**
   a channel or length of tubing through which rain is drained away from a road or from the roof of a building
   - cuneta; zanja en cada uno de los lados de un camino o carretera que canaliza el agua de la lluvia

5. **overjoyed**
   extremely happy
   - lleno de alegria; contento

6. passersby (**passerby**)
   someone who happens to be going past
   - transeúnte; alguien que transita o pasa por un lugar

7. **pavement**
   a hard material, such as concrete or asphalt, that is used to cover roads or sidewalks
   - pavimento; piso artificial de concreto o asfalto que cubre aceras o carreteras

8. profusely (**profuse**)
   plentiful or more than enough
   - abundantemente; generosamente; en gran cantidad

9. **ragged**
   old, torn, and worn out
   - harapiento, andrajoso; viejo y muy usado

10. **reward**
    something that is received for doing something good or useful
    - recompensa, se otorga para premiar un favor, virtud o mérito

11. **tattered**
    old and torn
    - andrajoso; viejo y roto

12. **wealthy**
    having a large amount of money or property
    - adinerado, rico; que posee gran cantidad de dinero o propiedades

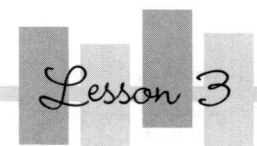
EXPAND MEANING:
Word Association

▼ **Review Vocabulary Review homework**

1. Ask students for answers.

2. Direct students to correct their own answers if needed.

▼ **Introduce the activity**

Say: *I am going to say a word or phrase that has something to do with one of the vocabulary words, kind of like a clue. Your job is to think about which vocabulary word goes with the clue.*

Give clues one at a time until the word is guessed. Say: *What vocabulary word do you think of when I say ――――――? Please explain why you think the vocabulary word goes with the clue.*

Accept any plausible answer that the student can justify.

Associated word	Vocabulary word
massive; fat; huge; stuffed	bulging
sidewalk; street; crash; cement	curb
rain; water; flood	gutter
happy; excited; fun	overjoyed
cement; asphalt; freeway	pavement
generously; abundantly	profusely
old; bum; rough-edged	ragged
comfortable; snuggle; toasty	cozy
money; prize; medal; trophy	reward
rich; well-to-do; money; abundant	wealthy
worn; well-used; ripped; shredded	tattered

Note: Encourage students to think of associated words for their classmates to guess, including synonyms and antonyms.

▼ **Word Wizard**

Motivate students to find sentences with this week's vocabulary. Say: *You are all going to continue being word wizards and even build your skills with this week's vocabulary words! Just like last week, I want you to demonstrate your wizardry in the following way: Each time you hear or read one of this week's words used at home, at school, or even on television, I want you to write the sentence on an index card (or sticky note). Write down where you heard or read it.*

Give students the Word Wizard List.

TOOLS TO DEVELOP VOCABULARY: Cognates

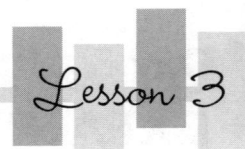

▼ **Prepare for activity**

1. Divide students into four heterogeneous language teams.
2. Give each team a Looking for Cognates worksheet.

▼ **Introduce the concept: Cognates**

Say: *Cognates are words that have similar spellings in English and Spanish and are related in meaning. For example, what do you think* **horrores** *(horrors) means in English?* **León** *(lion)?* **Océano** *(ocean)?* **However,** *there are also* **false cognates.** *False cognates are words that have similar spellings in English and Spanish but are* not *related in meaning. Sometimes people think of them as "false friends." For example, what do you think the Spanish word* **red** *means in English?* **Red** *means* **net** *in Spanish!*

▼ **Introduce the activity**

Say: *For this activity, I will give each team a passage from a fable that includes some cognates. Below the passage is a list of words in Spanish that have English cognates. Your job is to read the passage, looking for the English cognate. When you find the cognate, write it on the worksheet across from the Spanish word. Discuss the meanings of the English and Spanish words to make sure that they* **do** *have the same meanings.*

Allow students sufficient time to complete their worksheets.

▼ **Review the activity**

Ask students to compare the meanings of both words to decide if they are true or false cognates.

▼ **Cognates in the fable**

The Hen and the Apple Tree
delicious: delicioso
trunk: tronco
surprised: sorprendido
moment: momento

The Poor Old Dog
park: parque
magic: májico
buttons: botones
usual: usual
note: nota

Day 5
USING WORDS IN CONTEXT

Using Words in Context is designed to develop students' ability to decipher the meaning of a word by using clues in the surrounding text.

▼ Prepare for activity

Place students in heterogeneous language groups, ideally four to five students per group.

Materials: Using Words in Context worksheet for each student

If this activity is challenging for your students, then you may choose to complete it as a whole-group activity. It is helpful to make the worksheet into a transparency so that you can point out the context clues.

▼ Introduce the activity

Say: *Today's activity will help you practice using the target words in sentences. Your job is to figure out which word fits in the blank using the clues that are in the sentence. After you figure out the right word, think about **how** you figured it out; what were the clues in the rest of the sentence that helped you. When everyone in the group knows the correct word and **why it fits,** raise your hands.* The context clues are bold in some sentences to help students learn how to look for the clues in the text. *I'll call on one of the first groups ready. You will get a point if you get the correct answer* (you may choose not to use points). *Remember, everyone in your group must know the answer and why it is correct.*

Read the first sentence aloud to the class to illustrate the process.

▼ Review the activity

Ask one student at a table for the correct answer **and to explain how he or she figured it out**—which clues in the context helped. Explaining the thought process that led to the answer helps the students realize that they know how to use the clues in the text and will demonstrate the process to those students who have not yet developed the skill.

Continue until the lesson is completed, giving each group one point for each correct answer (you may choose not to use points).

Day 6
TOOLS TO DEVELOP VOCABULARY: Prefixes

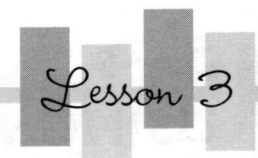

▼ **Prepare for activity**

1. Read "Teacher Tip: Promoting Word Play and Creativity with Words."
2. Divide the children into heterogeneous language groups of four to five students.

Materials: Prefixes worksheet

▼ **Introduce the concept: Prefixes**

Say: *Today we are going to learn about prefixes. Does anyone know what a prefix is? That's right, a* **prefix** *is a word part that is added to the beginning of a word to change its meaning, such as* **pre-** *in* **pre***view or* **pre***test. How does the prefix* **pre-** *change the meaning of test?*

▼ **Introduce the activity**

Say: *Today, each group will have a worksheet with a list of prefixes. Your job is to think of words that begin with each prefix. After you have filled out the worksheet, discuss what the prefix might mean, and write your definition in the space provided.*

▼ **Review the activity**

1. Ask students to share the words.
2. Discuss possible meanings of the prefixes. Ask students to justify their suggestions and explain their thought processes.
3. Elaborate on suggestions so that they are consistent with the following definitions:

   - re-:   back; again
     reelect: elect again
     return: turn back

   - tele-:   far away
     telephone: machine that lets you talk to someone far away
     telescope: instrument that allows you to see things that are far away

   - bi-:   occurring every two; having two
     bicycle: a vehicle having two wheels
     bilingual: able to speak two languages

   - pre-:   before
     prejudge: to judge before knowing the facts
     predict: say what you think will happen before it happens

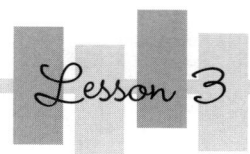

- auto-: of or by oneself
  autobiography: a book written by oneself
  automobile: a vehicle that can move by itself (without animals pulling it)

▼ **Assign homework**

Give students the crossword puzzle; review the instructions and the due date.

PROMOTING WORD PLAY AND CREATIVITY WITH WORDS

Children enjoy word play and games with words—witness the popularity of games such as Scrabble, Boggle, and Balderdash. There are a number of things that you can do to help children explore the meanings of words and use words in creative and imaginative ways while enriching their understanding.

1. *Have the class use words in original but legitimate ways.* For example, if you are trying to have children learn the meaning of *convention* for social studies, then you could ask children to make up "goofy" sentences with that word such as, "The gulls on the beach were having a convention."

2. *Have the class play with roots and affixes.* For example, have them think of all of the roots they can that allow *-ful* and *-less:*

thankful	thankless
useful	useless
graceful	graceless
thoughtful	thoughtless

Then, all the words that allow only *-ful:*

handful	handless (?)
playful	playless (?)
grateful	grateless (?)
awful	awless (?)

Then, all the words that allow only *-less:*

senseless	senseful (?)
baseless	baseful (?)
speechless	speechful (?)
formless	formful (?)

Day 7
WORD WIZARD REVIEW

▼ **Review the crossword puzzle homework**

1. Ask students for answers.

2. Direct students to correct their own answers if needed.

3. The crossword puzzle answer key for Lessons 1–5 can be found in the Teacher Answer Keys for Lesson 1.

▼ **Prepare for activity**

Instruct students to divide into their Word Wizard groups, taking the sentences they have collected throughout the 2 weeks.

▼ **Review Word Wizard**

• Allow students a few minutes to share sentences within their group and tell where they heard or read the word.

• Ask each group to share a few sentences with the class.

   Hint: the more enthusiasm you demonstrate and motivation you provide for this activity, the more the students will participate. Once the students are "hooked," it is rewarding to observe their enthusiasm and to know that they have incorporated the vocabulary activities into other areas of their lives. In the beginning, you may want to bring in a few examples of your own for extra motivation.

• Allow students to post their sentences on the Word Wizard Wall.

You may choose to give the teams points to encourage participation.

▼ Vocabulary assessment

Part 1: Instruct the students to circle the word that corresponds to the definition on the Vocabulary Assessment worksheet.

Part 2: Instruct students to write sentences that demonstrate their knowledge of the word's meaning on the Vocabulary Assessment Sentences worksheet.

Hint: You may need to provide examples of sentences that demonstrate knowledge of the meaning. For example, if the vocabulary word were **ring,** then the sentence "I have a ring" does not demonstrate knowledge of the meaning. **Nose, car, friend, house,** or any number of other words could be substituted for **ring** in the sentence. The sentence "I wear a ring on my finger" demonstrates knowledge of the meaning.

Teacher answer keys

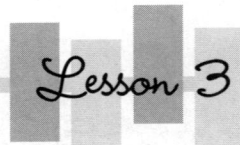

VOCABULARY REVIEW HOMEWORK

- Read the definitions.
- Find the word in the box that matches the definition.
- Write the correct word next to the definition.

pavement	curb	overjoyed	reward
profuse	bulge	wealthy	ragged
gutter	passerby	tattered	cozy

1. __**bulge**__ : to swell or curve outward

2. __**cozy**__ : comfortable or snug

3. __**curb**__ : a raised border along the edge of a paved street

4. __**gutter**__ : a channel or length of tubing through which rain is drained away from a road or from the roof of a building

5. __**overjoyed**__ : extremely happy

6. __**passerby**__ : someone who happens to be going past

7. __**pavement**__ : a hard material, such as concrete or asphalt, that is used to cover roads or sidewalks

8. __**profuse**__ : plentiful or more than enough

9. __**ragged**__ : old, torn, and worn out

10. __**reward**__ : something that is received for doing something good or useful

11. __**tattered**__ : old and torn

12. __**wealthy**__ : having a large amount of money or property

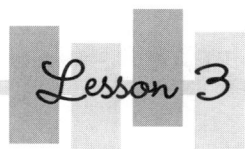

LOOKING FOR COGNATES WORKSHEET

- Read the bold section of the fable.
- Look for the English cognate for the Spanish word written below.
- Write each cognate on the line across from the Spanish word.
- Discuss the meanings of both words to make sure that they do have the same meanings.

THE HEN AND THE APPLE TREE

One October day, a Hen looked out her window. She saw an apple tree growing in her backyard.
"Now that is odd," said the Hen. "I am certain that there was no tree standing in that spot yesterday."
"There are some of us that grow fast," said the tree.
The Hen looked at the bottom of the tree.
"I have never seen a tree," she said, "that has ten furry toes."
"There are some of us that do," said the tree. "Hen come outside and enjoy the cool shade of my leafy branches."
The Hen looked at the top of the tree.
"I have never seen a tree," she said, "that has two long, pointed ears."

"There are some of us have," said the tree. "Hen, come outside and eat one of my delicious apples."

"Come to think of it," said the Hen, "I have never heard a tree speak from a mouth that is full of sharp teeth."

"There are some of us that can," said the tree. "Hen, come outside and rest your back against the bark of my trunk."

"I have heard," said the Hen, "that some of you trees lose all of your leaves at this time of the year."

"Oh, yes," said the tree, "there are some of us that will." The tree began to quiver and shake. All of its leaves quickly dropped off.

The Hen was not surprised to see a large Wolf in the place where an apple tree had been standing just a moment before. She locked her shutters and slammed her window closed.

The Wolf knew that he had been outsmarted. He stormed away in a hungry rage.
It is always difficult to pose as something that one is not.

Spanish word		English cognate
Delicioso	=	Delicious
Tronco	=	Trunk
Sorprendido	=	Surprised
Momento	=	Moment

From *Fables* by Arnold Lobel. © 1980 by Arnold Lobel. Reproduced by permission from HarperCollins Publishers.

LOOKING FOR COGNATES WORKSHEET

- Read the bold section of the fable.
- Look for the English cognate for the Spanish word written below.
- Write each cognate on the line across from the Spanish word.
- Discuss the meanings of both words to make sure that they do have the same meanings.

THE POOR OLD DOG

There was an old Dog who was very poor. The only coat he had to wear was mostly held together by ragged threads. He could feel the pebbles on the pavement through the thin soles in his tattered shoes.

He slept in the park because he had no home.

The Dog spent most of his time searching in garbage cans. He found bits of string and buttons. These he sold for pennies to passersby.

The Dog always walked with his nose close to the curb, looking for things to sell. That is how he came to find the gold ring that was lying in the gutter.

"My luck has changed," cried the Dog, "for I am sure that this is a magic ring!"

The Dog rubbed the ring and said, "I wish for a new coat. I wish for new shoes. I wish for a house to live in. I wish these wishes would come true right now!"

But nothing happened. The Dog felt the wind through the holes in his coat. He felt the pebbles under his thin shoes. That night he slept on his usual bench in the park. Several days later, the Dog saw a note on a lamppost.

The note said "Lost: gold ring. Large reward. Mr. Terrior. Ten Wealthy Lane."

The old Dog hurried to Wealthy Lane. Mr. Terrior was overjoyed to have his ring returned. He thanked the Dog profusely and gave him a bulging purse that was full of coins.

The Dog bought a warm fur coat. He bought a pair of good shoes with thick soles.

There was a large amount of money left over. The Dog used the rest as a down payment on a cozy little house. He moved right in and never had to sleep in the park again.

Wishes, on their way to coming true, will not be rushed.

Spanish word		English cognate
Parque	=	Park
Botones	=	Buttons
Májico	=	Magic
Usual	=	Usual
Nota	=	Note

From *Fables* by Arnold Lobel. © 1980 by Arnold Lobel. Reproduced by permission from HarperCollins Publishers.

Lesson 3

USING WORDS IN CONTEXT WORKSHEET

bulging	overjoyed	profusely	ragged	reward
curbed	tattered	wealth	wealthy	curb

1. The homeless old dog in the fable needed new clothes because his clothes were
   __**ragged**__ and __**tattered**__.

2. The boy tripped on the __**curb**__ when he tried to step up on the sidewalk.

3. The teacher __**curbed**__ our loud talking by threatening to take away recess.

4. Mr. Champlin is a __**wealthy**__ man who gives money to help city children go to
   summer camp in the country.

5. The little boy put so much candy in his mouth that his cheeks were __**bulging**__.

6. Some teachers give children points as a __**reward**__ for good behavior.

7. My grandma tells us that being healthy is more important than having a lot of money. She
   says, "Health is __**wealth**__."

8. Anna was __**overjoyed**__ to see her parents for the first time in 15 years. She
   __**profusely**__ thanked the social worker who helped them come to the United
   States of America.

USING WORDS IN CONTEXT WORKSHEET *(continued)*

cozy	gutter	passersby	paved	pavement
profusely	reward	profuse	wealthy	

9. The fire was warm and toasty; I felt very ___**cozy**___ sitting next to it.

10. The police found out about the accident from some ___**passersby**___ who saw the car crash and then called 911.

11. Tell the ambulance to hurry. She is bleeding ___**profusely**___.

12. My uncle's car got stuck in the mud when he parked off the ___**pavement**___ near the edge of the lake.

13. He couldn't tell from his map if the road was dirt or if it was ___**paved**___.

14. When I take my dog for a walk, he sniffs dirty things in the ___**gutter**___.

15. When my puppy makes a mess in the house, I punish him. When he is good, I give him a dog **treat** as a ___**reward**___.

16. On Halloween, my neighbor filled 20 big bags with candy. That is a ___**profuse**___ amount of candy!

17. Here's an old proverb, "Early to bed and early to rise makes a man healthy, ___**wealthy**___, and wise."

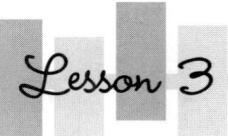

VOCABULARY ASSESSMENT WORKSHEET

- Circle the word that matches the definition.

1. Extremely happy

    ragged   (overjoyed)   passerby   reward

2. A channel or length of tubing through which rain is drained away from a road or from the roof of a building

    curb   profuse   bulge   (gutter)

3. Old, torn, and worn out

    pavement   (ragged)   wealthy   gutter

4. Someone who happens to be going past

    (passerby)   overjoyed   cozy   profuse

5. Something that is received for doing something good or useful

    wealthy   (reward)   cozy   ragged

6. A raised border along the edge of a paved street

    (curb)   bulge   pavement   profuse

7. To swell or curve outward

    tattered   cozy   (bulge)   pavement

8. Having a large amount of money or property

    ragged   (wealthy)   reward   profuse

9. A hard material, such as concrete or asphalt, that is used to cover roads or sidewalks

    profuse   passerby   overjoyed   (pavement)

10. Comfortable or snug

    wealthy   reward   (cozy)   gutter

11. Old and torn

    (tattered)   profuse   curb   overjoyed

12. Plentiful or more than enough

    ragged   reward   gutter   (profuse)

Reproducible materials

tattered

pavement

ragged

passersby

curb

gutter

overjoyed

wealthy

reward

cozy

bulging

profusely

VOCABULARY REVIEW HOMEWORK

- Read the definitions.
- Find the word in the box that matches the definition.
- Write the correct word next to the definition.

pavement	curb	overjoyed	reward
profuse	bulge	wealthy	ragged
gutter	passerby	tattered	cozy

1. _____: to swell or curve outward

2. _____: comfortable or snug

3. _____: a raised border along the edge of a paved street

4. _____: a channel or length of tubing through which rain is drained away from a road or from the roof of a building

5. _____: extremely happy

6. _____: someone who happens to be going past

7. _____: a hard material, such as concrete or asphalt, that is used to cover roads or sidewalks

8. _____: plentiful or more than enough

9. _____: old, torn, and worn out

10. _____: something that is received for doing something good or useful

11. _____: old and torn

12. _____: having a large amount of money or property

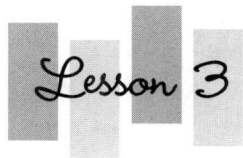

WORD WIZARD LIST

- Each time you hear or read one of these words used in a sentence at home, at school, on television, or on the radio, write the sentence on an index card or sticky note.

bulging (bulge): to swell or curve outward

cozy: comfortable or snug

curb: a raised border along the edge of a paved street

gutter: a channel or length of tubing through which rain is drained away from a road or from the roof of a building

overjoyed: extremely happy

passersby (passerby): someone who happens to be going past

pavement: a hard material, such as concrete or asphalt, that is used to cover roads or sidewalks

profusely (profuse): plentiful or more than enough

ragged: old, torn, and worn out

reward: something that is received for doing something good or useful

tattered: old and torn

wealthy: having a large amount of money or property

Vocabulary Improvement Program for English Language Learners and Their Classmates, 4th Grade, by Teresa Lively, Diane August, María Carlo, and Catherine Snow © 2003 Paul H. Brookes Publishing Co., Inc. All rights reserved.

LOOKING FOR COGNATES WORKSHEET

- Read the bold section of the fable.
- Look for the English cognate for the Spanish word written below.
- Write each cognate on the line across from the Spanish word.
- Discuss the meanings of both words to make sure that they do have the same meanings.

THE HEN AND THE APPLE TREE

One October day, a Hen looked out her window. She saw an apple tree growing in her backyard.
"Now that is odd," said the Hen. "I am certain that there was no tree standing in that spot yesterday."
"There are some of us that grow fast," said the tree.
The Hen looked at the bottom of the tree.
"I have never seen a tree," she said, "that has ten furry toes."
"There are some of us that do," said the tree. "Hen come outside and enjoy the cool shade of my leafy branches."
The Hen looked at the top of the tree.
"I have never seen a tree," she said, "that has two long, pointed ears."

"There are some of us have," said the tree. "Hen, come outside and eat one of my delicious apples."

"Come to think of it," said the Hen, "I have never heard a tree speak from a mouth that is full of sharp teeth."

"There are some of us that can," said the tree. "Hen, come outside and rest your back against the bark of my trunk."

"I have heard," said the Hen, "that some of you trees lose all of your leaves at this time of the year."

"Oh, yes," said the tree, "there are some of us that will." The tree began to quiver and shake. All of its leaves quickly dropped off.

The Hen was not surprised to see a large Wolf in the place where an apple tree had been standing just a moment before. She locked her shutters and slammed her window closed.

The Wolf knew that he had been outsmarted. He stormed away in a hungry rage.
It is always difficult to pose as something that one is not.

Spanish word		English cognate
Delicioso	=	
Tronco	=	
Sorprendido	=	
Momento	=	

Vocabulary Improvement Program for English Language Learners and Their Classmates, 4th Grade, by Teresa Lively, Diane August, María Carlo, and Catherine Snow © 2003 Paul H. Brookes Publishing Co., Inc. All rights reserved.

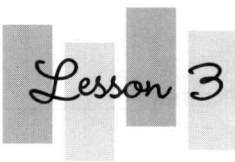
LOOKING FOR COGNATES WORKSHEET

- Read the bold section of the fable.
- Look for the English cognate for the Spanish word written below.
- Write each cognate on the line across from the Spanish word.
- Discuss the meanings of both words to make sure that they do have the same meanings.

THE POOR OLD DOG

There was an old Dog who was very poor. The only coat he had to wear was mostly held together by ragged threads. He could feel the pebbles on the pavement through the thin soles in his tattered shoes.

He slept in the park because he had no home.

The Dog spent most of his time searching in garbage cans. He found bits of string and buttons. These he sold for pennies to passersby.

The Dog always walked with his nose close to the curb, looking for things to sell. That is how he came to find the gold ring that was lying in the gutter.

"My luck has changed," cried the Dog, "for I am sure that this is a magic ring!"

The Dog rubbed the ring and said, "I wish for a new coat. I wish for new shoes. I wish for a house to live in. I wish these wishes would come true right now!"

But nothing happened. The Dog felt the wind through the holes in his coat. He felt the pebbles under his thin shoes. That night he slept on his usual bench in the park. Several days later, the Dog saw a note on a lamppost.

The note said "Lost: gold ring. Large reward. Mr. Terrior. Ten Wealthy Lane."

The old Dog hurried to Wealthy Lane. Mr. Terrior was overjoyed to have his ring returned. He thanked the Dog profusely and gave him a bulging purse that was full of coins.

The Dog bought a warm fur coat. He bought a pair of good shoes with thick soles.

There was a large amount of money left over. The Dog used the rest as a down payment on a cozy little house. He moved right in and never had to sleep in the park again.

Wishes, on their way to coming true, will not be rushed.

Spanish word		English cognate
Parque	=	
Botones	=	
Májico	=	
Usual	=	
Nota	=	

Vocabulary Improvement Program for English Language Learners and Their Classmates, 4th Grade, by Teresa Lively, Diane August, María Carlo, and Catherine Snow © 2003 Paul H Brookes Publishing Co., Inc. All rights reserved.

USING WORDS IN CONTEXT WORKSHEET

bulging	overjoyed	profusely	ragged	reward
curbed	tattered	wealth	wealthy	curb

1. The homeless old dog in the fable needed new clothes because his clothes were
   _____ and _____.

2. The boy tripped on the _____ when he tried to step up on the sidewalk.

3. The teacher _____ our loud talking by threatening to take away recess.

4. Mr. Champlin is a _____ man who gives money to help city children go to
   summer camp in the country.

5. The little boy put so much candy in his mouth that his cheeks were _____.

6. Some teachers give children points as a _____ for good behavior.

7. My grandma tells us that being healthy is more important than having a lot of money. She
   says, "Health is _____."

8. Anna was _____ to see her parents for the first time in 15 years. She
   _____ thanked the social worker who helped them come to the United
   States of America.

Vocabulary Improvement Program for English Language Learners and Their Classmates, 4th Grade, by Teresa Lively, Diane August, María Carlo, and Catherine
Snow © 2003 Paul H. Brookes Publishing Co., Inc. All rights reserved.

Name: _____

USING WORDS IN CONTEXT WORKSHEET *(continued)*

cozy	gutter	passersby	paved	pavement
profusely	reward	profuse	wealthy	

9. The fire was warm and toasty; I felt very _____ sitting next to it.

10. The police found out about the accident from some _____ who saw the car crash and then called 911.

11. Tell the ambulance to hurry. She is bleeding _____.

12. My uncle's car got stuck in the mud when he parked off the _____ near the edge of the lake.

13. He couldn't tell from his map if the road was dirt or if it was _____.

14. When I take my dog for a walk, he sniffs dirty things in the _____.

15. When my puppy makes a mess in the house, I punish him. When he is good, I give him a dog **treat** as a _____.

16. On Halloween, my neighbor filled 20 big bags with candy. That is a _____ amount of candy!

17. Here's an old proverb, "Early to bed and early to rise makes a man healthy, _____, and wise."

Vocabulary Improvement Program for English Language Learners and Their Classmates, 4th Grade, by Teresa Lively, Diane August, María Carlo, and Catherine Snow © 2003 Paul H. Brookes Publishing Co., Inc. All rights reserved.

PREFIXES WORKSHEET

• Write two words that begin with each prefix.

Prefix	Word that begins with the prefix

re-   1. _____
           2. _____

tele-   1. _____
           2. _____

bi-   1. _____
           2. _____

pre-   1. _____
           2. _____

auto-   1. _____
           2. _____

• Study the words. Think about how the prefix changes the meaning of the word.
• Discuss what it seems the prefixes might mean.
• Write what you think the prefix means on the line below.

1. re- _____

2. tele- _____

3. bi- _____

4. pre- _____

5. auto- _____

Name: _____

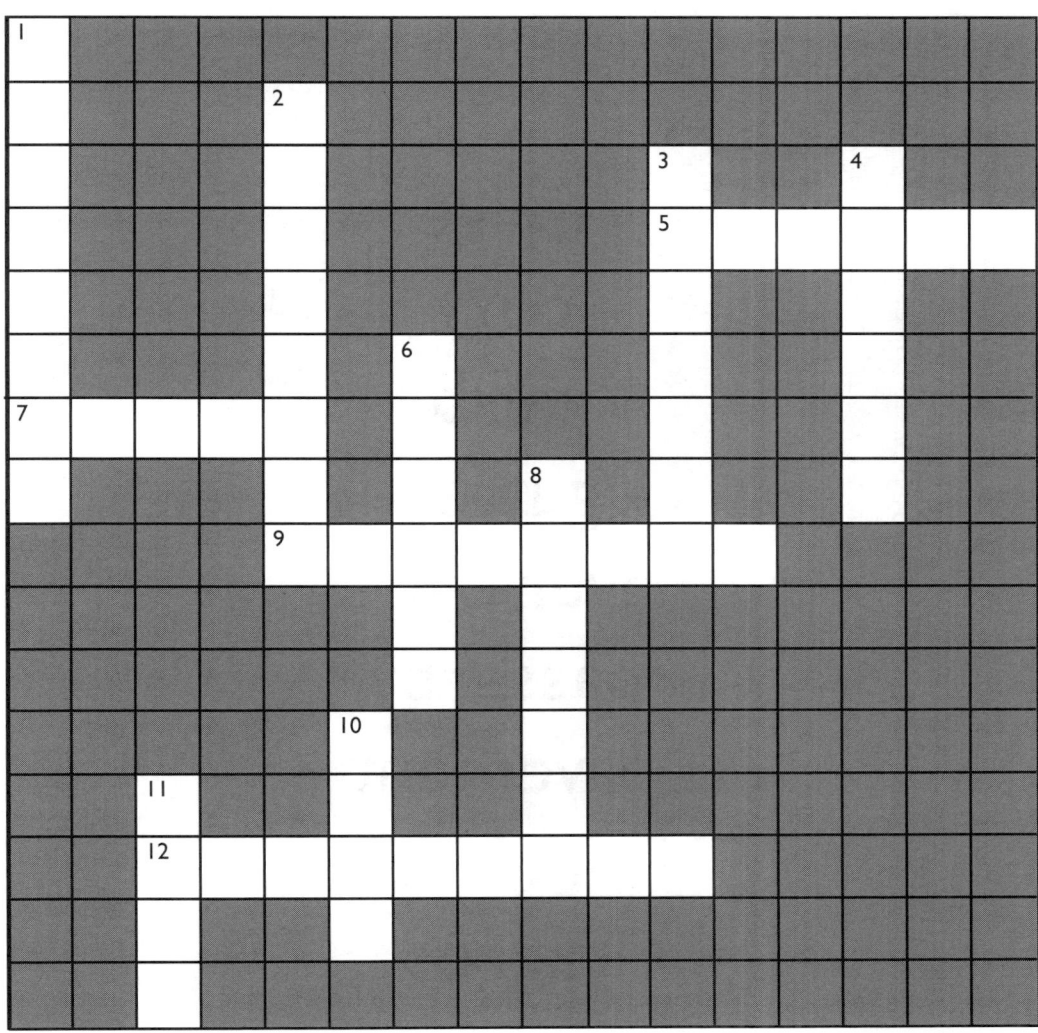

ACROSS

5. Something that is received for doing something good or useful
7. To swell or curve outwards
9. Old and torn
12. Extremely happy

DOWN

1. Someone who happens to be going past
2. A hard material, such as concrete or asphalt, that is used to cover roads or sidewalks
3. Plentiful or more than enough
4. Old, torn, and worn out
6. A channel or length of tubing through which rain is drained away from a road or from the roof of a building
8. Having a large amount of money or property
10. A raised border along the edge of a paved street
11. Comfortable or snug

bulge

cozy

curb

gutter

overjoyed

passerby

pavement

profuse

ragged

reward

tattered

wealthy

Name: _____

VOCABULARY ASSESSMENT WORKSHEET

• Circle the word that matches the definition.

1. Extremely happy

  ragged   overjoyed   passerby   reward

2. A channel or length of tubing through which rain is drained away from a road or from the roof of a building

  curb   profuse   bulge   gutter

3. Old, torn, and worn out

  pavement   ragged   wealthy   gutter

4. Someone who happens to be going past

  passerby   overjoyed   cozy   profuse

5. Something that is received for doing something good or useful

  wealthy   reward   cozy   ragged

6. A raised border along the edge of a paved street

  curb   bulge   pavement   profuse

7. To swell or curve outward

  tattered   cozy   bulge   pavement

8. Having a large amount of money or property

  ragged   wealthy   reward   profuse

9. A hard material, such as concrete or asphalt, that is used to cover roads or sidewalks

  profuse   passerby   overjoyed   pavement

10. Comfortable or snug

  wealthy   reward   cozy   gutter

11. Old and torn

  tattered   profuse   curb   overjoyed

12. Plentiful or more than enough

  ragged   reward   gutter   profuse

Name: _____

VOCABULARY ASSESSMENT
SENTENCES WORKSHEET

Write a sentence with each of these four vocabulary words to show that you know what the word means.

| ragged | reward | profusely | curb |

1. _____

_____

2. _____

_____

3. _____

_____

4. _____

_____

Vocabulary Improvement Program for English Language Learners and Their Classmates, 4th Grade, by Teresa Lively, Diane August, María Carlo, and Catherine Snow © 2003 Paul H. Brookes Publishing Co., Inc. All rights reserved.

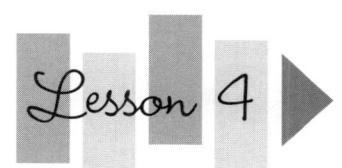

The Ostrich in Love

▼ OVERVIEW OF ACTIVITIES

Day 1	Day 2	Day 3	Day 4
TEXT INTRODUCTION • Predict storyline • Read fable • Discuss fable	**VOCABULARY INTRODUCTION** • Circle vocabulary • Extract definitions • Review cognates • Assign homework	**EXPAND MEANING** • Review homework • Related Words • Assign homework	**TOOLS TO DEVELOP VOCABULARY** • Multiple Meanings

Day 5	Day 6	Day 7	Day 8
USING WORDS IN CONTEXT • Contexting activity	**TOOLS TO DEVELOP VOCABULARY** • Word Roots • Assign homework	**WORD WIZARD REVIEW** • Review homework • Word Wizard review	**ASSESSMENT**

▼ WORD LIST

The word in bold is the base word, followed by its definition. If the word has more than one meaning, then we provide only the definition used in the text. *Please review the definitions prior to instruction.*

1. **beloved:** someone who is greatly loved
2. **compose:** to write music or poetry
3. **courage:** bravery or fearlessness
4. **fluff:** to make something appear larger by shaking or brushing
5. **flutter:** to move quickly and lightly
6. **gather:** to collect or pick things
7. **handsome:** attractive in appearance
8. **shy:** uncomfortable or nervous around people or with strangers
9. **surely:** certainly; without a doubt
10. **waltz:** to dance a smooth, gliding ballroom dance
11. **whirl:** to move around quickly in a circle
12. **wild:** not controlled; unruly

IDIOMATIC EXPRESSIONS

- **at once:** immediately

OTHER WORDS WORTH DEFINING

- **violets:** small purple flowers
- **ballroom:** very large room for dances or parties
- **alas:** unfortunately; sadly

▼ **Prepare for activity**

Post Classroom Word List.

Materials: Student Word Books, *Fables*

▼ **Predict storyline**

Show students the illustration for "The Ostrich in Love" in the color insert or turn to page 20 of *Fables*.

Say: *Today we are going to read the fable "The Ostrich in Love." What do you think this fable will be about when you look at the illustration and hear the title?*

Encourage a student discussion.

▼ **Ask the students to listen as you read the fable aloud**

▼ **Discuss the fable and moral; relate it to the students' lives**

- *Who are the main characters in this fable?*
- *Do you think ostriches really fall in love? Of course not, but it is fun to imagine!*
- *What did Ostrich do on Sunday that showed he was in love? On Monday? On Tuesday? And so forth.*
- *Why did Ostrich think he was too shy for love?*
- *Do you think it is a good idea to fall in love the first time you see someone?*

▼ **Reread the moral**

- *What do you think the moral means?*
- *Do you agree that some things are fun to think about even if you don't actually do them?*
- *Have you ever had such an experience?*

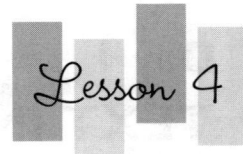

The Ostrich
in Love

On Sunday the ostrich saw a young lady walking in the park. He fell in love with her at once. He followed behind her at a distance, putting his feet in the very places she had stepped.

On Monday the Ostrich **gathered** violets as a gift to his **beloved.** He was too **shy** to give them to her. He left them at her door and ran away, but there was a great joy in his heart.

On Tuesday the Ostrich **composed** a song for his beloved. He sang it over and over. He thought it was the most beautiful music he had ever heard.

On Wednesday the Ostrich watched his beloved dining in a restaurant. He forgot to order supper for himself. He was too happy to be hungry.

On Thursday the Ostrich wrote a poem to his beloved. It was the first poem he had ever written, but he did not have the **courage** to read it to her.

On Friday the Ostrich bought a new suit of clothes. He **fluffed** his feathers, feeling fine and **handsome.** He hoped that his beloved might notice.

On Saturday the Ostrich dreamed that he was **waltzing** with his beloved in a great ballroom. He held her tightly as they **whirled** around and around to the music. He awoke feeling wonderfully alive.

On Sunday the Ostrich returned to the park. When he saw the young lady walking there, his heart **fluttered wildly,** but he said to himself, "Alas, it seems that I am much too shy for love. Yet, **surely** this has been a week well spent."

Love can be its own reward.

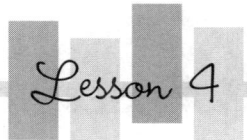
▼ Review the sections titled "Idiomatic Expressions" and "Other Words Worth Defining"

▼ Read posted target words to students, or ask students to read them

- Before you reread the fable, say: *Follow along in your Student Word Book as I read the fable again. Circle each target word when I read it. If you think you know what the word means* **without reading the definition,** *then raise your hand and I will call on you.* After students have suggested meanings, say: *Let's check the definition to see how close you were.*

    Note: The target words appear in the same order in the fable as on the word list. To help students find the words more easily, point out each target word on the list before looking for it in the text.

- Meaning can be inferred for **handsome** and **whirled**. When you reach **handsome,** say: *Sometimes you can figure out what a word means by skipping over it and finishing the sentence. Or, you can reread the sentence while thinking about what the word might mean. Let me show you how this works by reading the sentence with* **handsome** *in it. "He fluffed his feathers, feeling fine and handsome." Let's see, he fluffed his feathers and he felt fine. So, I wonder if it means that he thought he looked good. Let's look up the definition to see if that's what it means.*

- When you reach **whirled** (related to **around and around**), ask students to "think aloud" to explain how the clues in the fable helped them determine the word's meaning.

    You may need to continue modeling the strategy.

▼ Assign Vocabulary Review homework

Instruct students to write the correct vocabulary word in the space beside the definition.

▼ Cognates

If the students are bilingual, then you may wish to review the cognates from the fable.

English word		Spanish word	
park	order	parque	orden
once	poem	once (false)	poema
distance	fine	distancia	fino
violets		violetas	
composed		compuso	
music		música	
restaurant		restaurante	

TARGET WORD DEFINITIONS

- The base word is bold and is the word defined.
- If there is more than one meaning, then the bold definit on is the one used in the fable.
- The Spanish translation is provided for the meaning used in the fable.

1. **beloved**

   someone who is greatly loved

   • amado; alguien querido

2. composed (**compose**)

   a) **to write music or poetry**

   b) to make calm and quiet

   c) to be formed from (composed of)

   • componer; hacer versos o producir obras musicales

3. **courage**

   bravery or fearlessness

   • valor, valentía; sin miedo

4. fluffed (**fluff**)

   a) light down or fuzz, as on a young bird or dandelion

   b) **to make something appear larger by shaking or brushing**

   c) something that's not very important

   • sacudir

5. fluttered (**flutter**)

   to move quickly and lightly

   • revolotear; venir por el aire dando vueltas

6. gathered (**gather**)

   a) **to collect or pick things**

   b) to come together in a group

   c) to understand from something said or done

   d) to gain little by little

   • recoger; juntar o congregar cosas

7. handsome

   a) **attractive in appearance**

   b) large or generous

   • guapo; bien parecido

8. shy

   a) **uncomfortable or nervous around people or with strangers**

   b) lacking or falling short

   c) to draw back suddenly, as from fear or caution

   • tímido; temeroso de otras personas o extraños

9. **surely**

   a) with confidence; unhesitatingly

   b) **certainly; without a doubt**

   • seguramente; con certeza

10. waltzing (**waltz**)

    to dance a smooth, gliding ballroom dance

    • vals; baile de origen alemán que ejecutan las parejas con movimiento giratorio y de traslaciún

11. whirled (**whirl**)

    to move around quickly in a circle

    • arremolinar; moverse rápidamente y en círculos

12. wildly (**wild**)

    a) natural and not tamed by humans

    b) **not controlled; unruly**

    c) overcome with an emotion such as grief, anger, or happiness

    d) crazy, fantastic, or reckless

    • salvaje: sin control

▼ **Review Vocabulary Review homework**

1. Ask students for answers.

2. Direct students to correct their own answers if needed.

▼ **Prepare for activity**

1. Review "Teacher Tip: Rich Instruction" from Lesson 1, Day 3, before teaching the lesson.

2. Divide students into heterogeneous language pairs.

Materials: Related Words worksheet for each student

▼ **Introduce the concept: Related Words**

Say: *New words will mean more to you when you can relate them to other words that you already know and to experiences you've had in your life. For example, do you remember the word predicament from last lesson? Let's think about a predicament a little more. A predicament is a type of what? That's right, a predicament is a type of problem. Have you ever been in a predicament? What happened when you were in a predicament?* Encourage discussion. *Do you see how the word means more when you've thought about it in relationship to* **your** *life? You are more apt to remember it.*

▼ **Introduce the activity**

Say: *Today you will work in pairs and pretend that one of you is someone famous and the other is a reporter for a magazine. The reporter's job is to ask the questions on the Related Words worksheet and write down the answers. After a few minutes, you will change roles so that everyone will have a turn to be both the famous person and the reporter.*

Circulate among the groups providing guidance as needed. Allow the students to work together for 10–12 minutes before asking them to change roles.

Note: You may choose to have one of the pair answer questions 1–6 and have his or her partner answer questions 7–11.

▼ **Review the activity**

Say: *What was the most interesting thing you learned about your partner? Do you think differently about any of the words now? Do you understand them in a different way?*

Day 3: EXPAND MEANING

▼ Word Wizard

Motivate students to find sentences with this week's vocabulary. Say: *You are all going to continue being word wizards and even build your skills with this week's vocabulary words! Just like last week, I want you to demonstrate your wizardry in the following way: Each time you hear or read one of this week's words used at home, at school, or even on television, I want you to write the sentence on an index card (or sticky note). Write down where you heard or read it.*

Give students this week's Word Wizard List.

Day 4
TOOLS TO DEVELOP
VOCABULARY: Multiple Meanings

▼ **Prepare for activity**

Divide students into mixed language groups of four to five students.
Materials: Multiple Meanings worksheet

▼ **Introduce the activity**

PART 1

Say: *Today we are going to work with some of the words from the text that have more than one meaning. In the first part of the activity, we will discuss the different meanings for each word. Who knows one of the meanings for the word* —————————?

Continue until the students have provided the definitions they know. Then, introduce the remaining definitions.

compose	a) to write music or poetry
	b) to make calm and quiet
	c) to be formed from
fluff	a) light down or fuzz, as on a young bird or dandelion
	b) to make something appear larger by shaking or brushing
	c) something that's not very important
gather	a) to collect or pick things
	b) to come together in a group
	c) to understand from something said or done
	d) to gain little by little
shy	a) uncomfortable or nervous around people or with strangers
	b) lacking or falling short
	c) to draw back suddenly, as from fear or caution

PART 2

Say: *In the next part of the activity, you will see these same definitions in two boxes on the Multiple Meanings worksheet. Sentences that use the different meanings are below the boxes. Your job is to find the definition in the box that best fits the way the word is used in*

147

each sentence. You will then write the letter for that definition in the space at the end of the sentence. Let's try one together.

Write the following example on the board and complete it for practice.

A.	An interval of time
B.	A punctuation mark placed at the end of sentences and after many abbreviations

1. Remember to use a **period** after the middle initial in your name. _____

2. It was a terrible **period** in our country's history when we allowed slavery. _____

Allow students to work on the worksheets in their groups until finished.

▼ **Review the activity**

Ask students for the correct answers and for the clues that helped them choose the correct answers on the Multiple Meanings worksheet.

Day 5
USING WORDS IN CONTEXT

Lesson 4

Using Words in Context is designed to develop students' ability to decipher the meaning of a word by using clues in the surrounding text.

▼ Prepare for activity

Place students in heterogeneous language groups, ideally four to five students.

Materials: Using Words in Context worksheet for each student.

If this activity is challenging for your students, then you may choose to complete it as a whole-group activity. It is helpful to make the worksheet into a transparency so that you can point out the context clues.

▼ Introduce the activity

Say: *Today's activity will help you practice using the vocabulary words in sentences. Your job is to figure out which word fits in the blank using the clues that are in the sentence. After you figure out the right word, think about **how** you figured it out; what were the clues in the rest of the sentence that helped you. When everyone in the group knows the correct word and **why it fits,** raise your hands.* The context clues are bold in some sentences to help students learn how to look for the clues in the text. *I'll call on one of the first groups ready. You will get a point if you get the correct answer* (you may choose not to use points). *Remember, everyone in your group must know the answer and why it is correct.*

Read the first sentence aloud to the class to illustrate the process.

▼ Review the activity

- Ask one student at a table for the correct answer **and to explain how he or she figured it out**—which clues in the context helped. Explaining the thought process that led to the answer helps the students realize that they know how to use the clues in the text and will demonstrate the process to those students who have not yet developed the skill.

- Continue until the lesson is completed, giving each group one point for the correct answer (you may choose not to use points).

TOOLS TO DEVELOP VOCABULARY: Roots

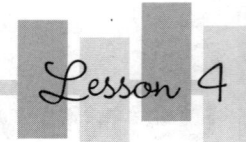

▼ **Prepare for activity**

1. Read "Teacher Tip: Using Roots" before teaching the lesson.
2. Place students in mixed language groups of four students.

Materials: Root Words and Find the Roots worksheets for each group.

▼ **Introduce the concept: Word Roots**

Say: *Have you ever thought about where words come from?* Pause to let a few students respond. *Do you know that words have roots?* **The base part of a word—the part from which it originally came—is called the root.** *Today we are going to study the roots of a few words. You may not have realized that words have a history, but they do! Most of the words that we use when we talk to each other come from words that were first used* **hundreds of years ago.** *The letters in a word may have changed (some may have been added or subtracted), but if you really study a word, you can usually discover where it came from. By studying* **a few** *roots, you will be able to figure out* **a lot of** *words because many words come from the same root.*

▼ **Introduce the activity**

Say: *I am going to give each group a worksheet with some words on it. Your job is to:*

1. *Read all of the words, and look for the parts that are the same in the different words; these are the roots. Clue: there are four different roots.*
2. *Figure out what the root is in each of these words, and then circle it.*
3. *Write one root at the top of each box on the worksheet.*
4. *Write the words in the box below their root.*
5. *Read each list of words, and study them with the other people in your group.*
6. *Discuss what the root might mean.*

▼ **Review roots with class**

1. Ask students to name the roots they found and read the words that share each root.
2. Call on students from the different groups to suggest possible meanings for each root. Ask them to justify their suggestions. Say: *Good thinking! Let's see how close you were.*

3. Read the root definition for the students from the page titled "Definitions of the Roots."

4. Discuss the meaning of each of the words.

▼ Assign homework

Give students the crossword puzzle; review the instructions and the due date.

   If you notice that students are simply matching the number of spaces with the number of letters in a word, then remind them that this activity will not give them practice with the words and definitions if it becomes a counting exercise. Counting is useful for students to check their answers.

DEFINITIONS OF THE ROOTS

Word root: bio   *The root "bio" comes from a Greek word meaning "life."*

biography: the study of a person's *life*

biodegradable: able to be broken down by the natural action of *living* things

biology: the scientific study of *living* things

biopsy: the removal and study of cells or tissue from the *living* body

biorhythms: the regular changes in the *life* processes of people or animals

Word root: pel   *The root "pel" comes from a Latin word meaning "to push."*

com**pel:** *push* a person to do something

ex**pel:** to *push* out

pro**pel:** to *push* forward

re**pel:** to *push* back or away

pro**pel**ler: something that *pushes* something else forward

Word root: dyna   *The root word "dyna" comes from a Greek word meaning "power."*

dynamic: relating to physical force or *power*

dynamite: a *powerful* explosive

dynamo: a forceful or *powerful* individual

dynasty: a *powerful* group or family that holds its *power* for a long time

Word root: ject   *The root "ject" comes from a Latin word meaning "to throw."*

e**ject:** to *throw* out

in**ject:** to *throw*, drive, or force into something

pro**ject:** to *throw* forward (project the film onto the wall or project your voice)

re**ject:** to cast off or *throw* off

Teacher Tip

USING ROOTS

One of the best ways to expand a child's vocabulary is through *structural analysis*. This means children learn to figure out the parts of words—how they are structured. For example, the word *unfruitful* has the prefix *un-,* the base *fruit,* and the suffix *-ful.* Other words, such as *snowman,* are compounds of two words.

The first step in structural analysis is to help students learn what is a **meaningful unit** in a word. They need to avoid "phantom prefixes" such as *re* in *reality.* They will need help so they do not look for "little words in big words." This will lead to mistakes such as finding *moth* in *mother* and *fat* in *father.*

Such problems can be overcome by explicit instructions and modeling. You will need to convey clearly to students when and how to apply structural analysis. During the school day, when you come across a new word to which structural analysis can be applied, "think aloud," explaining as thoroughly as possible how to apply knowledge of structural analysis. Anderson and Nagy (1992) suggested saying something like the following:

> Here's a word we haven't seen before. The first thing I'll do is see whether I recognize any familiar parts—a prefix, root, or suffix—or maybe it might be a compound word. Okay, I see that I can divide this word into a root I know, and a suffix. So the meaning of this word must have something to do with . . . Now I'll see if the meaning makes any sense in this sentence. (pp. 14–16, 44–48)

It is helpful to reinforce this skill by giving students guided practice with other paragraphs while you provide prompts and questions as needed. As students learn how to apply what they have learned, your prompts can be less frequent.

It is important to rely more on examples than on abstract rules, principles, or definitions. It will help students to know the meaning of concepts such as *prefix, suffix, root,* and *compound.* However, you will have to illustrate the concepts with numerous examples. It helps to begin with words that are already familiar to the students.

It is also important to recognize the diversity of English word structure. Some suffixes are relatively easy to teach, such as *-ness* and *-ity.* Others, such as *-tion,* have meanings that are more abstract and are difficult to convey.

Structural analysis has its limitations, but if students can be taught to recognize familiar words and parts of words in new words, then they can make rapid strides in vocabulary development.

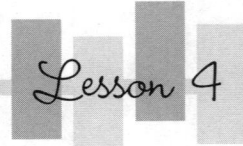

Day 7
WORD WIZARD REVIEW

▼ **Review the crossword puzzle homework**

1. Ask students for answers.

2. Direct students to correct their own answers if needed.

3. The crossword puzzle answer key for Lessons 1–5 can be found in the Teacher Answer Keys for Lesson 1.

▼ **Prepare for activity**

Instruct students to divide into their Word Wizard groups, taking the sentences they have collected throughout the 2 weeks.

▼ **Review Word Wizard**

- Allow students a few minutes to share sentences within their group and tell where they heard or read the word.

- Ask each group to share a few sentences with the class.

   Hint: The more enthusiasm you demonstrate and motivation you provide for this activity, the more the students will participate. Once the students are "hooked," it is most rewarding to observe their enthusiasm and to know that they have incorporated the vocabulary activities into other areas of their lives. In the beginning, you may want to bring in a few examples of your own for extra motivation.

- Allow students to post their sentences on the Word Wizard Wall.

You may choose to give the teams points to encourage participation.

▼ Vocabulary assessment

Part 1: Instruct the students to circle the word that corresponds to the definition on the Vocabulary Assessment worksheet.

Part 2: Instruct students to write sentences that demonstrate their knowledge of the word's meaning on the Vocabulary Assessment Sentences worksheet.

Hint: You may need to provide examples of sentences that demonstrate knowledge of the meaning. For example, if the vocabulary word were **ring,** then the sentence "I have a ring" does not demonstrate knowledge of the meaning. **Nose, car, friend, house,** or any number of other words could be substituted for **ring** in the sentence. The sentence "I wear a ring on my finger" demonstrates knowledge of the meaning.

Teacher answer keys

VOCABULARY REVIEW HOMEWORK

- Read the definitions.
- Find the word in the box that matches the definition.
- Write the correct word next to the definition.

flutter	surely	gather	wild
compose	whirl	waltz	fluff
shy	handsome	beloved	courage

1. _____**fluff**_____: to make something appear larger by shaking or brushing

2. _____**whirl**_____: to move around quickly in a circle

3. _____**compose**_____: to write music or poetry

4. _____**surely**_____: certainly; without a doubt

5. _____**flutter**_____: to move quickly and lightly

6. _____**shy**_____: uncomfortable or nervous around people or with strangers

7. _____**courage**_____: bravery or fearlessness

8. _____**gather**_____: to collect or pick things

9. _____**waltz**_____: to dance a smooth, gliding ballroom dance

10. _____**handsome**_____: attractive in appearance

11. _____**wild**_____: not controlled; unruly

12. _____**beloved**_____: someone who is greatly loved

Lesson 4

MULTIPLE MEANINGS WORKSHEET

- Read each sentence below.
- Choose the meaning for each bold word from the definition in the box.
- Write the letter for that meaning in the space at the end of the sentence.
- The sentences contain clues that will help you figure out which meaning is used for words with more than one meaning.

A. Light down or fuzz, as on a young bird or dandelion

B. To make calm and quiet

C. Something that's not very important

D. To write music or poetry

E. To make something appear larger by shaking or brushing

F. To be formed from

---

1. I will **compose** a poem for you for Valentine's Day. __D__

2. It is hard to **compose** yourself when you are extremely upset. __B__

3. Water is **composed** of hydrogen and oxygen. __F__

4. I made a wish as I blew the dandelion **fluff**. __A__

5. Sometimes birds **fluff** their feathers so that they look bigger to their enemies. __E__

6. The newspaper article wasn't very meaningful; it was just a piece of **fluff**. __C__

MULTIPLE MEANINGS WORKSHEET *(continued)*

G. To gain little by little

H. Uncomfortable or nervous around people

I. To collect or pick things

J. To draw back suddenly, as from fear or caution

K. To understand from something said or done

L. Lacking or falling short

M. To come together in a group

7. In the spring, I like to **gather** wildflowers. __I__

8. We will **gather** together tonight to sing songs. __M__

9. His attitude is so cold that I **gather** we are not welcome here. __K__

10. The storm **gathered** force as it approached. __G__

11. I feel **shy** and want to stay close to my mom when we go somewhere new. __H__

12. I don't have quite enough money to buy a new bike; I'm just a few dollars **shy**. __L__

13. Deer usually **shy** away from people. __J__

USING WORDS IN CONTEXT WORKSHEET

Alasᵃ	beloved	composers	courage	fluffy
flutter	gather	handsome	wildly	shy

Note: ᵃ means another word worth defining.

1. In *The Wizard of Oz*, there is a cowardly lion who wants to be **brave**. He asks the wizard to give him ___**courage**___.

2. Amadeus Mozart started **writing music** when he was a young child. He was one of the most brilliant ___**composers**___ in the world.

3. When we go camping in the desert, there aren't many trees, so it takes a long time to ___**gather**___ enough wood to make a campfire.

4. In *Beauty and the Beast*, Beauty kissed the **ugly** Beast and he **changed** back into a ___**handsome**___ prince.

5. In *Sleeping Beauty*, the Prince kissed the sleeping princess and her eyelids began to ___**flutter**___. Then she opened her eyes and awoke from her long sleep.

6. My heart was beating ___**wildly**___ when I found out I won the lotto.

7. We are writing a play about the Middle Ages. How would a knight say, "**Oh no!** My **girlfriend** has gone"? He'd say, "___**Alas**___! My ___**beloved**___ has gone."

8. Baby ducklings have **soft**, ___**fluffy**___ feathers.

9. When my rabbit was a baby, he was very **timid**, and he hid in the corner of his cage. Now he comes out and looks around; he's not so ___**shy**___.

beloved	composition	fluff	courageous	gathered
fluttering	surely	shy	waltz	whirled

10. The **courageous** girl jumped into the deep lake to save her baby brother.

11. My friend won first prize in an **essay** contest. She wrote the best **composition** in the school.

12. A crowd of people **gathered** around the juggler at the street fair.

13. I painted a picture of a garden with yellow butterflies **fluttering** over blue flowers.

14. I spent so much time studying that I will **surely** pass the test.

15. The author of the book said, "I dedicate this book to my **beloved** grandfather who told me so many wonderful stories."

16. If your pillow gets too flat, you can shake it to **fluff** it up.

17. When we saw the new girl standing by herself and watching us, we called out, "Come play with us. Don't be **shy**."

18. At the wedding, everyone watched the bride and groom **dance** the first **waltz** together.

19. The swings **whirled** **around and around** because the kids had twisted the chains.

VOCABULARY ASSESSMENT WORKSHEET

• Circle the word that matches the definition.

1. Uncomfortable or nervous around people or with strangers

    whirl   (shy)   handsome   surely

2. Someone who is greatly loved

    fluff   courage   (beloved)   waltz

3. Attractive in appearance

    (handsome)   gather   wild   whirl

4. To move around quickly in a circle

    gather   compose   flutter   (whirl)

5. To make something appear larger by shaking or brushing

    compose   (fluff)   courage   shy

6. Not controlled; unruly

    (wild)   shy   waltz   beloved

7. To collect or pick things

    fluff   courage   (gather)   surely

8. To write music or poetry

    waltz   (compose)   shy   flutter

9. Certainly; without a doubt

    wild   handsome   whirl   (surely)

10. To dance a smooth, gliding ballroom dance

    (waltz)   flutter   wild   fluff

11. Bravery or fearlessness

    wild   shy   (courage)   handsome

12. To move quickly and lightly

    waltz   (flutter)   fluff   surely

Reproducible materials

The Ostrich in Love

CLASSROOM WORD LIST

gathered

beloved

shy

composed

courage

fluffed

handsome

waltzing

whirled

fluttered

wildly

surely

VOCABULARY REVIEW HOMEWORK

- Read the definitions.
- Find the word in the box that matches the definition.
- Write the correct word next to the definition.

flutter	surely	gather	wild
compose	whirl	waltz	fluff
shy	handsome	beloved	courage

1. _____: to make something appear larger by shaking or brushing

2. _____: to move around quickly in a circle

3. _____: to write music or poetry

4. _____: certainly; without a doubt

5. _____: to move quickly and lightly

6. _____: uncomfortable or nervous around people or with strangers

7. _____: bravery or fearlessness

8. _____: to collect or pick things

9. _____: to dance a smooth, gliding ballroom dance

10. _____: attractive in appearance

11. _____: not controlled; unruly

12. _____: someone who is greatly loved

Vocabulary Improvement Program for English Language Learners and Their Classmates, 4th Grade, by Teresa Lively, Diane August, María Carlo, and Catherine Snow © 2003 Paul H. Brookes Publishing Co., Inc. All rights reserved.

WORD WIZARD LIST

- Each time you hear or read one of these words used in a sentence at home, at school, on television, or on the radio, write the sentence on an index card or sticky note.

beloved: someone who is greatly loved

composed (compose): to write music or poetry

courage: bravery or fearlessness

fluffed (fluff): to make something appear larger by shaking or brushing

fluttered (flutter): to move quickly and lightly

gathered (gather): to collect or pick things

handsome: attractive in appearance

shy: uncomfortable or nervous around people or with strangers

surely: certainly; without a doubt

waltzing (waltz): to dance a smooth, gliding ballroom dance

whirled (whirl): to move around quickly in a circle

wildly (wild): not controlled; unruly

RELATED WORDS WORKSHEET

1. Name three things you would like to **gather**.

_____

_____

_____

2. Do you ever feel **shy**? When?

_____

_____

_____

3. Have you ever read a poem someone **composed** for their **beloved**? What did you think about it?

_____

_____

_____

4. Name three situations in which you have shown **courage**.

_____

_____

_____

_____

Name: _____

RELATED WORDS WORKSHEET *(continued)*

5. What are two words that mean about the same (synonyms) as **handsome**?

_____

_____

6. Describe two ways something could **whirl**?

_____

_____

7. What are two things you have seen **flutter**?

_____

_____

8. What are two words that mean the opposite (antonyms) of **wild**?

_____

_____

9. What is something you would **surely** like to do?

_____

_____

10. Describe two ways you could **fluff** something.

_____

_____

11. Have you ever seen someone **waltz**? How is a waltz different from today's dances?

_____

_____

_____

Vocabulary Improvement Program for English Language Learners and Their Classmates, 4th Grade, by Teresa Lively, Diane August, María Carlo, and Catherine Snow © 2003 Paul H. Brookes Publishing Co., Inc. All rights reserved.

MULTIPLE MEANINGS WORKSHEET

- Read each sentence below.
- Choose the meaning for each bold word from the defin tion in the box.
- Write the letter for that meaning in the space at the end of the sentence.
- The sentences contain clues that will help you figure out which meaning is used for words with more than one meaning.

A. Light down or fuzz, as on a young bird or dandelion

B. To make calm and quiet

C. Something that's not very important

D. To write music or poetry

E. To make something appear larger by shaking or brushing

F. To be formed from

---

1. I will **compose** a poem for you for Valentine's Day. _____

2. It is hard to **compose** yourself when you are extremely upset. _____

3. Water is **composed** of hydrogen and oxygen. _____

4. I made a wish as I blew the dandelion **fluff**. _____

5. Sometimes birds **fluff** their feathers so that they look bigger to their enemies. _____

6. The newspaper article wasn't very meaningful; it was just a piece of **fluff**. _____

MULTIPLE MEANINGS WORKSHEET *(continued)*

G. To gain little by little

H. Uncomfortable or nervous around people

I. To collect or pick things

J. To draw back suddenly, as from fear or caution

K. To understand from something said or done

L. Lacking or falling short

M. To come together in a group

---

7. In the spring, I like to **gather** wildflowers. _____

8. We will **gather** together tonight to sing songs. _____

9. His attitude is so cold that I **gather** we are not welcome here. _____

10. The storm **gathered** force as it approached. _____

11. I feel **shy** and want to stay close to my mom when we go somewhere new. _____

12. I don't have quite enough money to buy a new bike; I'm just a few dollars **shy**. _____

13. Deer usually **shy** away from people. _____

Name: _____

Lesson 4

USING WORDS IN CONTEXT WORKSHEET

Alas[a]	beloved	composers	courage	fluffy
flutter	gather	handsome	wildly	shy

Note: [a] means another word worth defining.

1. In *The Wizard of Oz*, there is a cowardly lion who wants to be **brave**. He asks the wizard to give him _____.

2. Amadeus Mozart started **writing music** when he was a young child. He was one of the most brilliant _____ in the world.

3. When we go camping in the desert, there aren't many trees, so it takes a long time to _____ enough wood to make a campfire.

4. In *Beauty and the Beast*, Beauty kissed the **ugly** Beast and he **changed** back into a _____ prince.

5. In *Sleeping Beauty*, the Prince kissed the sleeping princess and her eyelids began to _____. Then she opened her eyes and awoke from her long sleep.

6. My heart was beating _____ when I found out I won the lotto.

7. We are writing a play about the Middle Ages. How would a knight say, "**Oh no!** My **girlfriend** has gone"? He'd say, "_____! My _____ has gone."

8. Baby ducklings have **soft**, _____ feathers.

9. When my rabbit was a baby, he was very **timid**, and he hid in the corner of his cage. Now he comes out and looks around; he's not so _____.

Vocabulary Improvement Program for English Language Learners and Their Classmates, 4th Grade, by Teresa Lively, Diane August, María Carlo, and Catherine Snow © 2003 Paul H. Brookes Publishing Co., Inc. All rights reserved.

Name: _____

USING WORDS IN CONTEXT WORKSHEET *(continued)*

beloved fluttering	composition surely	fluff shy	courageous waltz	gathered whirled

10. The _____ girl jumped into the deep lake to save her baby brother.

11. My friend won first prize in an **essay** contest. She wrote the best _____ in the school.

12. A crowd of people _____ around the juggler at the street fair.

13. I painted a picture of a garden with yellow butterflies _____ over blue flowers.

14. I spent so much time studying that I will _____ pass the test.

15. The author of the book said, "I dedicate this book to my _____ grand-father who told me so many wonderful stories."

16. If your pillow gets too flat, you can shake it to _____ it up.

17. When we saw the new girl standing by herself and watching us, we called out, "Come play with us. Don't be _____."

18. At the wedding, everyone watched the bride and groom **dance** the first _____ together.

19. The swings _____ **around and around** because the kids had twisted the chains.

Vocabulary Improvement Program for English Language Learners and Their Classmates, 4th Grade, by Teresa Lively, Diane August, María Carlo, and Catherine Snow © 2003 Paul H. Brookes Publishing Co., Inc. All rights reserved.

FIND THE ROOTS WORKSHEET

• Find the word roots and circle them.

biography   inject

dynasty   repel

compel   dynamite

eject   propel

expel   project

biodegradable   biopsy

dynamic   biology

biorhythms   propeller

reject   dynamo

ROOT WORDS WORKSHEET

- Write one word root at the top of each list.
- Write the words that you circled on the Find the Roots worksheet in the list for the matching root.
- Study the words and discuss what the root might mean. Be sure that everyone in your group knows what the root means.

Root: _____

_____ _____
_____ _____
_____ _____
_____ _____

Root: _____

_____ _____
_____ _____
_____ _____
_____ _____

Root: _____

_____ _____
_____ _____
_____ _____
_____ _____

Root: _____

_____ _____
_____ _____
_____ _____
_____ _____

Name: _____

Lesson 4

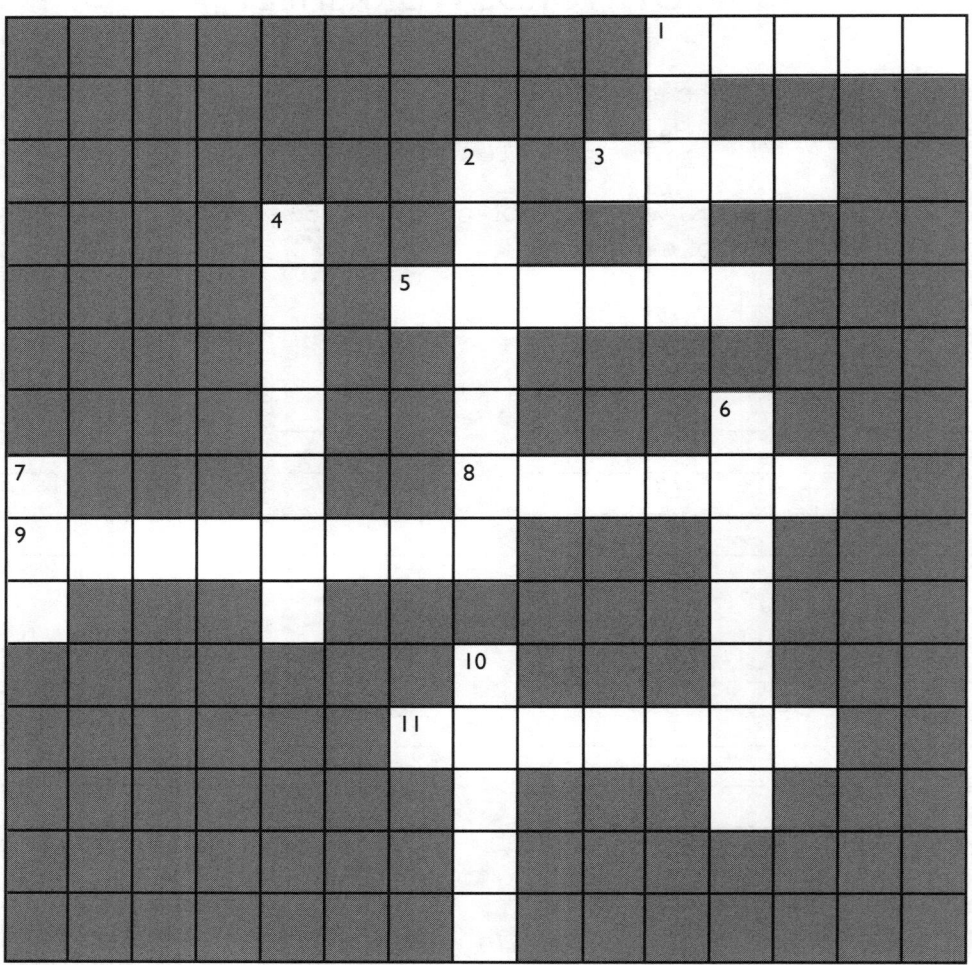

ACROSS

1. To dance a smooth, gliding ballroom dance
3. Not controlled; unruly
5. Certainly; without a doubt
8. To collect or pick things
9. Attractive in appearance
11. To move quickly and lightly

DOWN

1. Move around quickly in a circle
2. Bravery or fearlessness
4. To write music or poetry
6. Someone who is greatly loved
7. Uncomfortable or nervous around people or with strangers
10. To make something appear larger by shaking or brushing

Lesson 4

beloved

compose

courage

fluff

flutter

gather

handsome

shy

surely

waltz

whirl

wild

Name: _____

VOCABULARY ASSESSMENT WORKSHEET

• Circle the word that matches the definition.

1. Uncomfortable or nervous around people or with strangers

    whirl   shy   handsome   surely

2. Someone who is greatly loved

    fluff   courage   beloved   waltz

3. Attractive in appearance

    handsome   gather   wild   whirl

4. To move around quickly in a circle

    gather   compose   flutter   whirl

5. To make something appear larger by shaking or brushing

    compose   fluff   courage   shy

6. Not controlled; unruly

    wild   shy   waltz   beloved

7. To collect or pick things

    fluff   courage   gather   surely

8. To write music or poetry

    waltz   compose   shy   flutter

9. Certainly; without a doubt

    wild   handsome   whirl   surely

10. To dance a smooth, gliding ballroom dance

    waltz   flutter   wild   fluff

11. Bravery or fearlessness

    wild   shy   courage   handsome

12. To move quickly and lightly

    waltz   flutter   fluff   surely

Name: _____

VOCABULARY ASSESSMENT
SENTENCES WORKSHEET

Write a sentence with each of these four vocabulary words to show that you know what the word means.

surely   compose   whirl   gather

1. _____

_____

2. _____

_____

3. _____

_____

4. _____

_____

Vocabulary Improvement Program for English Language Learners and Their Classmates, 4th Grade, by Teresa Lively, Diane August, María Carlo, and Catherine Snow © 2003 Paul H. Brookes Publishing Co., Inc. All rights reserved.

Review Week

▼ OVERVIEW OF ACTIVITIES

Review Day 1
20 QUESTIONS
• Assign homework

Review Day 2
WORD BEE

Review Day 3
CHARADES
• Assign homework

Review Day 4
ANTONYMS/ SYNONYMS
• Review homework

Review Day 5
POSTTEST

▼ Introduce review week

Say: *This week, we will play several games to help us review **all** of the vocabulary words that we studied during the past four lessons. That may sound like a lot of work, but I think we will have a lot of fun!*

If you review the words and definitions from the past four lessons, then you will find this week's activities more fun.

It will help the students with the week's activities if they study the words and definitions as homework on the first day.

Post the Classroom Word Lists from the past four lessons for the students to use as a reference throughout the week.

The objective of this game is to teach the students to eliminate or focus on words that share a particular semantic feature.

▼ Prepare for activity

Cut small pieces of paper for the students to write on.

▼ Introduce the activity

Say: *Today we will begin to review by playing a thinking game that includes all of the animals that we have read about in the fables. One student will write the name of an animal from any of the fables on a piece of paper and show it to me. Other students will ask questions to find out what features this particular animal has or doesn't have. When you think that you have heard enough about the animal to know what it is, raise your hand and ask.* For example:

Student 1: I'm thinking of an animal from a fable.

Student 2: Does it have fur?

Student 1: No.

Student 3: Is it a bird?

Student 1: Yes.

Student 4: Does it like to swim?

Student 1: Yes.

Student 5: Is it a duck?

Student 1: Yes.

Say: *How did you figure that out?* You may need to prompt for details by asking leading question such as, *Why didn't you think it was a crow?*

Focus on the students' thought processes.

▼ Assign homework

Review the words and definitions from the previous four lessons.

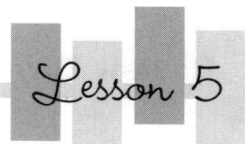
▼ Prepare for activity

1. Cut apart the Word Bee Cards.

2. Display target word lists from Lessons 1–4.

3. Divide students into heterogeneous language groups of four to five students.

4. Provide paper and pencils to each team.

▼ Introduce the activity: Word Bee

Say:

1. *The objective of this game is for team members to work together to give a good definition for each vocabulary word.*

2. *Each team will be given a card with a vocabulary word and will have 2 minutes to work together to write a definition for the word.*

3. *You may not use your Student Word Books. I want to see what you remember.*

4. *When you have finished writing the definition, one team member will present the definition to the class.*

5. *The remainder of the class will judge the accuracy of the definition.*

   • *If you think the definition is right, then put your thumbs up.*

   • *if you think the definition is wrong, then put your thumbs down, and another team can try to define the word.*

You may choose to give points to the teams.

If a team is unable to give an accurate definition, then please give the correct definition.

▼ Begin play

1. Give each team one Word Bee Card (all teams will work on their definitions simultaneously).

2. Play continues between the teams until all cards have been used and all definitions presented.

Word	Definition
advice	a suggestion about what someone should do
bark	the hard covering on the outside of a tree
cozy	comfortable or snug
curb	a raised border along the edge of a paved street
flutter	to move quickly and lightly

fur	the soft, thick, hairy coat of an animal
gather	to collect or pick things
handsome	attractive in appearance
jungle	land in warm, tropical areas near the equator covered with trees, vines, and bushes
outsmart	to defeat by being clever
predicament	an awkward or difficult situation
profuse	plentiful or more than enough
tattered	old and torn

Review Day 3
CHARADES

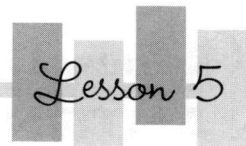

▼ **Prepare for activity**

1. Display target word lists from Lessons 1–4.
2. Cut apart the Charades Cards.
3. Students may use their Word Books to review word meanings.
4. Divide the class into heterogeneous language teams of six to eight students each.

▼ **Introduce the concept**

Say: *Has anyone ever played Charades? Who can tell us what the object of Charades is?*

*That's right, Charades is a game in which students act out a word **without talking** while the other students on their own team try to guess what word they are acting out.*

▼ **Introduce the activity: Charades**

1. Divide the Charades Cards evenly between the teams.
2. Two teams will compete while the others observe.
3. Students on Team A choose a word and give it to three students on Team B.
4. The students on Team B act out the word for their team **without talking.**
5. Team B has three chances to guess the correct word. If they fail, then Team A tells them the word and defines it.
6. Team B then selects a word for Team C to act out. After Team C has its turn, they select the word for Team D to act out. The last team picks a word for team A.

Play continues until time or words run out.

▼ **Assign homework**

Instruct students to complete the crossword puzzle; review the instructions and the due date.

ANTONYMS/SYNONYMS

▼ **Review the crossword puzzle homework**

1. Ask students for answers.
2. Direct students to correct their own answers if needed.
3. The crossword puzzle answer key for Lessons 1–5 can be found in the Teacher Answer Keys for Lesson 1.

▼ **Expanding meaning: Antonyms/Synonyms**

Students will identify a vocabulary word when given either its synonym or antonym. This will help students to develop their understanding of synonyms and antonyms as well as reinforce the meanings of the vocabulary words.

▼ **Introduce the concept: Antonyms/Synonyms**

1. Say: *I am going to say a word or phrase that will help you think of one of the vocabulary words, kind of like a clue. Your job is to think about which vocabulary word goes with the clue. The clues I give you will be either synonyms or antonyms.*

   Does anyone remember what synonyms are? That's right, **synonyms** *are words that have the same meanings, such as* **furious** *and* **angry.**

   Does anyone remember what antonyms are? That's right, **antonyms** *are words that have opposite meanings, such as* **hot** *and* **cold.**

   Who can give me an example of a pair of antonyms? Who can give me an example of a pair of synonyms? Elicit several examples from students before proceeding with the lesson.

2. Say: *What vocabulary word do you think of when I say* _____? Provide an associated word. *Please explain why you think the vocabulary word goes with the clue. Is it a synonym or an antonym?*

Give the associated words one at a time. Accept any plausible answer that the student can justify.

Associated word	Vocabulary word	Synonym/antonym
fearful; cowardly	courage	antonym
dear; darling	beloved	synonym
penniless; needy; poor	wealthy	antonym
usual; regular; normal	odd	antonym
pleasant; enjoyable	delightful	synonym
slow	quick	antonym
shabby; tattered	ragged	synonym
answer	solution	synonym
irritated	annoyed	synonym
unsure	certain	antonym
calmly; controlled	wildly	antonym

Direct students to think of antonyms, synonyms, or words otherwise associated for the vocabulary words.

POSTTEST FOR LESSONS 1–4

▼ **Prepare for activity**

- Separate students so that they will work individually.

- Hand out the extra copy of the assessment forms that you made when you gave the pretest.

▼ **Introduce the activity**

Say: *In this lesson, you will complete three worksheets to see which of the target words you have learned. You have probably done activities like these before. I will show you examples of each of the three different activities again before you begin.*

1. Write the following example on the board.

fun	big	happy

I am _____ when the sun is shining.

Say: *The first worksheet has a box at the top with words in it. Sentences below the box have a line in them to show that a word is missing. First, you will read a sentence. Then, you will look in the box for a word that makes sense if you write it in the space.*

Who can read the sentence on the board? Good, now what word makes the most sense if we put it in the space? That's right, so I am going to write **happy** *in the space.*

Note: Be sure that students know they are to **use each word only one time.**

2. Again, please write the example on the board.

A toy that spins

sled   **top**   **puzzle**   **kite**

Say: *The second worksheet has definitions and four words from which to choose. Who can raise their hand to read the definition on the board? Good, now who can read the four words below the definition? Which word goes with the definition? That's right, so now I will draw a circle around the word* **top.**

3. Say: *For the last worksheet, you are going to work with words that have more than one meaning. For example, let's think about the word top again. Who can think of one meaning of top? You can tell me either a definition or a sentence.*

Write responses on the board, eliciting examples of both definitions and meaningful sentences for the word *top.* For example:

1. Mar'a stood on *top* of the table.

2.   A *top* is a toy that spins around quickly.

3.   José was the *top* student in his class.

4.   Jenny wore a new *top*.

5.   I collect bottle *tops*.

Say: *In this activity, you will see four words that have more than one meaning. Think about the different meanings of each word. Write one sentence for each of the meanings that you know, or write the definition if that is easier for you. Write as many meanings as you can, but do not feel bad if you cannot think of all of the meanings.*

•   Distribute the activity.

•   Leave the examples on the board as a reference for the students.

•   Monitor the students as they work to be certain they understand the activity.

Reproducible materials

Please cut words apart.

advice	handsome
bark	jungle
cozy	outsmart
curb	predicament
flutter	profuse
fur	tattered
gather	

CHARADES CARDS

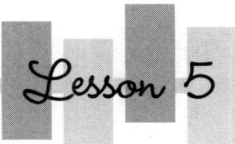

Please cut words apart.

delicious	bulge
quiver	overjoyed
rage	passerby
baboon	fluffed
scissors	waltzing
underneath	whirled

Name: _____

ACROSS

6. Uncooperative; bad tempered
9. The main stem of a tree
10. To write music or poetry
11. A channel or length of tubing through which rain is drained away from a road or from the roof of a building

DOWN

1. Certainly; without a doubt
2. Something that is received for doing something good or useful
3. Area sheltered from light
4. A small ape with long, slender arms and no tail that lives mainly in Southeast Asia
5. The flat and usually green parts of a plant or tree that grow out from a stem, twig, or branch
7. Fixed in a particular position
8. A hard material, such as concrete or asphalt, that is used to cover roads or sidewalks

compose

disagreeable

gibbon

gutter

leaf

pavement

reward

shade

stuck

surely

trunk

Lessons 6–9
PRETEST FOR LESSONS 6–9

▼ **Prepare for activity**

- Separate students so that they will work individually.

- Make two copies of each of the three Lessons 6–9 assessment forms and save one copy for the posttest.

▼ **Introduce the activity**

Say: *In this lesson, you will complete three worksheets to find out which of the words that we will study in the next lessons you already know and which you don't know. You have probably done activities like these before. I will show you examples of each of the three different activities to review.*

1. Write the following example on the board.

fun	big	happy

I am _____ when the sun is shining.

Say: *The first worksheet has a box at the top with words in it. Sentences below the box have a line in them to show that a word is missing. First, you will read a sentence. Then, you will look in the box for a word that makes sense if you write it in the space.*

*Who can read the sentence on the board? Good, now what word makes the most sense if we put it in the space? That's right, so I am going to write **happy** in the space.*

Note: Be sure that students know they are to **use each word only one time.**

2. Again, please write the example on the board.

A toy that spins

sled   **top**   **puzzle**   **kite**

Say: *The second worksheet has definitions and four words from which to choose. Who can raise their hand to read the definition on the board? Good, now who can read the four words below the definition? Which word goes with the definition? That's right, so now I will draw a circle around the word **top**.*

3. Say: *For the last worksheet, you are going to work with words that have more than one meaning. For example, let's think about the word top again. Who can think of one meaning of top? You can tell me either a definition or a sentence.*

Write responses on the board, eliciting examples of both definitions and meaningful sentences for the word *top*. For example:

1. María stood on *top* of the table.

2. A *top* is a toy that spins around quickly.
3. José was the *top* student in his class.
4. Jenny wore a new *top*.
5. I collect bottle *tops*.

Say: *In this activity, you will see four words that have more than one meaning. Think about the different meanings of each word. Write one sentence for each of the meanings that you know, or write the definition if that is easier for you. Write as many meanings as you can, but do not feel bad if you cannot think of all of the meanings.*

• Distribute the activity.

• Leave the examples on the board as a reference for the students.

• Monitor the students as they work to be certain they understand the activity.

Teacher answer keys

VOCABULARY ASSESSMENT 1

dawn	morsel	contained	temptation	glamorous
regret	flattery	adorned	alarmed	gazed
budge	sprouted	enormously	alluring	contentment
several				

- Find the word that **best** fits in the sentence.
- Use each word only **one** time.

1. When I left home and heard my puppy crying, I was filled with ___**regret**___ .

2. The ___**temptation**___ to spend my lunch money on comic books was too much for me, and now I have no money for lunch.

3. Paolo was ___**enormously**___ happy when his band was invited to perform at the festival.

4. David ___**sprouted**___ up another 2 inches this year.

5. Ana gets up early every morning.
   Some days she wakes up before ___**dawn**___ .

6. Maureen was satisfied after she finished her meal.
   She was filled with ___**contentment**___ .

7. José ___**adorned**___ the room with brightly colored balloons.

8. When I tell my teacher how much I like his hair, he tells me that ___**flattery**___ will get me nowhere.

9. The little mouse ate every last ___**morsel**___ of the crumbs from dinner.

10. The ___**alluring**___ smell of our food brought six bears into our campsite!

11. Teresa was _____**alarmed**_____ when she learned she had only one day to finish all her work.

12. Joleen's lunchbox _____**contained**_____ a sandwich, an apple, and juice.

13. My sister looked _____**glamorous**_____ in her fancy dress and with a new hairstyle.

14. The ocean view was so spectacular, I could have _____**gazed**_____ at it all day.

15. I was scared because we could not _____**budge**_____ the huge rock that fell and blocked the entrance to the cave in which we were playing.

16. It took me _____**several**_____ days of practicing to learn the long poem.

Lessons 6–9

VOCABULARY ASSESSMENT 2

- Circle the word that matches the definition.

1. The wish to have what someone else has
   adorn   flatter   (envy)   stare

2. To give off a steady, low light
   (glow)   heartburn   contain   sprout

3. Sad or lonely
   dab   satisfy   gaze   (forlorn)

4. A man or woman who sells goods or services
   teacher   dancer   (salesperson)   parent

5. To think of or look at with pleasure and respect
   (admire)   disapprove   stare   tug

6. To refuse to accept; oppose
   support   regret   (resist)   twinkle

7. To shine with quick flashes of light
   regret   (twinkle)   budge   satisfy

8. A long trip
   proposal   (journey)   admiration   decision

9. Persuade someone not to do something
   flatter   inspire   journey   (discourage)

10. A serving of food
    (portion)   envy   gaze   delicious

11. To touch a surface lightly with something soft
    frown   stare   (dab)   glow

12. A dark and depressing atmosphere
    decide   glow   alarm   (gloom)

13. Something that causes very great fear

    (terror)   bravery   content   dawn

14. Barely enough; almost not enough

    content   dawn   plenty   (narrow)

15. To have a very strong effect

    decide   calm   (overwhelm)   tangle

16. To make up one's mind about something

    (decide)   alarm   dawn   overwhelm

VOCABULARY ASSESSMENT 3

- In this activity, you will see four different words that have more than one meaning.
- Think about the different meanings of each word.
- Write one sentence for each of the meanings that you know, or write the definitions.

1. firm

1) strong and solid (firm mattress); 2) definite and not easily changed; 3) strong (a firm voice); 4) a business or company

2. roll

1) to move forward by turning over and over; 2) to make something into the shape of a ball or tube; 3) to flatten something by pushing a rounded object over it; 4) a small piece of baked bread; 5) a list of names; 6) to start (let's get rolling); 7) to make a deep, loud sound (drum roll); 8) to move in a side-to-side or up-and-down way (ship rolls)

3. spin

1) to make thread by twisting fine fibers together; 2) to make a web or cocoon from a liquid that hardens into thread; 3) to rotate or whirl around; 4) to tell or relate

4. dawn

1) the beginning of the day; 2) the start of something new; 3) to begin to be understood

Reproducible materials

VOCABULARY ASSESSMENT I

dawn	morsel	contained	temptation	glamorous
regret	flattery	adorned	alarmed	gazed
budge	sprouted	enormously	alluring	contentment
several				

- Find the word that **best** fits in the sentence.
- Use each word only **one** time.

1. When I left home and heard my puppy crying, I was filled with _____.

2. The _____ to spend my lunch money on comic books was too much for me, and now I have no money for lunch.

3. Paolo was _____ happy when his band was invited to perform at the festival.

4. David _____ up another 2 inches this year.

5. Ana gets up early every morning.
   Some days she wakes up before _____.

6. Maureen was satisfied after she finished her meal.
   She was filled with _____.

7. José _____ the room with brightly colored balloons.

8. When I tell my teacher how much I like his hair, he tells me that _____ will get me nowhere.

9. The little mouse ate every last _____ of the crumbs from dinner.

10. The _____ smell of our food brought six bears into our campsite!

Name: _____

VOCABULARY ASSESSMENT 1 *(continued)*

11. Teresa was _____ when she learned she had only one day to finish all her work.

12. Joleen's lunchbox _____ a sandwich, an apple, and juice.

13. My sister looked _____ in her fancy dress and with a new hairstyle.

14. The ocean view was so spectacular, I could have _____ at it all day.

15. I was scared because we could not _____ the huge rock that fell and blocked the entrance to the cave in which we were playing.

16. It took me _____ days of practicing to learn the long poem.

Vocabulary Improvement Program for English Language Learners and Their Classmates, 4th Grade, by Teresa Lively, Diane August, María Carlo, and Catherine Snow © 2003 Paul H Brookes Publishing Co., Inc. All rights reserved.

VOCABULARY ASSESSMENT 2

• Circle the word that matches the definition.

1. The wish to have what someone else has

    adorn   flatter   envy   stare

2. To give off a steady, low light

    glow   heartburn   contain   sprout

3. Sad or lonely

    dab   satisfy   gaze   forlorn

4. A man or woman who sells goods or services

    teacher   dancer   salesperson   parent

5. To think of or look at with pleasure and respect

    admire   disapprove   stare   tug

6. To refuse to accept; oppose

    support   regret   resist   twinkle

7. To shine with quick flashes of light

    regret   twinkle   budge   satisfy

8. A long trip

    proposal   journey   admiration   decision

9. Persuade someone not to do something

    flatter   inspire   journey   discourage

10. A serving of food

    portion   envy   gaze   delicious

11. To touch a surface lightly with something soft

    frown   stare   dab   glow

12. A dark and depressing atmosphere

    decide   glow   alarm   gloom

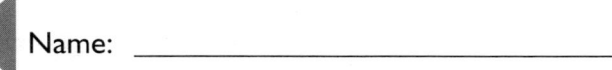
VOCABULARY ASSESSMENT 2 *(continued)*

13. Something that causes very great fear

| terror | bravery | content | dawn |

14. Barely enough; almost not enough

| content | dawn | plenty | narrow |

15. To have a very strong effect

| decide | calm | overwhelm | tangle |

16. To make up one's mind about something

| decide | alarm | dawn | overwhelm |

VOCABULARY ASSESSMENT 3

- In this activity, you will see four different words that have more than one meaning.
- Think about the different meanings of each word.
- Write one sentence for each of the meanings that you know, or write the definitions.

1. firm

_____

_____

2. roll

_____

_____

3. spin

_____

_____

4. dawn

_____

_____

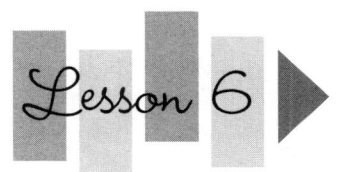
Lesson 6

Madame Rhinoceros and Her Dress

OVERVIEW OF ACTIVITIES

Day 1	Day 2	Day 3	Day 4
TEXT INTRODUCTION	**VOCABULARY INTRODUCTION**	**EXPAND MEANING**	**TOOLS TO DEVELOP VOCABULARY**
• Predict storyline • Read fable • Discuss fable	• Circle vocabulary • Extract definitions • Review cognates • Assign homework	• Review homework • Word Substitution • Assign homework	• Infer Meaning

Day 5	Day 6	Day 7	Day 8
USING WORDS IN CONTEXT	**TOOLS TO DEVELOP VOCABULARY**	**WORD WIZARD REVIEW**	**ASSESSMENT**
• Contexting activity	• Word Webs • Assign homework	• Review homework • Word Wizard review	

WORD LIST

The word in bold is the base word, followed by its definition. If the word has more than one meaning, then we provide only the definition used in the text. *Please review the definitions prior to instruction.*

1. **absolutely:** certainly
2. **admire:** to think of or look at with pleasure and respect
3. **adorn:** to make more beautiful or interesting by decorating
4. **allure:** to attract
5. **complete:** total; in every way
6. **envy:** the wish to have what someone else has
7. **flatter:** to praise too much and often insincerely, especially in order to get a favor
8. **frown:** to wrinkle the forehead when one is unhappy
9. **glamour:** attractive and exciting quality of something special
10. **resist:** to refuse to accept; to oppose
11. **salesperson:** a man or woman who sells goods or services
12. **stare:** to look directly at someone or something for a long time without moving the eyes

IDIOMATIC EXPRESSIONS

- **you have my word:** I promise

OTHER WORDS WORTH DEFINING

- **lace:** a delicate fabric made of yarn or thread in an open web-like pattern
- **madame:** a formal title for a woman
- **polka dots:** circular spots that form a pattern

▼ **Prepare for activity**

Post Classroom Word List.

Materials: Student Word Books, *Fables*

▼ **Predict storyline**

Show students the illustration for "Madame Rhinoceros and Her Dress" in the color insert or turn to page 27 of *Fables*.

Say: *Today we are going to read the fable "Madame Rhinoceros and Her Dress." What do you think this fable will be about when you look at the illustration and hear the title?*

Encourage a student discussion.

▼ **Ask the students to listen as you read the fable aloud**

▼ **Discuss the fable and moral; relate it to the students' lives**

- *Who are the main characters in this fable?*
- *Have you ever imagined a rhinoceros wearing a dress?*
- *What was Madame Rhinoceros' first reaction when she saw herself in the dress?*
- *How did the salesperson respond to Madame Rhinoceros?*
- *Why do you think the salesperson said that Madame Rhinoceros looked good in the dress?*
- *Why do you think Madame Rhinoceros believed the salesperson?*
- *Why do you think it is sometimes hard to trust your own opinions?*
- *Do you think Madame Rhinoceros will trust her own opinions in the future?*

▼ **Reread the moral**

- *What do you think the moral means?*
- *Have you ever had someone tell you something that was not true so that you would do them a favor? What did you do?*

Madame Rhinoceros and Her Dress

Madame Rhinoceros saw a dress in the window of a shop. It was covered with polka dots and flowers. It was **adorned** with ribbons and lace. She admired it for a moment and then entered the shop.

"That dress in the window," said Madame Rhinoceros to a **salesperson,** "I would like to try it on."

Madame Rhinoceros put on the dress. She looked at herself in the mirror. "I do not think this dress is at all attractive on me," she said.

"But Madame," said the salesperson, "you are **completely** wrong. This dress makes you look **glamorous** and **alluring**."

"If only I were sure," said Madame Rhinoceros.

"Ah, Madame," said the salesperson, "everyone who sees you wearing this dress will be filled with **admiration** and **envy**."

"Do you really think so?" asked Madame Rhinoceros, turning around and around in front of the mirror.

"**Absolutely**," said the salesperson. "You have my word."

"Very well," said Madame Rhinoceros, "I will buy the dress, and I will wear it now."

Madame Rhinoceros left the shop. As she walked up the avenue, she saw that people were smiling and laughing at her.

"Admiration," thought Madame Rhinoceros.

She saw some people who were shaking their heads and **frowning.**

"Envy," thought Madame Rhinoceros.

She continued up the avenue. Everyone who saw her stopped and **stared.** Madame Rhinoceros felt more glamorous and alluring every step.

*Nothing is harder to **resist** than a bit of **flattery.***

From *Fables* by Arnold Lobel. © 1980 by Arnold Lobel. Reproduced by permission from HarperCollins Publishers.

▼ Review the sections titled "Idiomatic Expressions" and "Other Words Worth Defining"

▼ Read posted target words to students, or ask students to read them

- Before you reread the fable, say: *Follow along in your Student Word Book as I read the fable again. Circle each target word when I read it. If you think you know what the word means **without reading the definition,** then raise your hand and I will call on you.* After students have suggested meanings, say: *Let's check the definition to see how close you were.*

    Note: The target words appear in the same order in the fable as on the word list. To help students find the words more easily, point out each target word on the list before looking for it in the text.

- There are no target words for which meaning can be inferred this week.

▼ Assign Vocabulary Review homework

Instruct students to write the correct vocabulary word in the space beside the definition.

▼ Cognates

If the students are bilingual, then you may wish to review the cognates from the fable.

English word	Spanish word
adorned	adornado
admired	admiró
moment	momento
attractive	atractivo
completely	completamente
glamorous	glamoroso
admiration	admiración
envy	envidia
avenue	avenida
resist	resistir

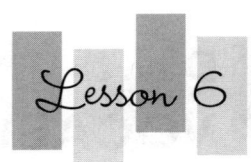
- The base word is bold and is the word defined.
- If there is more than one meaning, then the bold definition is the one used in the fable.
- The Spanish translation is provided for the meaning used in the fable.

1. **absolutely**
   certainly
   - absolutamente; de manera segura

2. admiration (**admire**)
   to think of or look at with pleasure and respect
   - admiración; contemplar o considerar con estima o agrado

3. adorned (**adorn**)
   to make more beautiful or interesting by decorating
   - adornar; engalanar con adornos que dan mejor parecer a personas o cosas

4. alluring (**allure**)
   to attract
   - fascinar; atraer irresistiblemente

5. completely (**complete**)
   a) having all necessary or normal parts
   b) to finish something
   c) total; in every way
   - completo; acabado; perfecto

6. **envy**
   the wish to have what someone else has
   - envidia; deseo de algo que no se posee

7. flattery (**flatter**)
   a) **to praise too much and often insincerely, especially in order to get a favor**
   b) to make a person look better or more beautiful
   - halagar; adular o decir a uno insinceramente cosas que le agraden

8. frowning (**frown**)
   to wrinkle the forehead when one is unhappy
   - fruncir el entrecejo

9. glamorous (**glamour**)
   attractive and exciting quality of something special
   - encantador; que hace muy viva y grata impresión en el alma o los sentidos

10. **resist**
    a) **to refuse to accept; to oppose**
    b) to fight back
    c) to stop oneself from doing something that one would like to do
    - resistir; rechazar; contrariar; contradecir

11. **salesperson**
    a man or woman who sells goods or services
    - vendedor o vendedora; que vende bienes o servicios

12. stared (**stare**)
    to look directly at someone or something for a long time without moving the eyes
    - mirar fijamente

EXPAND MEANING:
Word Substitution

▼ **Review Vocabulary Review homework**

1. Ask students for answers.

2. Direct students to correct their own answers if needed.

▼ **Prepare for activity**

Give a copy of the Word Substitution worksheet to each student or each group.

You might choose to have students work together in heterogeneous language groups to create new sentences that replace the underlined word with a synonymous word or phrase.

▼ **Introduce the concept: Word Substitution**

Say: _In today's activity, you will figure out how to substitute your own words for a target word in a sentence. This will encourage you to think deeply about what each word means._

▼ **Introduce the activity**

Say: _Now we are going to read sentences that use a target word. I want you to think about what the bold target word means. Then, figure out how to **replace** the bold word with another word or phrase that means about the same thing. I will call on you to read the sentence again, substituting the new word or phrase for the vocabulary word. You may use your Student Word Book._

> _For example: When you see ducks walk, they **waddle.**_
>
> _When you see ducks walk, they **take short steps and move from side to side.**_

Read each sentence on the Word Substitution worksheet.

Encourage all students to respond.

▼ **Review the activity**

Say: _Was it hard to figure out a way to replace the word? Do you think it helped you understand the word better by thinking about it, even if you weren't called on?_

▼ **Word Wizard**

Motivate students to find sentences with this week's vocabulary. Say: _You are all going to continue being word wizards and even build your skills with this week's vocabulary words! Just like last week, I want you to demonstrate your wizardry in the following way: Each time_ *you hear or read one of the target words used at home, at school, or even on television, I want you to write the sentence on an index card (or sticky note). Write down where you heard or read it.*

Give students the Word Wizard List.

TOOLS TO DEVELOP
VOCABULARY: Infer Meaning

▼ **Prepare for activity**

1. Read "Teacher Tip: Inferring Meaning from Text" before teaching the activity.

2. Divide students into mixed language groups of four to five students.

3. Write the example on the board.

Materials: Mystery Words worksheet for each group

▼ **Introduce the activity**

Say: *Who can tell me what a mystery is? How many of you like to solve mysteries? What is a detective? In this activity, you are going to solve mysteries about words. You will be* **word detectives!** *As detectives, your assignment is to figure out the meaning of the bold mystery words.*

Good detectives look for clues while gathering information about the mystery they are trying to solve. So, you will look for clues in the words and sentences that surround the mystery word. Use these clues to help pick a definition from the box that might go with the bold word. Follow the steps on the inside back cover of your Word Book (Hints for Solving Mystery Words) to help you decide if the definition you chose is the correct one.

These are pretty difficult words—that's why they're called mystery words! Many grown-ups don't even know these words, so you will need to use good detective skills to find the clues to the meanings! Let's try one.

Use the example below to illustrate the process using the following steps:

1. Pick a definition from the box that might go with the bold word.

2. Write the number for the definition in the space beside the word.

3. Check the definition you chose using the steps listed on the Hints for Solving Mystery Words page in your Student Word Book.

A.   Courageous and bold

B.   Difficult to control

C.   Having very great desire for money

---

1. The **intractable** ——————— dog would not stop jumping on everyone no matter what I did.

• Use the Hints for Solving Mystery Words sheet in the Student Word Books to determine the correct answer.

• Direct the groups to complete the Mystery Words worksheet in a similar manner.

Day 4: TOOLS TO DEVELOP VOCABULARY

▼ **Review the activity**

Help students infer meaning from the text. Say: *Sometimes you can figure out what a word means by skipping over it and finishing the sentence. Or, you can reread the sentence while thinking about what the word might mean. Let's see how this works by reading the first paragraph.*

Ask students to "think aloud" to explain how the clues in the paragraph helped them figure out what the words mean. You may need to model the strategy.

Teacher Tip

INFERRING MEANING FROM TEXT

Each lesson of this program begins with an exercise in which students are to infer the meaning of specific words from the text. We have deliberately selected words for which there are enough cues for students to determine the meaning. On the fifth day of the program, the students further develop their inferencing skills.

However, context does not always give a lot of information about the meaning of new words. In a study by Beck, McKeown, and Omanson (1987), only 3% of adults could define *grudgingly* in the following passage:

(1) Sandra had won a dance contest and the audience's cheers brought her to the stage for an encore. "Every step she takes is so perfect and graceful," Ginny said *grudgingly*, as she watched Sandra dance.

Twenty-seven percent could define *lumbering* in this passage:

(2) Dan heard the door open and wondered who had arrived. He couldn't make out the voices. Then he recognized the *lumbering* footsteps on the stairs and knew it was Aunt Grace.

Yet, 86% could define *commotion* in this passage:

(3) The animals ran past Wendy, tripping her. She cried out and fell to the floor. As the noise and confusion mounted, Mother hollered upstairs, "What's all that *commotion?*"

The differing number and quality of context clues in the passages determined the readers' ability to figure out the meaning of the word. The context is actually misleading in the first passage, but there is enough information from the text in the third passage to make a good guess as to the meaning. There is little information in the second passage.

You might want to ask students to tell you whether there are enough context clues in passages such as the three given previously. Help them by having them think aloud as they try to figure out the words' meaning. Some other examples include:

(4) John wanted to know how long dinosaurs slept. He read every book he could find in the school library. He looked in encyclopedias. He asked his teachers. After *extensive* research, he finally found the answer. (Good context)

223

(5) The man was skilled in wood carving. He had labored many hours and had produced one of his finest bird carvings. "This is my best work," he said somewhat *lackadaisically.* (Misleading)

(6) Maria was somewhat worried. She had not seen her cat for several days. He did not return at night. She asked her mother, but she could not tell her where he was. In her *tribulation,* she prayed her hardest that he would soon return. (Good context)

USING WORDS IN CONTEXT

Using Words in Context is designed to develop students' ability to decipher the meaning of a word by using clues in the surrounding text.

▼ Prepare for activity

Place students in heterogeneous language groups, ideally four to five students.

Materials: Using Words in Context worksheet for each student

If this activity is challenging for your students, then you may choose to complete it as a whole-group activity. It is helpful to make the worksheet into a transparency so that you can point out the context clues.

▼ Introduce the activity

Say: *Today's activity will help you practice using the target words in sentences. Your job is to figure out which word fits in the blank using the clues that are in the sentence. After you figure out the right word, think about* **how** *you figured it out; what were the clues in the rest of the sentence that helped you. When everyone in the group knows the correct word and* **why it fits,** *raise your hands. I'll call on one of the first groups ready. You will get a point if you get the correct answer (you may choose not to use points). Remember, everyone in your group must know the answer and why it is correct.*

Read the first sentence aloud to the class to illustrate the process.

▼ Review the activity

Ask one student at a table for the correct answer **and to explain how he or she figured it out**—which clues in the context helped. Explaining the thought process that led to the answer helps the students realize that they know how to use the clues in the text and will demonstrate the process to those students who have not yet developed the skill.

Continue until the lesson is completed, giving each group one point for each correct answer (you may choose not to use points).

Lesson 6

TOOLS TO DEVELOP
VOCABULARY: Word Webs

▼ **Prepare for activity**

Divide students into heterogeneous language groups of four to five students.

Materials: one blank copy of a Word Web worksheet for each group, dictionaries, Student Word Books

    Note: You may choose to make the Word Webs into transparencies and complete the activity as a whole group.

▼ **Introduce the concept**

The objective of this lesson is for students to study word meanings, usage, and relationships by completing a Word Web.

    Say: *Today you will complete an activity that will help you think carefully about words in order to understand them better. Each group will study one vocabulary word from this week's lesson and see if they can find synonyms, antonyms, other forms of the word, and other meanings and write a new sentence with the word.*

    You will analyze three words from the text: **admire, allure,** and **complete.**

1. Begin by writing the target word in the center box.

2. Locate the target word in the text in the Student Word Book.

3. Record the sentence containing the target word in the appropriate box (i.e., "Sentence from the fable").

4. Write the definition in the appropriate box (i.e., "Definition"); students may refer to their Student Word Book definitions if needed.

5. Complete the remaining information boxes on the Word Web using dictionaries as needed.

▼ **Review the activity**

Ask each group to share their completed Word Web.

▼ **Assign homework**

Give students the crossword puzzle; review the instructions and the due date. If you notice that students are simply matching the number of spaces with the number of letters in a word, then remind them that this activity will not give them practice with the words and definitions if it becomes a counting exercise. Counting is useful to check their answers.

WORD WIZARD REVIEW

▼ **Review the crossword puzzle homework**

1. Ask students for answers.

2. Direct students to correct their own answers if needed.

▼ **Prepare for activity**

Instruct students to divide into their Word Wizard groups, taking the sentences they have collected throughout the 2 weeks.

▼ **Review Word Wizard**

- Allow students a few minutes to share sentences within their group and tell where they heard or read the word.

- Ask each group to share a few sentences with the class.

   Hint: The more enthusiasm you demonstrate and motivation you provide for this activity, the more the students will participate. Once the students are "hooked," it is most rewarding to observe their enthusiasm and to know that they have incorporated the vocabulary activities into other areas of their lives. You may want to bring in a few examples of your own for extra motivation.

- Allow students to post their sentences on the Word Wizard Wall.

You may choose to give the teams points to encourage participation.

▼ Vocabulary assessment

Part 1: Instruct the students to circle the word that corresponds to the definition on the Vocabulary Assessment worksheet.

Part 2: Instruct students to write sentences that demonstrate their knowledge of the word's meaning on the Vocabulary Assessment Sentences worksheet.

Hint: You may need to provide examples of sentences that demonstrate knowledge of the meaning. For example, if the vocabulary word were **ring,** then the sentence "I have a ring" does not demonstrate knowledge of the meaning. **Nose, car, friend, house,** or any number of other words could be substituted for **ring** in the sentence. The sentence "I wear a ring on my finger" demonstrates knowledge of the meaning.

Teacher answer keys

VOCABULARY REVIEW HOMEWORK

- Read the definitions.
- Find the word in the box that matches the definition.
- Write the correct word next to the definition.

glamour	adorn	flatter	absolutely
salesperson	frown	allure	resist
envy	admire	stare	complete

1. _____**flatter**_____ : to praise too much and often insincerely, especially in order to get a favor

2. _____**adorn**_____ : to make more beautiful or interesting by decorating

3. _____**absolutely**_____ : certainly

4. _____**stare**_____ : to look directly at someone or something for a long time without moving the eyes

5. _____**complete**_____ : total; in every way

6. _____**frown**_____ : to wrinkle the forehead when one is unhappy

7. _____**admire**_____ : to think of or look at with pleasure and respect

8. _____**glamour**_____ : attractive and exciting quality of something special

9. _____**resist**_____ : to refuse to accept; to oppose

10. _____**envy**_____ : the wish to have what someone else has

11. _____**allure**_____ : to attract

12. _____**salesperson**_____ : a man or woman who sells goods or services

MYSTERY WORDS WORKSHEET

- Pick a definition from the box that might go with the bold word.
- Write the number for the definition in the space beside the word.
- Check the cefinition you chose using the steps listed on the Hints for Solving Mystery Words sheet in your Student Word Book.

---

1. Settled; not moving from one place to another
2. One who collects stamps
3. Having to do with birds
4. Having to do with night
5. The point at which something is likely to begin
6. Animals that live by hunting other animals for food

THE KIWI

Everyone in New Zealand knows the kiwi. It is an **avian** __3__ species often found in that

country. It has very short wings and cannot fly. The kiwi's picture is on New Zealand's

stamps, which makes it a **philatelist's** __2__ delight.

    The kiwi is **nocturnal** __4__ —it likes to eat and play when it is dark outside. Some of

the kiwi's **predators** __6__ , such as owls and rats, are also nocturnal. These animals have

brought the kiwi to the **brink** __5__ of extinction; however, the kiwi is a strong fighter, so it

has not died out completely.

    The kiwi lays only one egg at a time. The male sits on the egg. He is very **sedentary**

__1__ —he doesn't leave the nest even for food and water.

USING WORDS IN CONTEXT WORKSHEET

Admiration	adorned	Envy	flatter	frown
glamorous	glamorous	resist	salespeople	

1. When you smile, your mouth and eyebrows go up; they **go down** when you __**frown**__.

2. During the holidays, a lot of stores are so busy that they need more __**salespeople**__
to wait on customers.

3. Madame Rhinoceros looked silly in the dress, but the salesperson **told her that it made her look attractive.** Salespeople sometimes __**flatter**__ customers so that they will buy something.

4. When people smiled at Madame Rhinoceros in her new dress, she thought that they **liked** it. "__**Admiration**__," thought Madame Rhinoceros.

5. When people frowned at Madame Rhinoceros in her new dress, she thought that they were **jealous.** "__**Envy**__," thought Madame Rhinoceros.

6. Actors put on make-up and **fancy** costumes to look __**glamorous**__ in movies.

7. At my sister's wedding, the tables were beautifully **decorated.** They were __**adorned**__ with flowers, candles, and lace doilies.

8. Madame Rhinoceros felt **attractive** in her new dress; she thought the dress made her look __**glamorous**__.

9. If muggers want your money, don't **argue.** They might hurt you if you __**resist**__.

Absolutely	adorned	admires	complete	stare
completely	envy	flattering	frown	

10. It is alright to **look at** people you don't know, but it is not polite to _____**stare**_____ at them **for a long time.**

11. I **look up to** my brother because he is intelligent, kind, generous, strong, and handsome. Everyone in our neighborhood _____**admires**_____ him.

12. I _____**envy**_____ Juan for having cookies when I **wish I had some.**

13. The dancer **made** her costume **more beautiful** when she _____**adorned**_____ it with feathers and scarves.

14. Some people's **faces** change when they are angry; they _____**frown**_____.

15. My friend has **every** *Goosebumps* book ever published. He has the _____**complete**_____ series.

16. Are you sure that you have **entirely** finished all your work? Yes, I am _____**completely**_____ finished. Now may I go?

17. When our teacher asked, "Would you like to have recess all day?" The class answered, "_____**Absolutely**_____!"

18. The dress didn't **make** Madame Rhinoceros **look prettier.** It wasn't a _____**flattering**_____ dress at all.

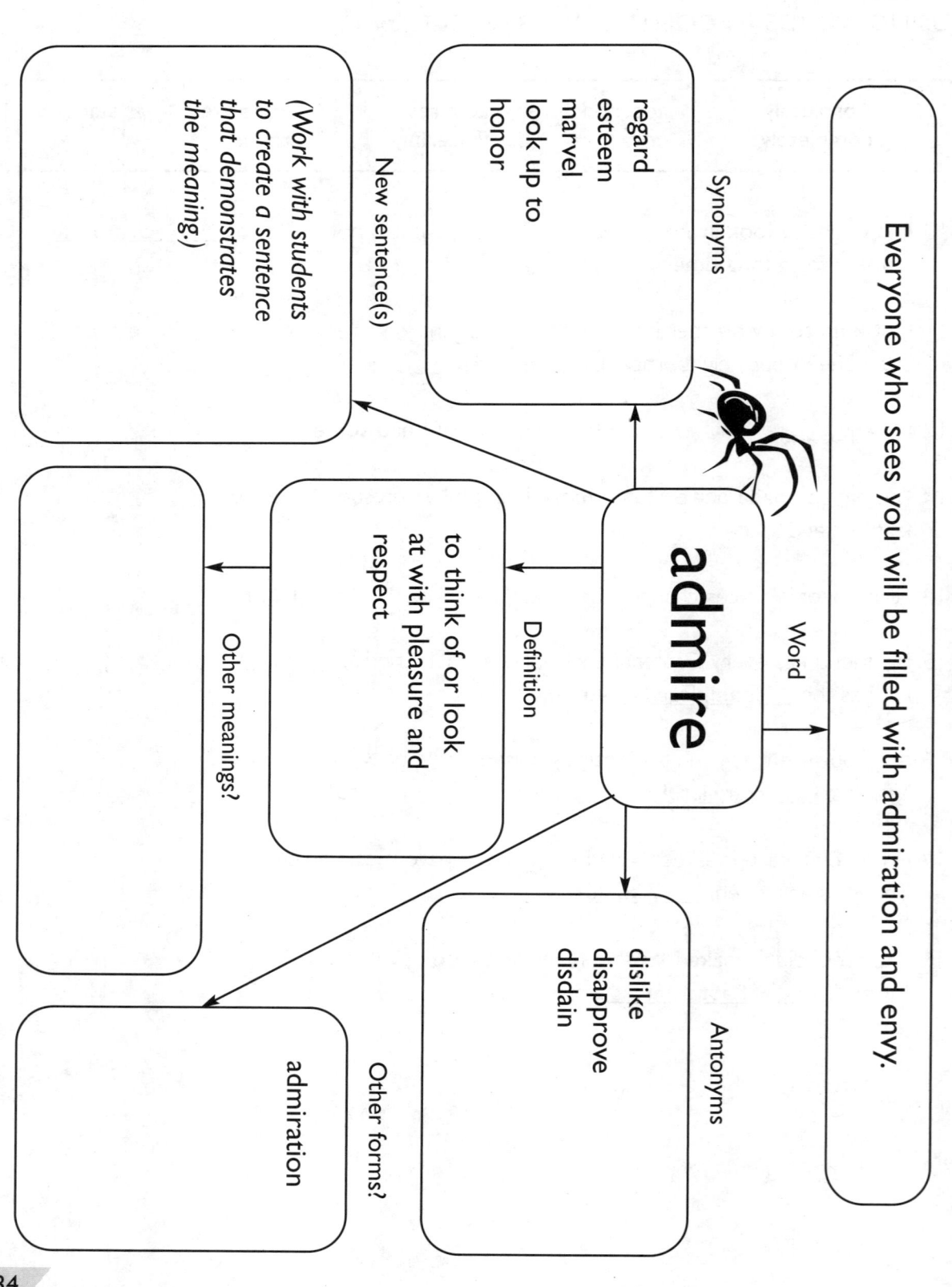

Sentence from fable

Everyone who sees you will be filled with admiration and envy.

Word

admire

Synonyms

regard
esteem
marvel
look up to
honor

Definition

to think of or look at with pleasure and respect

New sentence(s)

(Work with students to create a sentence that demonstrates the meaning.)

Other meanings?

Antonyms

dislike
disapprove
disdain

Other forms?

admiration

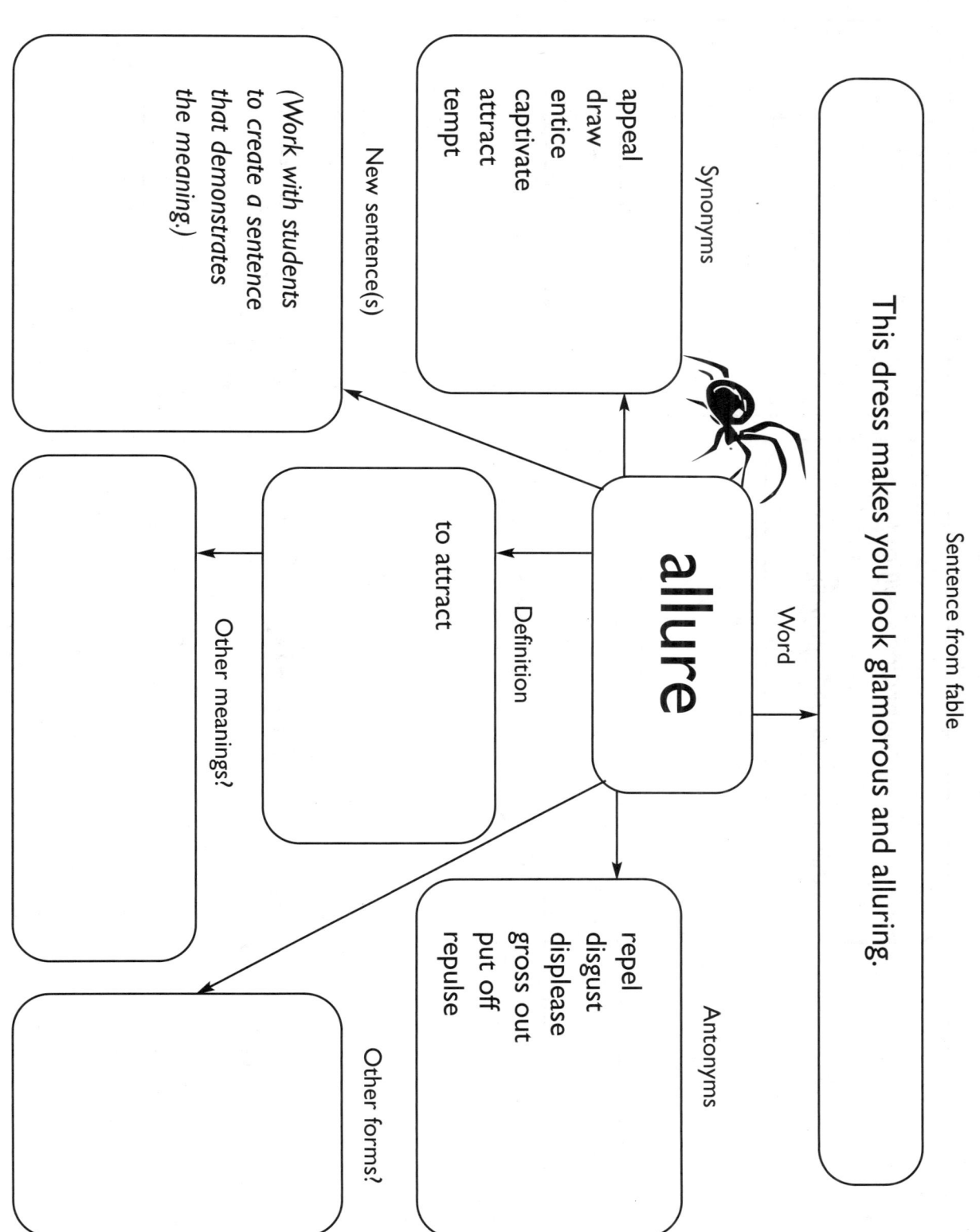

Sentence from fable

This dress makes you look glamorous and alluring.

Word

allure

Synonyms

appeal
draw
entice
captivate
attract
tempt

Antonyms

repel
disgust
displease
gross out
put off
repulse

Definition

to attract

New sentence(s)

(Work with students to create a sentence that demonstrates the meaning.)

Other meanings?

Other forms?

complete

Word → But Madame, you are completely wrong.

Sentence from fable

Synonyms

finish
entire
ended
totally
wholly

New sentence(s)

(Work with students
to create a sentence
that demonstrates
the meaning.)

Definition

total; in every way

Other meanings?

a) to have all necessary or normal parts
b) to finish something

Antonyms

begin
start
partial
unfinished
incomplete

Other forms?

completion

LESSON 6

```
                    G
        F       G       F
        L       L       R
C O M P L E T E A       O W
        A       M           N
    S A L E S P E R S O N
        T   R   O   N
        T   R   U   V       A
        E   R   R   Y       D
        R           S       O
      R E S I S T   T       R
                A   A       E
              A D M I R E   N
                R   R
    A B S O L U T E L Y
```

LESSON 7

```
                        S
    T       G           P
    W I L L P O W E R   R
    I       O       H   O
    N       W       E   U
    K           H E A R T B U R N
    L           J   L   T
    E           O   F   E
                U   W   M
  D I S C O U R A G E   P
                R   Y   T
C O N T A I N       S P I N
                E       T
    L I K E L Y
```

LESSON 8

```
S
A
T U G               M
I   A   P O R T I O N
S   Z           R
F   E N O R M O U S
Y       E       E   F
    B U D G E   G L O O M
        R           R
    D   E           L
    A P P E T I T E O
    B               R
                    N
```

LESSON 9

```
    S
    E           C O N T E N T
    V           A
    E   B   T E R R O R
    R O L L   R
    A   O   D O       A
    L   O V E R W H E L M
        D   C       A
    F   Y   I       R
    I       D A W N M
B R U I S E
    M
```

LESSON 10

```
                A   L
                L   I
                L   K
                U   E
    G       C   R   L
    A B S O L U T E L Y   P
    Z       N           O
    E       T       B   R
            A     D U   T
        T W I N K L E D I
            N     C   G L O W
              A D M I R E N
                  D
        O V E R W H E L M
```

Lesson 6

VOCABULARY ASSESSMENT WORKSHEET

- Circle the word that matches the definition.

1. To praise too much and often insincerely, especially in order to get a favor

    allure   admire   (flatter)   stare

2. To refuse to accept; to oppose

    (resist)   glamour   complete   salesperson

3. A man or woman who sells goods or services

    flatter   adorn   (salesperson)   frown

4. To attract

    envy   (allure)   stare   complete

5. Attractive and exciting quality of something special

    adorn   (glamour)   absolutely   resist

6. The wish to have what someone else has

    resist   frown   allure   (envy)

7. To think of or look at with pleasure and respect

    (admire)   salesperson   envy   frown

8. To wrinkle the forehead when one is unhappy

    glamour   resist   (frown)   stare

9. Total; in every way

    allure   (complete)   resist   flatter

10. To make more beautiful or interesting by decorating

    stare   flatter   (adorn)   allure

11. To look directly at someone or something for a long time without moving the eyes

    (stare)   adorn   envy   frown

12. Certainly

    resist   flatter   (absolutely)   glamour

Reproducible materials

Madame Rhinoceros and Her Dress

Lesson 6

CLASSROOM WORD LIST

adorned

salesperson

completely

admiration

alluring

glamorous

envy

absolutely

frowning

flattery

resist

stared

Name: _____

VOCABULARY REVIEW HOMEWORK

- Read the definitions.
- Find the word in the box that matches the definition.
- Write the correct word next to the definition.

glamour	adorn	flatter	absolutely
salesperson	frown	allure	resist
envy	admire	stare	complete

1. _____: to praise too much and often insincerely, especially in order to get a favor

2. _____: to make more beautiful or interesting by decorating

3. _____: certainly

4. _____: to look directly at someone or something for a long time without moving the eyes

5. _____: total; in every way

6. _____: to wrinkle the forehead when one is unhappy

7. _____: to think of or look at with pleasure and respect

8. _____: attractive and exciting quality of something special

9. _____: to refuse to accept; to oppose

10. _____: the wish to have what someone else has

11. _____: to attract

12. _____: a man or woman who sells goods or services

WORD WIZARD LIST

• Each time you hear or read one of these words used in a sentence at home, at school, on television, or on the radio, write the sentence on an index card or sticky note.

absolutely: certainly

admiration (admire): to think of or look at with pleasure and respect

adorned (adorn): to make more beautiful or interesting by decorating

alluring (allure): to attract

completely (complete): total; in every way

envy: the wish to have what someone else has

flattery (flatter): to praise too much and often insincerely, especially in order to get a favor

frowning (frown): to wrinkle the forehead when one is unhappy

glamorous (glamour): attractive and exciting quality of something special

resist: to refuse to accept; to oppose

salesperson: a man or woman who sells goods or services

stared (stare): to look at something for a long time without moving the eyes

Name: _____

WORD SUBSTITUTION WORKSHEET

1. I like to **adorn** my house for the holidays.

2. The **salesperson** tried to convince my mom to buy a 72-inch television.

3. I am **completely** certain that I would not miss it if I never had to do homework again!

4. My older sister felt **glamorous** when she was dressed up for the prom.

5. Some people know how to make bird calls to **allure** birds.

6. I **admire** my friends who do their homework when they first come home from school.

7. I **envy** people who don't have to study very much for tests.

8. My brother **absolutely** does not want to go into the haunted house.

9. Babies are so cute when they **frown**; older people are not!

10. My dad always tells me that it isn't nice to **stare**.

11. At times it is hard for me to **resist** watching television, even when I have a test the next day.

12. My grandma often tells me, "**Flattery** will not get you anywhere!"

MYSTERY WORDS WORKSHEET

- Pick a definition from the box that might go with the bold word.
- Write the number for the definition in the space beside the word.
- Check the definition you chose using the steps listed on the Hints for Solving Mystery Words sheet in your Student Word Book.

---

1. Settled; not moving from one place to another
2. One who collects stamps
3. Having to do with birds
4. Having to do with night
5. The point at which something is likely to begin
6. Animals that live by hunting other animals for food

THE KIWI

Everyone in New Zealand knows the kiwi. It is an **avian** _____ species often found in that country. It has very short wings and cannot fly. The kiwi's picture is on New Zealand's stamps, which makes it a **philatelist's** _____ delight.

The kiwi is **nocturnal** _____—it likes to eat and play when it is dark outside. Some of the kiwi's **predators** _____, such as owls and rats, are also nocturnal. These animals have brought the kiwi to the **brink** _____ of extinction; however, the kiwi is a strong fighter, so it has not died out completely.

The kiwi lays only one egg at a time. The male sits on the egg. He is very **sedentary** _____—he doesn't leave the nest even for food and water.

Vocabulary Improvement Program for English Language Learners and Their Classmates, 4th Grade, by Teresa Lively, Diane August, María Carlo, and Catherine Snow © 2003 Paul H. Brookes Publishing Co., Inc. All rights reserved.

USING WORDS IN CONTEXT WORKSHEET

| Admiration | adorned | Envy | flatter | frown |
| glamorous | glamorous | resist | salespeople | |

1. When you smile, your mouth and eyebrows go up; they **go down** when you _____.

2. During the holidays, a lot of stores are so busy that they need more _____ **to wait on customers**.

3. Madame Rhinoceros looked silly in the dress, but the salesperson **told her that it made her look attractive**. Salespeople sometimes _____ customers so that they will buy something.

4. When people smiled at Madame Rhinoceros in her new dress, she thought that they **liked it**. "_____," thought Madame Rhinoceros.

5. When people frowned at Madame Rhinoceros in her new dress, she thought that they were **jealous**. "_____," thought Madame Rhinoceros.

6. Actors put on makeup and **fancy** costumes to look _____ in movies.

7. At my sister's wedding, the tables were beautifully **decorated**. They were _____ with flowers, candles, and lace doilies.

8. Madame Rhinoceros felt **attractive** in her new dress; she thought the dress made her look _____.

9. If muggers want your money, don't **argue**. They might hurt you if you _____.

Name: _____

USING WORDS IN CONTEXT WORKSHEET (continued)

Absolutely	adorned	admires	complete	stare
completely	envy	flattering	frown	

10. It is alright to **look at** people you don't know, but it is not polite to _____ at them **for a long time**.

11. I **look up to** my brother because he is intelligent, kind, generous, strong, and handsome. Everyone in our neighborhood _____ him.

12. I _____ Juan for having cookies when I **wish I had some**.

13. The dancer made her costume **more beautiful** when she _____ it with feathers and scarves.

14. Some people's **faces** change when they are angry; they _____.

15. My friend has **every** *Goosebumps* book ever published. He has the _____ series.

16. Are you sure that you have **entirely** finished all your work? Yes, I am _____ finished. Now may I go?

17. When our teacher asked, "Would you like to have recess all day?" The class answered, "_____!"

18. The dress didn't **make** Madame Rhinoceros **look prettier**. It wasn't a _____ dress at all.

Vocabulary Improvement Program for English Language Learners and Their Classmates, 4th Grade, by Teresa Lively, Diane August, María Carlo, and Catherine Snow © 2003 Paul H. Brookes Publishing Co., Inc. All rights reserved.

WORD WEB

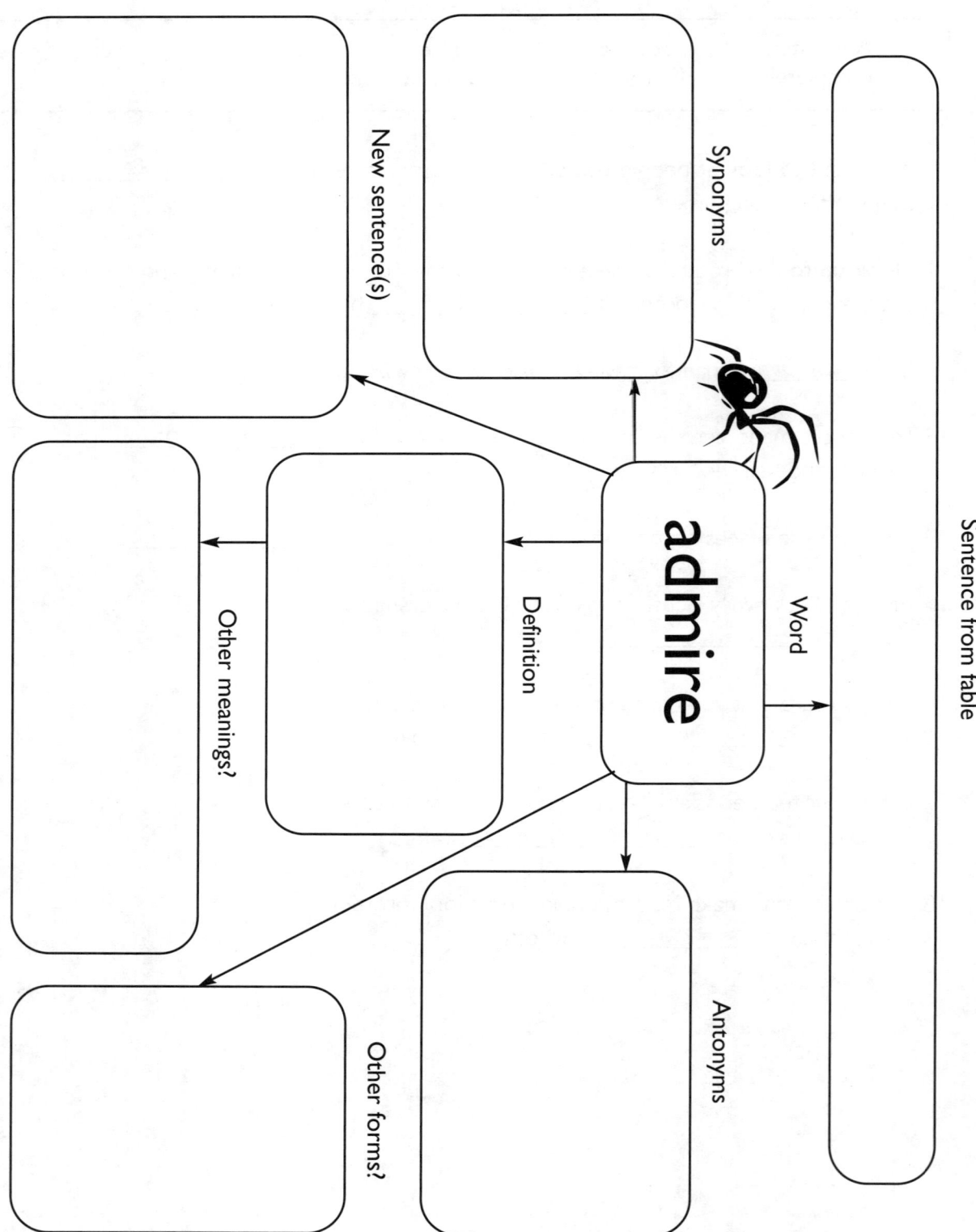

New sentence(s)

Synonyms

Sentence from fable

Other meanings?

Definition

admire

Word

Other forms?

Antonyms

WORD WEB

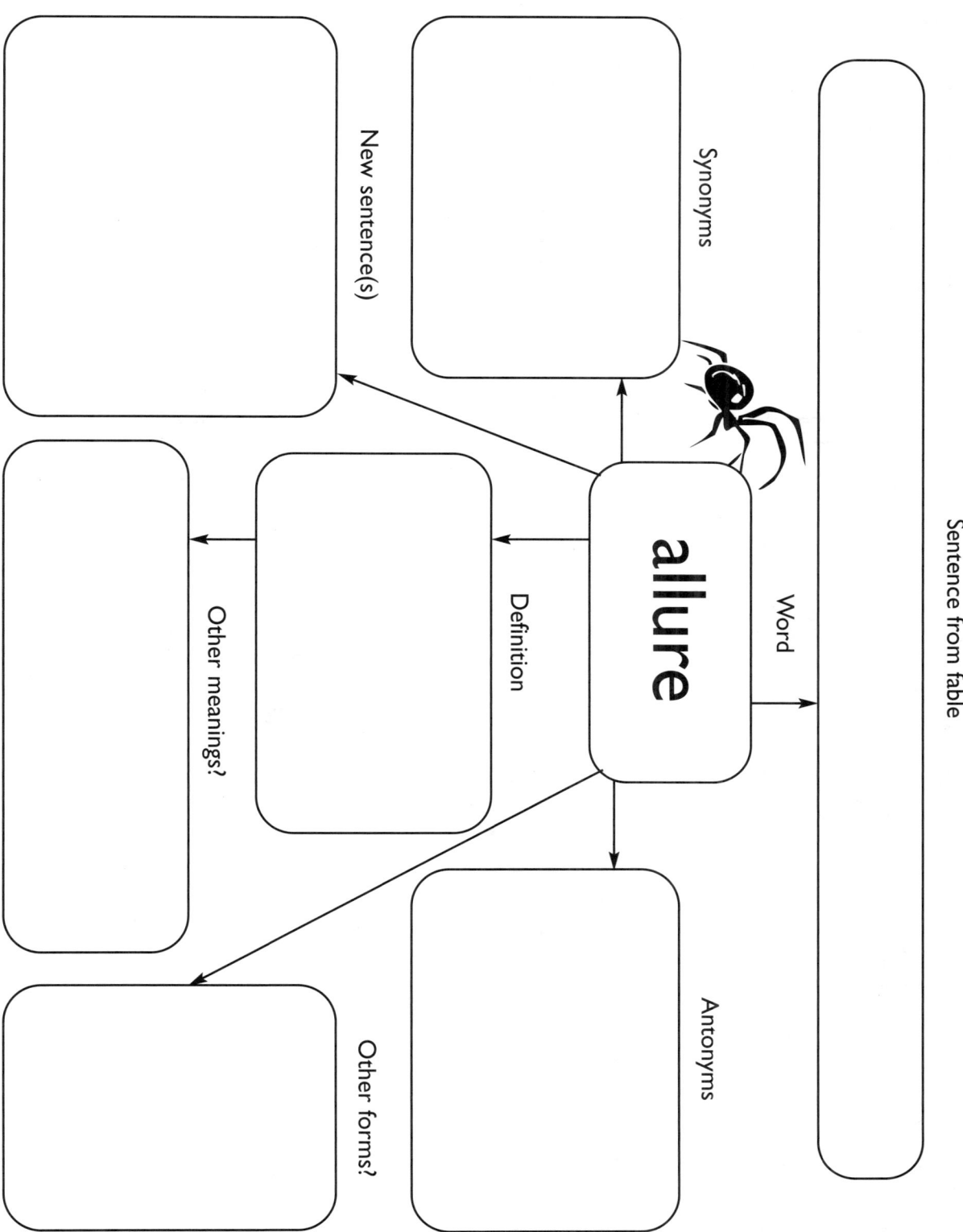

New sentence(s)

Synonyms

Definition

allure

Word

Sentence from fable

Other meanings?

Other forms?

Antonyms

WORD WEB

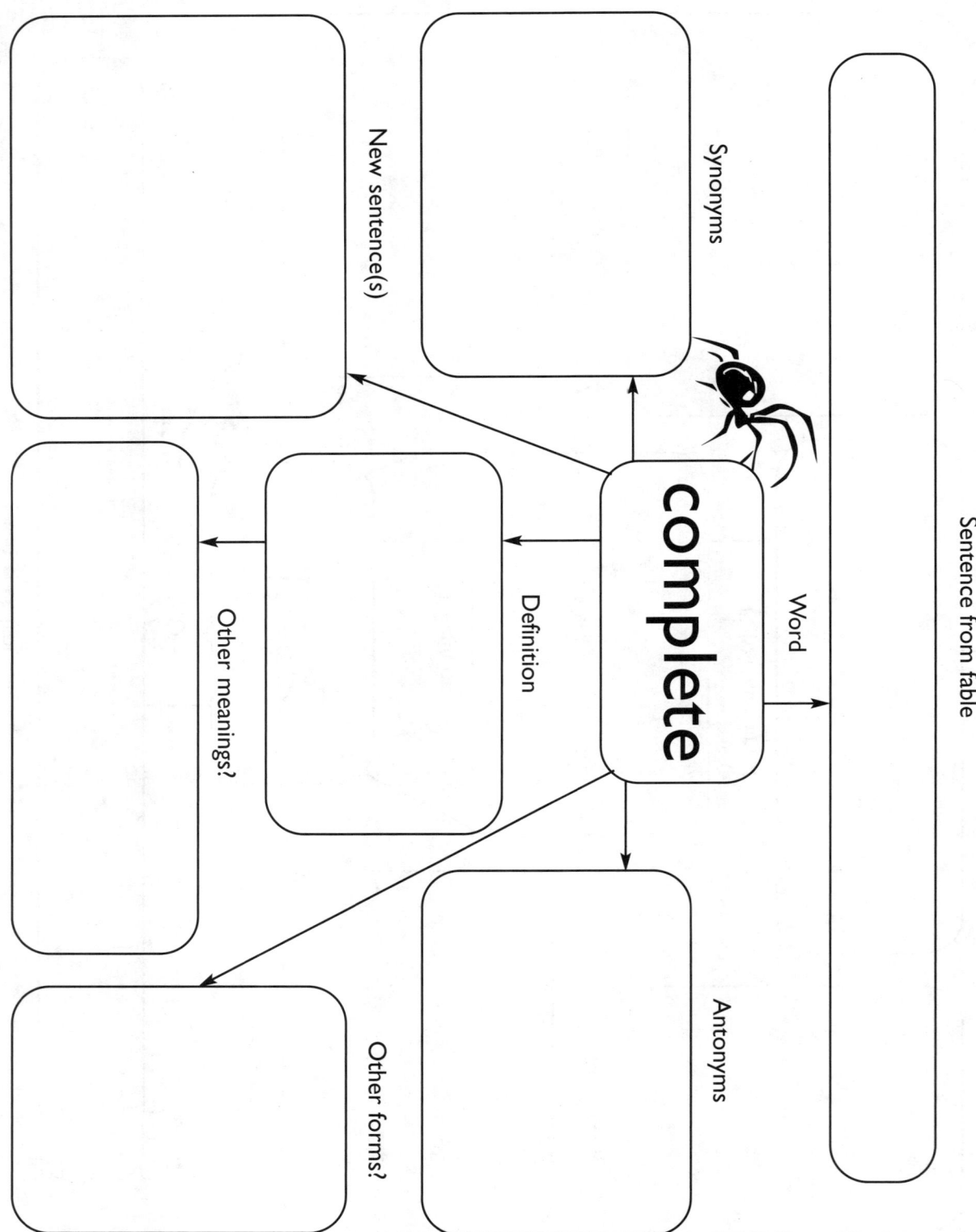

New sentence(s)

Synonyms

Sentence from fable

Other meanings?

Definition

complete

Word

Other forms?

Antonyms

Name: _____

ACROSS

4. Total; in every way
5. A man or woman who sells goods or services
10. To refuse to accept; to oppose
11. To think of, or look at, with pleasure and respect
12. Certainly

DOWN

1. Attractive and exciting quality of something special
2. To praise too much and often insincerely, especially in order to get a favor
3. To wrinkle the forehead when one is unhappy
6. To attract
7. The wish to have what someone else has
8. To make more beautiful or interesting by decorating
9. To look directly at someone or something for a long time without moving the eyes

Lesson 6

absolutely

admire

adorn

allure

complete

envy

flatter

frown

glamour

resist

salesperson

stare

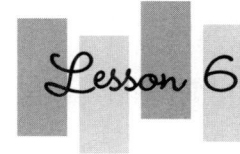

VOCABULARY ASSESSMENT WORKSHEET

• Circle the word that matches the definition.

1. To praise too much and often insincerely, especially in order to get a favor

    allure   admire   flatter   stare

2. To refuse to accept; to oppose

    resist   glamour   complete   salesperson

3. A man or woman who sells goods or services

    flatter   adorn   salesperson   frown

4. To attract

    envy   allure   stare   complete

5. Attractive and exciting quality of something special

    adorn   glamour   absolutely   resist

6. The wish to have what someone else has

    resist   frown   allure   envy

7. To think of or look at with pleasure and respect

    admire   salesperson   envy   frown

8. To wrinkle the forehead when one is unhappy

    glamour   resist   frown   stare

9. Total; in every way

    allure   complete   resist   flatter

10. To make more beautiful or interesting by decorating

    stare   flatter   adorn   allure

11. To look directly at someone or something for a long time without moving the eyes

    stare   adorn   envy   frown

12. Certainly

    resist   flatter   absolutely   glamour

VOCABULARY ASSESSMENT
SENTENCES WORKSHEET

• Write a sentence with each of these four vocabulary words to show that you know what the word means.

resist	adorn	envy	stare

1. _____

_____

2. _____

_____

3. _____

_____

4. _____

_____

Vocabulary Improvement Program for English Language Learners and Their Classmates, 4th Grade, by Teresa Lively, Diane August, María Carlo, and Catherine Snow © 2003 Paul H. Brookes Publishing Co., Inc. All rights reserved.

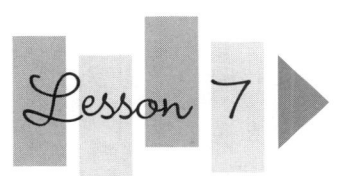

The Pig at the Candy Store

OVERVIEW OF ACTIVITIES

Day 1	Day 2	Day 3	Day 4
TEXT INTRODUCTION	**VOCABULARY INTRODUCTION**	**EXPAND MEANING**	**TOOLS TO DEVELOP VOCABULARY**
• Predict storyline • Read fable • Discuss fable	• Circle vocabulary • Extract definitions • Review cognates • Assign homework	• Review homework • Word Associations • Assign homework	• Multiple Meanings

Day 5	Day 6	Day 7	Day 8
USING WORDS IN CONTEXT	**TOOLS TO DEVELOP VOCABULARY**	**WORD WIZARD REVIEW**	**ASSESSMENT**
• Contexting activity	• Affixes • Assign homework	• Review homework • Word Wizard review	

WORD LIST

The word in bold is the base word, followed by its definition. If the word has more than one meaning, then we provide only the definition used in the text. *Please review the definitions prior to instruction.*

1. **contain:** to have inside; hold
2. **discourage:** persuade someone not to do something
3. **glow:** give off a steady, low light
4. **halfway:** half the distance from one place to another
5. **heartburn:** an unpleasant burning in the chest caused by acid acting on food in the stomach
6. **journey:** a long trip
7. **likely:** probable
8. **spin:** to make thread by twisting fine fibers together
9. **sprout:** to emerge (come out) and develop rapidly
10. **tempt:** to try to convince someone to do something wrong
11. **twinkle:** to shine with quick flashes of light
12. **willpower:** the strength to control one's actions

IDIOMATIC EXPRESSIONS

- **on second thought:** when one stops to think about something again

OTHER WORDS WORTH DEFINING

- **marzipan:** candy made of almonds
- **marshmallow:** spongy, white candy
- **chocolate kisses:** chocolate candy
- **peppermints:** mint-flavored candy
- **gumdrops:** small, colored, chewy candy coated with coarse sugar
- **foil:** thin, silvery sheets of metal
- **wrappers:** paper that protects candy

▼ **Prepare for activity**

Post Classroom Word List.

Materials: Student Word Books, *Fables*

▼ **Predict storyline**

Show students the illustration for "The Pig in the Candy Store" in the color insert or turn to page 30 of *Fables*.

Say: *Today we are going to read the fable "The Pig at the Candy Store." What do you think this fable will be about when you look at the illustration and hear the title?*

Encourage a student discussion.

▼ **Ask the students to listen as you read the fable aloud**

▼ **Discuss the fable and moral; relate it to the students' lives**

- *Who is the main character in this fable?*
- *What were Pig's dreams?*
- *Do you think pigs really dream? How would we know?*
- *What did Pig do when he woke up?*
- *Have your dreams ever affected your actions after you woke up?*
- *Why did Pig hesitate before going to the candy store?*
- *Why didn't the pig buy any candy?*
- *Do you think he enjoyed his healthy dinner?*

▼ **Reread the moral**

- *What do you think the moral means?*
- *What have you been tempted to do that you knew you should not do?*
- *Have you ever had something keep you from giving in to your temptation?*
- *How did you feel?*

The Pig at the Candy Store

All night long, the sleeping Pig dreamed of candy. He **sprouted** wings of **spun** sugar. He flew through marshmallow clouds to a **glowing** marzipan moon. The stars that **twinkled** in the sky were chocolate kisses wrapped in shiny foil.

The Pig woke up with his mouth watering.

"Candy," he cried. "I must have some this minute!"

The Pig ran to the candy dish. It was empty. The box of chocolate creams in the cupboard **contained** nothing but paper wrappers.

"I will go to the candy store," said the Pig, as he put on his clothes and rushed out of his house.

"On second thought," said the Pig, "I must remember that candy is bad for me. It makes me fatter than I already am. It gives me gas and **heartburn**."

Then the Pig remembered his sweet dreams. He decided that since he was **halfway** to the candy store, he might as well finish the **journey.**

"Just a few peppermints will not hurt me," he said.

As the Pig came near the store, his mouth began to water again. "Maybe I will buy a small bag of gumdrops as well."

But the candy store was closed. A sign on the door said "On Vacation."

The Pig went back home.

"What wonderful **willpower** I have!" he cried happily. "I did not eat a single piece of candy!"

That night the Pig had a vegetable salad for supper. He drank a glass of cold, fresh milk. He felt thin and had neither gas nor heartburn.

*A locked door is very **likely** to **discourage temptation**.*

Day 2
VOCABULARY INTRODUCTION

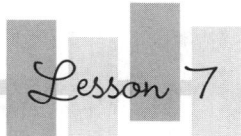

Lesson 7

▼ Review the sections titled "Idiomatic Expressions" and "Other Words Worth Defining"

▼ Read posted target words to students, or ask students to read them

- Before you reread the fable, say: *Follow along in your Student Word Book as I read the fable again. Circle the target word when I read it. If you think you know what the word means* **without reading the definition,** *then raise your hand and I will call on you.* After students have suggested meanings, say: *Let's check the definition to see how close you were.*

  Note: The target words appear in the same order in the fable as on the word list. To help students find the words more easily, point out each target word on the list before looking for it in the text.

- There are no target words for which meaning can be inferred this week.

▼ Assign Vocabulary Review homework

Instruct students to write the correct vocabulary word in the space beside the definition.

▼ Cognates

If the students are bilingual, then you may wish to review the cognates from the fable.

English word	Spanish word
marzipan	marzapán
chocolate	chocolate
minute	minuto
creams	cremas
contained	contenía
paper	papel
gas	gas
vacation	vacaciones
vegetable	vegetal

TARGET WORD DEFINITIONS

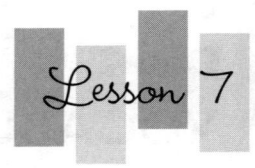

- The base word is bold and is the word defined.
- If there is more than one meaning, then the bold definition is the one used in the fable.
- The Spanish translation is provided for the meaning used in the fable.

1. contained (**contain**):
   a) to have inside; hold
   b) to include or be a part of
   c) to hold or keep within limits; restrain
   - contener; tener dentro de si, sugetar

2. **discourage:**
   a) to take away someone's courage or confidence
   b) persuade someone not to do something
   - desalentar; quitar el ánimo, acobardar

3. glowing (**glow**):
   a) give off a steady, low light
   b) to show a bright, warm, or healthy color
   c) to show a warm feeling
   - candente; que emana luz

4. **halfway:**
   a) half the distance from one place to another
   b) not thorough or complete
   - a medio camino

5. **heartburn:**
   an unpleasant burning in the chest caused by acid acting on food in the stomach
   - acidez; exceso de ácido en el estómago

6. **journey:**
   a long trip
   - jornada; viaje

7. **likely:**
   probable
   - probable; hay buenas razones para creer que suceder

8. sprouted (**sprout**):
   a) to begin to grow; give off shoots or buds (as in plants)
   b) to emerge (come out) and develop rapidly
   - germinar; brotar y comenzar a crecer

9. spun (**spin**):
   a) to make thread by twisting fine fibers together
   b) to make a web or cocoon from a liquid that hardens into thread
   c) to rotate or whirl around
   d) to tel or relate
   - hilar; reducir a hilo el lino, lana, seda, algodón, etc.

10. temptation (**tempt**):
    a) to try to convince someone to do something wrong
    b) to appeal strongly to
    - tentación; que induce o persuade a una cosa mala

11. twinkled (**twinkle**):
    to shine with quick flashes of light
    - centellear o titular; que despide rayos de luz de intensidad o coloración variables

12. **willpower:**
    the strength to control one's actions
    - fuerza de voluntad

▼ **Review Vocabulary Review homework**

1. Ask students for answers.

2. Direct students to correct their own answers if needed.

▼ **Introduce the activity**

1. Say: *I am going to say a word or phrase that has something to do with one of the vocabulary words, kind of like a clue. Your job is to think about which vocabulary word goes with the clue.*

2. Give clues one word at a time until the word is guessed. Say: *What vocabulary word do you think of when I say _____? Please explain why you think the vocabulary word goes with the clue.*

Accept any plausible answer that the student can justify.

Associated word	Vocabulary word
hold; lunch box; chest	contain
sad; fail	discourage
happy; moon; kryptonite; neon	glowing
partially; almost; in-between	halfway
Tums; greasy food; stomachache	heartburn
far; travel; voyage; Oregon Trail	journey
probably; for sure; possible	likely
seeds; grew; corn; alfalfa	sprouted
Rumpelstiltskin; wool; dizzy; lottery	spin
money on the floor; chocolate cake; resist	temptation
jewels; sparkle; star; eye; flash	twinkle
strong; resist; motivation	willpower

Note: Encourage students to think of associated words for their classmates to guess, including synonyms and antonyms.

▼ **Word Wizard**

Motivate students to find sentences with this week's vocabulary. Say: *You are all going to continue being word wizards and even build your skills with this week's vocabulary words! Just like last week, I want you to demonstrate your wizardry in the following way: Each time you hear or read one of this week's words used at home, at school, or even on television, I want you to write the sentence on an index card (or sticky note). Write down where you heard or read it.*

Give students the Word Wizard List.

TOOLS TO DEVELOP
VOCABULARY: Multiple Meanings

▼ **Prepare for activity**

Divide students into mixed language groups of four to five students.
Materials: Multiple Meanings worksheet

▼ **Introduce the activity**

PART 1

Say: *Today we are going to work with some of the words from the text that have more than one meaning. In the first part of the activity, we will discuss the different meanings for each word. Who knows one of the meanings for the word* _____ ?

Continue until the students have provided the definitions they know; then introduce the remaining definitions.

contain	a) to have inside; hold
	b) to include or be a part of
	c) to hold or keep within limits; restrain
glow	a) give off a steady, low light
	b) to show a bright, warm or healthy color
	c) to show a warm feeling
spin	a) to make thread by twisting fine fibers together
	b) to make a web or cocoon from a liquid that hardens into thread
	c) to rotate or whirl around
	d) to tell or relate
discourage	a) to take away someone's courage or confidence
	b) persuade someone not to do something
long	a) more than the average length
	b) throughout the length or duration of
	c) to want something very much
halfway	a) half the distance from one place to another
	b) not thorough or complete

PART 2

Say: *In the next part of the activity, you will see these same definitions in two boxes on the Multiple Meanings worksheet. Sentences below the boxes use the different meanings. Your job is to find the definition in the box that best fits the way the word is used in each sentence. You will then write the letter for that definition in the space at the end of the sentence. Let's try one together.*

Write the following example on the board and complete for practice.

A. An interval of time

B. A punctuation mark placed at the end of sentences and after many abbreviations

---

1. Remember to use a **period** after the middle initial in your name. _____

2. It was a terrible **period** in our country's history when we allowed slavery. _____

Allow students to work on the worksheets in their groups until finished.

▼ Review the activity

Ask students for the correct answers and for the clues that helped them choose the correct answers.

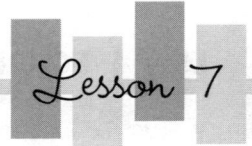

Day 5
USING WORDS IN CONTEXT

Using Words in Context is designed to develop students' ability to decipher the meaning of a word by using clues in the surrounding text.

▼ Prepare for activity

Place students in heterogeneous language groups, ideally four to five students.

Materials: Using Words in Context worksheet for each student

If this activity is challenging for your students, then you may choose to complete it as a whole-group activity. It is helpful to make the worksheet into a transparency so that you can point out the context clues.

▼ Introduce the activity

Say: *Today's activity will help you practice using the target words in sentences. Your job is to figure out which word fits in the blank using the clues that are in the sentence. After you figure out the right word, think about* **how** *you figured it out; what were the clues in the rest of the sentence that helped you. When everyone in the group knows the correct word and* **why it fits,** *raise your hands. I'll call on one of the first groups ready. You will get a point if you get the correct answer (you may choose not to use points). Remember, everyone in your group must know the answer and why it is correct.*

Read the first sentence aloud to the class to illustrate the process.

▼ Review the activity

- Ask one student at a table for the correct answer **and to explain how he or she figured it out**—which clues in the context helped. Explaining the thought process that led to the answer helps the students realize that they know how to use the clues in the text and will demonstrate the process to those students who have not yet developed the skill.

- Continue until the lesson is completed, giving each group one point for each correct answer (you may choose not to use points).

Day 6
TOOLS TO DEVELOP
VOCABULARY: Affixes

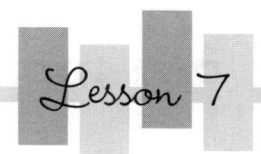

▼ **Prepare for activity**

Divide students into heterogeneous language groups of four to six students.
Materials: Affixes worksheet

▼ **Review the concept**

Say: *Today we're going to practice using affixes again. Who remembers what the two kinds of affixes are? That's right, prefixes and suffixes.*

> ***Prefixes*** *are letters added to the beginning of a word that change its meaning. For example, if you add the prefix* **un-** *to* **important,** *how does the meaning change?*

> ***Suffixes*** *are letters added to the end of a word that change its meaning. For example, if you add the suffix* **-less** *to* **friend,** *how does the meaning change?*

> *For example, if you did not know the meaning of the word* **beloved** *but you knew that the prefix* **be-** *means completely, and you could see that the root word is* **love,** *you could figure out that beloved is someone who is loved completely.*

> *You may want to provide more examples for the students.*

> *Remember, when you're working with affixes, keep it in the back of your mind that you are practicing with a tool that you might be able to use when you read or hear a word that you don't know.*

▼ **Introduce the activity: Affixes**

Say: *Today you will work with four prefixes and five suffixes. Let's look at the affixes and their meanings.*

PREFIXES

re-: again
mis-: wrong, wrongly
un-: not
dis-: opposite of

SUFFIXES

-less: without
-er: someone who _____ ; something that _____
-ful: full of _____
-ly: in the stated way
-y: full of or covered with

Allow students to work in their groups until they have completed the worksheet.

Day 6: TOOLS TO DEVELOP VOCABULARY

▼ **Review the activity**

Ask students to explain how they chose their answers.

▼ **Assign homework**

Give students the crossword puzzle; review the instructions and the due date.

▼ **Review the crossword puzzle homework**

1. Ask students for answers.

2. Direct students to correct their own answers if needed.

3. The crossword puzzle answer key for Lessons 6–10 can be found in the Teacher Answer Keys for Lesson 6.

▼ **Prepare for activity**

1. Instruct students to divide into their Word Wizard groups, taking the sentences they have collected throughout the 2 weeks.

▼ **Review Word Wizard**

• Allow students a few minutes to share sentences within their group and tell where they heard or read the word.

• Ask each group to share a few sentences with the class.

   Hint: The more enthusiasm you demonstrate and motivation you provide for this activity, the more the students will participate. Once the students are "hooked," it is most rewarding to observe their enthusiasm and to know that they have incorporated the vocabulary activities into other areas of their lives. You may want to bring in a few examples of your own for extra motivation.

• Allow students to post their sentences on the Word Wizard Wall.

You may choose to give the teams points to encourage participation.

▼ **Vocabulary assessment**

Part 1: Instruct the students to circle the word that corresponds to the definition on the Vocabulary Assessment worksheet.

Part 2: Instruct students to write sentences that demonstrate their knowledge of the word's meaning on the Vocabulary Assessment Sentences worksheet.

Hint: You may need to provide examples of sentences that demonstrate knowledge of the meaning. For example, if the vocabulary word were **ring,** then the sentence "I have a ring" does not demonstrate knowledge of the meaning. **Nose, car, friend, house,** or any number of other words could be substituted for **ring** in the sentence. The sentence "I wear a ring on my finger" demonstrates knowledge of the meaning.

Teacher answer keys

Lesson 7

VOCABULARY REVIEW HOMEWORK

• Read the definitions.
• Find the word in the box that matches the definition.
• Write the correct word next to the definition.

journey	twinkle	tempt	willpower
spin	heartburn	likely	contain
glow	discourage	sprout	halfway

1. _____glow_____ : give off a steady, low light

2. _____spin_____ : to make thread by twisting fine fibers together

3. _____journey_____ : a long trip

4. _____discourage_____ : persuade someone not to do something

5. _____sprout_____ : to emerge (come out) and develop rapidly

6. _____heartburn_____ : an unpleasant burning in the chest caused by acid acting on food in the stomach

7. _____contain_____ : to have inside; hold

8. _____twinkle_____ : to shine with quick flashes of light

9. _____likely_____ : probable

10. _____willpower_____ : the strength to control one's actions

11. _____halfway_____ : half the distance from one place to another

12. _____tempt_____ : to try to convince someone to do something wrong

Lesson 7

MULTIPLE MEANINGS WORKSHEET

- Read each sentence below.
- Choose the meaning for each bold word from the definition in the box.
- Write the letter for that meaning in the space at the end of the sentence.
- The sentences contain clues that will help you figure out which meaning is used for words with more than one meaning.

A. To show a bright, warm, or healthy color

B. To take away someone's courage or confidence

C. To hold or keep within limits; restrain

D. Give off a steady, low light

E. To include or be a part of

F. To show a warm feeling

G. To have inside; hold

---

1. That box **contains** my favorite toys. ___G___

2. Yogurt **contains** mostly milk. ___E___

3. If someone is mean to my friend, I have a hard time **containing** my temper. ___C___

4. It is fun to see the candle **glow** in a jack-o'-lantern's face. ___D___

5. After eating and sleeping, my sister's face **glowed**. ___A___

6. My dad **glowed** with pride when I told him that I got an A on the science test. ___F___

7. I was **discouraged** after I practiced for 3 hours and still could not do the dance. ___B___

H. Persuade someone not to do something

I. To tell or relate

J. More than the average length

K. Half the distance from one place to another

L. To rotate or whirl around

M. Throughout the length or duration of

N. Not thorough or complete

O. To make thread by twisting fine fibers together

P. To want something very much

8. My big brother **discouraged** me from quitting school. __H__

9. My grandmother **spins** wool from her sheep into yarn. __O__

10. I get dizzy at the fair when I go on rides that **spin**. __L__

11. My aunt can **spin** wonderful stories about our family. __I__

12. I walk a **long** way to get to school. __J__

13. My stomach hurt all night **long** after eating an entire banana split by myself. __M__

14. After not seeing her parents for 2 years, my mom **longs** to visit them. __P__

15. We must be more than **halfway** there; it seems we have walked for miles. __K__

16. Dad made me rewrite my homework because I did a **halfway** job the first time. __N__

USING WORDS IN CONTEXT WORKSHEET

contained	discourages	Journey	sprouted
tempted	spun	twinkles	willpower
likely			

1. It is hard to get up early every morning to jog when other people are still asleep. It takes great __willpower__ to make myself do it.

2. It's very cloudy. It is __likely__ to rain.

3. I jog every morning because it's good for me. But when it's cold and rainy, I am __tempted__ to stay in bed.

4. Dan's father __discourages__ him from going to the video arcade because kids sometimes get in trouble there.

5. The old pirate trunk __contained__ gold and silver coins.

6. We saw a movie about a young girl who travels across the country to find her father. It's called The __Journey__ of Natty Gann.

7. In science class, we planted seeds and watered them. They __sprouted__ in a few days.

8. I know a song about a little star that __twinkles__ like a diamond.

9. Cotton candy is made from __spun__ sugar.

contain	discouraged	Journey	likely
sprouted	temptation	tempting	willpower
glow			

10. My brother has all A's and B's, so it is __likely__ that he will be accepted at a good college.

11. My mom said, "No dessert, thank you," but then she changed her mind because the strawberry shortcake looked so __tempting__.

12. If the teacher leaves the classroom during a test, then some students might feel the __temptation__ to cheat.

13. The skater fell down three times and felt so __discouraged__ that she wanted to quit the competition.

14. The skater made herself get up and keep skating. She has strong __willpower__.

15. We heard the fire engines and saw the __glow__ of the fire lighting up the sky.

16. Vegetables are a healthy food because they __contain__ vitamins and minerals.

17. We read an exciting science fiction story by Jules Verne about people who traveled inside the earth. The title is __Journey__ *to the Center of the Earth.*

18. I grew so much that my teacher said, "You really __sprouted__ up over vacation."

AFFIXES WORKSHEET

- Review the affixes and their meanings.
- Read the sentences.
- Discuss which affix can be added to the word to fit in the sentence.
- Write the affix in the blank.
- Be sure that you can explain why the affix fits in the sentence.

PREFIXES	SUFFIXES
re-: again	**-less:** without
mis-: wrong, wrongly	**-er:** someone who ____; something that ____
un-: not	**-ful:** full of _____
dis-: opposite of	**-ly:** in the stated way
	-y: full of or covered with

1. If someone __**mis**__remembers a spelling word, they will get it wrong on the test.

2. I am such a dream**_er_** ; the teacher always reminds me to pay attention.

3. I was glad that I had a dream**_less_** night after watching the horror movie.

4. After all of the hot weather, it was nice to have a cloud**_y_** day.

5. I hope my mom left the door __**un**_locked because I forgot my key.

6. I had to __**re**_lock the door after my little cousin unlocked it.

7. It was hurt**_ful_** when the neighbor wouldn't let me play with her dog anymore.

8. My brother happi**_ly_** mopped the floor after my sister said she would pay him $5.

9. My friend felt __**dis**_couraged after he fell off the skateboard for the fifth time.

10. I need a contain**_er_** for the soup my dad made for my lunch.

11. To see the stars clearly, it helps to have a cloud**_less_** night.

12. The candy store buy**_er_** didn't think it was a good idea for the shop to carry licorice because not many people liked it.

VOCABULARY ASSESSMENT WORKSHEET

• Circle the word that matches the definition.

1. To emerge (come out) and develop rapidly

contain   (sprout)   tempt   glow

2. Half the distance from one place to another

journey   likely   (halfway)   discourage

3. To shine with quick flashes of light

(twinkle)   willpower   spine   glow

4. A long trip

sprout   twinkle   heartburn   (journey)

5. To try to convince someone to do something wrong

discourage   willpower   halfway   (tempt)

6. To have inside; hold

likely   (contain)   twinkle   journey

7. Persuade someone not to do something

glow   tempt   (discourage)   sprout

8. The strength to control one's actions

(willpower)   heartburn   glow   discourage

9. Probable

spin   journey   (likely)   halfway

10. Give off a steady, low light

contain   willpower   sprout   (glow)

11. To make thread by twisting fine fibers together

twinkle   (spin)   journey   discourage

12. An unpleasant burning in the chest caused by acid acting on food in the stomach

willpower   glow   (heartburn)   tempt

Reproducible materials

glowing

spun

sprouted

heartburn

contained

twinkled

willpower

journey

halfway

temptation

discourage

likely

Name: _____

VOCABULARY REVIEW HOMEWORK

- Read the definitions.
- Find the word in the box that matches the definition.
- Write the correct word next to the definition.

journey	twinkle	tempt	willpower
spin	heartburn	likely	contain
glow	discourage	sprout	halfway

1. _____ : give off a steady, low light

2. _____ : to make thread by twisting fine fibers together

3. _____ : a long trip

4. _____ : persuade someone not to do something

5. _____ : to emerge (come out) and develop rapidly

6. _____ : an unpleasant burning in the chest caused by acid acting on food in the stomach

7. _____ : to have inside; hold

8. _____ : to shine with quick flashes of light

9. _____ : probable

10. _____ : the strength to control one's actions

11. _____ : half the distance from one place to another

12. _____ : to try to convince someone to do something wrong

WORD WIZARD LIST

- Each time you hear or read one of these words used in a sentence at home, at school, on television, or on the radio, write the sentence on an index card or sticky note.

contained (contain): to have inside; hold

discourage: persuade someone not to do something

glowing (glow): give off a steady, low light

halfway: half the distance from one place to another

heartburn: an unpleasant burning in the chest caused by acid acting on food in the stomach

journey: a long trip

likely: probable

sprouted (sprout): to emerge (come out) and develop rapidly

spun (spin): to make thread by twisting fine fibers together

temptation (tempt): to try to convince someone to do something wrong

twinkles (twinkle): to shine with quick flashes of light

willpower: the strength to control one's actions

Vocabulary Improvement Program for English Language Learners and Their Classmates, 4th Grade, by Teresa Lively, Diane August, María Carlo, and Catherine Snow © 2003 Paul H. Brookes Publishing Co., Inc. All rights reserved.

MULTIPLE MEANINGS WORKSHEET

- Read each sentence below.
- Choose the meaning for each bold word from the definition in the box.
- Write the letter for that meaning in the space at the end of the sentence.
- The sentences contain clues that will help you figure out which meaning is used for words with more than one meaning.

A. To show a bright, warm, or healthy color

B. To take away someone's courage or confidence

C. To hold or keep within limits; restrain

D. Give off a steady, low light

E. To include or be a part of

F. To show a warm feeling

G. To have inside; hold

---

1. That box **contains** my favorite toys. _____

2. Yogurt **contains** mostly milk. _____

3. If someone is mean to my friend, I have a hard time **containing** my temper. _____

4. It is fun to see the candle **glow** in a jack-o'-lantern's face. _____

5. After eating and sleeping, my sister's face **glowed**. _____

6. My dad **glowed** with pride when I told him that I got an A on the science test. _____

7. I was **discouraged** after I practiced for 3 hours and still could not do the dance. _____

Vocabulary Improvement Program for English Language Learners and Their Classmates, 4th Grade, by Teresa Lively, Diane August, María Carlo, and Catherine Snow © 2003 Paul H. Brookes Publishing Co., Inc. All rights reserved.

MULTIPLE MEANINGS WORKSHEET *(continued)*

H. Persuade someone not to do something

I. To tell or relate

J. More than the average length

K. Half the distance from one place to another

L. To rotate or whirl around

M. Throughout the length or duration of

N. Not thorough or complete

O. To make thread by twisting fine fibers together

P. To want something very much

---

8. My big brother **discouraged** me from quitting school. _____

9. My grandmother **spins** wool from her sheep into yarn. _____

10. I get dizzy at the fair when I go on rides that **spin**. _____

11. My aunt can **spin** wonderful stories about our family. _____

12. I walk a **long** way to get to school. _____

13. My stomach hurt all night **long** after eating an entire banana split by myself. _____

14. After not seeing her parents for 2 years, my mom **longs** to visit them. _____

15. We must be more than **halfway** there; it seems we have walked for miles. _____

16. Dad made me rewrite my homework because I did a **halfway** job the first time. _____

Name: _____

Lesson 7

USING WORDS IN CONTEXT WORKSHEET

contained	discourages	Journey	sprouted
tempted	spun	twinkles	willpower
likely			

1. It is hard to get up early every morning to jog when other people are still asleep. It takes great _____ to make myself do it.

2. It's very cloudy. It is _____ to rain.

3. I jog every morning because it's good for me. But when it's cold and rainy, I am _____ to stay in bed.

4. Dan's father _____ him from going to the video arcade because kids sometimes get in trouble there.

5. The old pirate trunk _____ gold and silver coins.

6. We saw a movie about a young girl who travels across the country to find her father. It's called *The* _____ *of Natty Gann.*

7. In science class, we planted seeds and watered them. They _____ in a few days.

8. I know a song about a little star that _____ like a diamond.

9. Cotton candy is made from _____ sugar.

USING WORDS IN CONTEXT WORKSHEET *(continued)*

contain	discouraged	Journey	likely
sprouted	temptation	tempting	willpower
glow			

10. My brother has all A's and B's, so it is _____ that he will be accepted at a good college.

11. My mom said, "No dessert, thank you," but then she changed her mind because the strawberry shortcake looked so _____.

12. If the teacher leaves the classroom during a test, then some students might feel the _____ to cheat.

13. The skater fell down three times and felt so _____ that she wanted to quit the competition.

14. The skater made herself get up and keep skating. She has strong _____.

15. We heard the fire engines and saw the _____ of the fire lighting up the sky.

16. Vegetables are a healthy food because they _____ vitamins and minerals.

17. We read an exciting science fiction story by Jules Verne about people who traveled inside the earth. The title is _____ *to the Center of the Earth.*

18. I grew so much that my teacher said, "You really _____ up over vacation."

Name: _____

AFFIXES WORKSHEET

- Review the affixes and their meanings.
- Read the sentences.
- Discuss which affix can be added to the word to fit in the sentence.
- Write the affix in the blank.
- Be sure that you can explain why the affix fits in the sentence.

PREFIXES	SUFFIXES
re-: again	**-less:** without
mis-: wrong, wrongly	**-er:** someone who _____; something that _____
un-: not	**-ful:** full of _____
dis-: opposite of	**-ly:** in the stated way
	-y: full of or covered with

1. If someone _____ remembers a spelling word, they will get it wrong on the test.

2. I am such a dream_____; the teacher always reminds me to pay attention.

3. I was glad that I had a dream_____ night after watching the horror movie.

4. After all of the hot weather, it was nice to have a cloud_____ day.

5. I hope my mom left the door _____locked because I forgot my key.

6. I had to _____lock the door after my little cousin unlocked it.

7. It was hurt_____ when the neighbor wouldn't let me play with her dog anymore.

8. My brother happi_____ mopped the floor after my sister said she would pay him $5.

9. My friend felt _____couraged after he fell off the skateboard for the fifth time.

10. I need a contain_____ for the soup my dad made for my lunch.

11. To see the stars clearly, it helps to have a cloud_____ night.

12. The candy store buy_____ didn't think it was a good idea for the shop to carry licorice because not many people liked it.

Vocabulary Improvement Program for English Language Learners and Their Classmates, 4th Grade, by Teresa Lively, Diane August, María Carlo, and Catherine Snow © 2003 Paul H. Brookes Publishing Co., Inc. All rights reserved.

ACROSS

4. The strength to control one's actions
6. An unpleasant burning in the chest caused by acid acting on food in the stomach
9. Persuade someone not to do something
10. To have inside; hold
11. To make thread by twisting fine fibers together
12. Probable

DOWN

1. To emerge and develop rapidly
2. To shine with quick flashes of light
3. Give off a steady, low light
5. Half the distance from one place to another
7. A long trip
8. To try to get (someone) to do wrong, especially by a promise of reward

contain

discourage

glow

halfway

heartburn

journey

likely

sprout

spin

tempt

twinkle

willpower

VOCABULARY ASSESSMENT WORKSHEET

• Circle the word that matches the definition.

1. To emerge (come out) and develop rapidly

    contain   sprout   tempt   glow

2. Half the distance from one place to another

    journey   likely   halfway   discourage

3. To shine with quick flashes of light

    twinkle   willpower   spine   glow

4. A long trip

    sprout   twinkle   heartburn   journey

5. To try to convince someone to do something wrong

    discourage   willpower   halfway   tempt

6. To have inside; hold

    likely   contain   twinkle   journey

7. Persuade someone not to do something

    glow   tempt   discourage   sprout

8. The strength to control one's actions

    willpower   heartburn   glow   discourage

9. Probable

    spin   journey   likely   halfway

10. Give off a steady, low light

    contain   willpower   sprout   glow

11. To make thread by twisting fine fibers together

    twinkle   spin   journey   discourage

12. An unpleasant burning in the chest caused by acid acting on food in the stomach

    willpower   glow   heartburn   tempt

VOCABULARY ASSESSMENT
SENTENCES WORKSHEET

• Write a sentence with each of these four vocabulary words to show that you know what the word means.

sprout   twinkle   contain   tempt

1. _____

_____

2. _____

_____

3. _____

_____

4. _____

_____

The Hippopotamus at Dinner

OVERVIEW OF ACTIVITIES

Day 1	Day 2	Day 3	Day 4
TEXT INTRODUCTION	**VOCABULARY INTRODUCTION**	**EXPAND MEANING**	**TOOLS TO DEVELOP VOCABULARY**
• Predict storyline • Read fable • Discuss fable	• Circle vocabulary • Extract definitions • Assign homework	• Review homework • Related Words • Assign homework	• Infer Meaning

Day 5	Day 6	Day 7	Day 8
USING WORDS IN CONTEXT	**TOOLS TO DEVELOP VOCABULARY**	**WORD WIZARD REVIEW**	**ASSESSMENT**
• Contexting activity	• Semantic Features Analysis • Assign homework	• Review homework • Word Wizard review	

WORD LIST

The word in bold is the base word, followed by its definition. If the word has more than one meaning, then we provide only the definition used in the text. *Please review the definitions prior to instruction.*

1. **appetite:** desire for food
2. **budge:** to start or cause to move
3. **dab:** to touch a surface gently with something soft
4. **enormous:** having great size, number, or degree
5. **forlorn:** sad or lonely
6. **gaze:** to look at something steadily
7. **gloom:** a dark and depressing atmosphere
8. **morsel:** a small piece of food
9. **portion:** a serving of food
10. **regret:** to be sad or sorry about something
11. **satisfy:** to please someone by giving them enough
12. **tug:** to pull hard

IDIOMATIC EXPRESSIONS

- **the hour grew late:** it became late

OTHER WORDS WORTH DEFINING

- **Brussels sprouts:** a vegetable that looks like miniature cabbages
- **mashed:** changed into a soft mixture
- **glare:** to look in a very angry way

▼ **Prepare for activity**

Post Classroom Word List.

Materials: Student Word Books, *Fables*

▼ **Predict storyline**

Show students the illustration for "The Hippopotamus at Dinner" in the color insert or turn to page 39 of *Fables*.

Say: *Today we are going to read the fable "The Hippopotamus at Dinner." What do you think this fable will be about when you look at the illustration and hear the title?*

Encourage a student discussion.

▼ **Ask the students to listen as you read the fable aloud**

▼ **Discuss the fable and moral; relate it to the students' lives**

- *Who are the main characters in this fable?*
- *Why did Hippopotamus glare at his plate?*
- *What did the waiter bring to Hippopotamus after he complained?*
- *Do you think that even a hippopotamus could eat a bathtub of bean soup, a bucket of Brussels sprouts, and a mountain of mashed potatoes?*
- *Why do you think the author decided to say that Hippopotamus ate such an extremely large amount of food?*
- *What happened after Hippopotamus finished eating?*

▼ **Reread the moral**

- *What do you think the moral means?*
- *Do you think Hippopotamus regretted eating so much food? Why?*
- *Have you ever done too much of something, even if it was something you thought would be fun?*

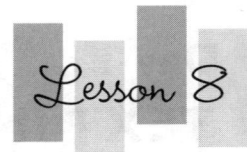

The Hippopotamus at Dinner

The Hippopotamus went into a restaurant. He sat at his favorite table.

"Waiter!" called the Hippopotamus. "I will have the bean soup, the Brussels sprouts, and the mashed potatoes. Please hurry, I am **enormously** hungry tonight!"

In a short while, the waiter returned with the order. The Hippopotamus glared down at his plate.

"Waiter," he said, "do you call this a meal? These **portions** are much too small. They would not **satisfy** a bird. I want a *bathtub* of bean soup, a *bucket* of Brussels sprouts, and a *mountain* of mashed potatoes. I tell you I have an **APPETITE**!"

The waiter went back into the kitchen. He returned carrying enough bean soup to fill a bathtub, enough Brussels sprouts to fill a bucket, and a mountain of mashed potatoes. In no time, the Hippopotamus had eaten every last **morsel.**

"Delicious!" said the Hippopotamus, as he **dabbed** his mouth with a napkin and prepared to leave.

To his surprise, he could not move. His stomach, which had grown considerably larger, was caught between the table and the chair. He pulled and **tugged,** but it was no use. He could not **budge.**

The hour grew late. The other customers in the restaurant finished their dinners and left. The cooks took off their aprons and put away their pots. The waiters cleared the dishes and turned out the lights. They all went home.

The Hippopotamus remained there, sitting **forlornly** at the table.

"Perhaps I should not have eaten quite so many Brussels sprouts," he said, as he **gazed** into the **gloom** of the darkened restaurant. Occasionally, he burped.

Too much of anything often leaves one with a feeling of **regret.**

▼ Review the sections titled "Idiomatic Expressions" and "Other Words Worth Defining"

▼ Read posted target words to students, or ask students to read them

- Before you reread the fable, say: *Follow along in your Student Word Book as I read the fable again. Circle each target word when I read it. If you think you know what the word means* **without reading the definition,** *then raise your hand and I will call on you.* After students have suggested meanings, say: *Let's check the definition to see how close you were.*

   Note: The target words appear in the same order in the fable as on the word list. To help students find the words more easily, point out each target word on the list before looking for it in the text.

- Meaning can be inferred for **portions**, **tugged**, and **budge**. When you reach **portions**, say: *Sometimes you can figure out what a word means by skipping over it and finishing the sentence. Or, you can reread the sentence while thinking about what the word might mean. Let me show you how this works by reading the sentence with portions in it. "These portions are much too small." Let's see, it sounds like he is com-plaining about* **small** *portions and then he goes on to say that he wants a* **bathtub** *of beans, a* **bucket** *of Brussels sprouts, and a* **mountain** *of mashed potatoes. That's a lot! So, he's unhappy with the small portions and wants big ones. I wonder if a por-tion is an amount of food? Let's look up the definition to see if that's what it means.*

- When you reach **tugged** (related to **pulled**) and **budge** (related to **could not move; but it was no use**), ask students to "think aloud" to explain how the clues in the fable can help them figure out what the words mean. You may need to model the strategy.

▼ Assign Vocabulary Review homework

Instruct students to write the correct vocabulary word in the space beside the definition.

▼ Cognates

If the students are bilingual, then you may wish to review the cognates from the fable.

English word	Spanish word
restaurant	restaurante
favorite	favorito
enormously	enormemente
order	orden
plate	plato
portions	porciones
satisfy	satisfacer
appetite	apetito
delicious	delicioso
considerably	considerablemente
late	late (false)
occasionally	ocasionalmente

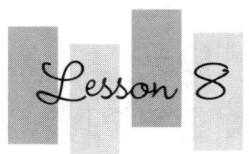
- The base word is bold and is the word defined.
- If there is more than one meaning, then the bold definition is the one used in the fable.
- The Spanish translation is provided for the meaning used in the fable.

1. **appetite**
   a) **desire for food**
   b) great enjoyment of something
   - apetito; deseo de alimento

2. **budge**
   to start or cause to move
   - moverse

3. dabbed (**dab**)
   to touch a surface gently with something soft
   - tocar suavemente

4. enormously (**enormous**)
   having great size, number, or degree
   - enorme; de gran tamaño o cantidad

5. forlornly (**forlorn**)
   sad or lonely
   - abandonado o desamparado; solo

6. gazed (**gaze**)
   to look at something steadily
   - contemplar; fijar la vista

7. **gloom**
   a) a sense of hopelessness
   b) **a dark and depressing atmosphere**
   - tenebrosidad; ambiente depresivo

8. **morsel**
   a small piece of food
   - bocado de comida

9. portions (**portion**)
   a) a part or piece of something
   b) a share of something that is divided among two or more people
   c) **a serving of food**
   - porción; pedazo

10. **regret**
    to be sad or sorry about something
    - remordimiento; sentir, tener pena

11. **satisfy**
    a) **to please someone by giving them enough**
    b) to convince or to free from doubt
    - satisfacer; agradar; saciar un apetito

12. tugged (**tug**)
    a) **to pull hard**
    b) a small, powerful boat that tows or pushes ships and barges
    - tirón; halar con fuerza

EXPAND MEANING:
Related Words

▼ **Review Vocabulary Review homework**

1. Ask students for answers.

2. Direct students to correct their own answers if needed.

▼ **Prepare for activity**

1. Place students in heterogeneous language groups of three to four students.

2. Write the following example on the board:

happy is to sad

as

cold is to _____

Materials: Related Words worksheet for each student

▼ **Introduce the concept: Related Words**

Words can be related to each other in many ways. They can be antonyms or synonyms, or can be related in another way.

Review the following concepts with the students

- Synonyms: words that have the same or similar meanings (happy and joyful)
- Antonyms: words that have opposite meanings (happy and sad)
- Related words: words that are associated in another way (happy and smile)

▼ **Introduce the activity**

Say: *In this activity, your job is to find relationships between pairs of words. For example, the first part of the sentence gives a pair of words that are antonyms, synonyms, or related in another way.*

Point to the example on the board. *For example, happy is to sad: happy is* **the opposite of** *sad. In the second part of the sentence there is another word and a space to be filled in with a vocabulary word. The words are related in the same way as the words in the first part of the sentence. Happy* **is the opposite of** *sad, and cold* **is the opposite of** _____?

You will work in your groups to figure out which vocabulary word fits in the space on the Related Words worksheet.

▼ **Review the activity**

Ask students to state the relationship between the word pairs: Are they synonyms, antonyms, or related in another way?

▼ **Word Wizard**

Motivate students to find sentences with this week's vocabulary. Say: *You are all going to continue being word wizards and even build your skills with this week's vocabulary words! Just like last week, I want you to demonstrate your wizardry in the following way: each time you hear or read one of this week's words used at home, at school, or even on television, I want you to write the sentence on an index card (or sticky note). Write down where you heard or read it.*

Give students the Word Wizard List.

TOOLS TO DEVELOP
VOCABULARY: Infer Meaning

▼ Prepare for activity

1. Divide students into mixed language groups of four to five students.

2. Write the example on the board.

Materials: Mystery Words worksheet for each group

▼ Introduce the lesson

Say: *Who can remember what a word detective is? Today you will be **word detectives** again! As detectives, your assignment is to figure out the meaning of the bold mystery words.*

Remember, good detectives look for clues while gathering information about the mystery they are trying to solve. Look for clues in the words and sentences that surround the mystery word. Use these clues to help pick a definition from the box that might go with the bold word. Follow the steps in the Hints for Solving Mystery Words page on the inside back cover of your Student Word Book to help you decide if the definition you chose is the correct one.

These are pretty difficult words—that's why they're called mystery words! Many grown-ups don't even know these words, so you will need to use good detective skills to find the clues to the meanings! Let's try one.

Use the example to illustrate the process using the following steps:

1. Pick a definition from the box that might go with the bold word.

2. Write the number for the definition in the space beside the word.

3. Check the definition you chose using the steps listed on the Hints for Solving Mystery Words page in your Student Word Book.

> A. An instrument that measures how high a person can jump
>
> B. An instrument that measures how deep the water is in the ocean
>
> C. An instrument that measures cloudiness

The **nephelometer** _____ showed us that it would probably rain soon.

• Use Hints for Solving Mystery Words in Student Word Books to help students figure out the correct answer to the example.

• Direct the groups to complete the Mystery Words worksheet in a similar manner.

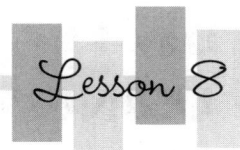

▼ **Review the activity**

Help students infer meaning from the text. Say: *Sometimes you can figure out what a word means by skipping over it and finishing the sentence. Or, you can reread the sentence while thinking about what the word might mean. Let's see how this works by reading the first paragraph.*

Ask students to "think aloud" to explain how the clues in the paragraph help them figure out what the word means. You may need to model the strategy.

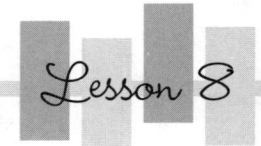
Using Words in Context is designed to develop students' ability to decipher the meaning of a word by using clues in the surrounding text.

▼ Prepare for activity

Place students in heterogeneous language groups, ideally four to five students.

Materials: Using Words in Context worksheet for each student.

If this activity is challenging for your students, then you may choose to complete it as a whole-group activity. It is helpful to make the worksheet into a transparency so that you can point out the context clues.

▼ Introduce the activity

Say: *Today's activity will help you practice using the target words in sentences. Your job is to figure out which word fits in the blank using the clues that are in the sentence. After you figure out the right word, think about **how** you figured it out; what were the clues in the rest of the sentence that helped you. When everyone in the group knows the correct word and **why it fits,** raise your hands. I'll call on one of the first groups ready. You will get a point if you get the correct answer (you may choose not to use points). Remember, everyone in your group must know the answer and why it is correct.*

Read the first sentence aloud to the class to illustrate the process.

▼ Review the activity

- Ask one student at a table for the correct answer **and to explain how he or she figured it out**—which clues in the contexts helped. Explaining the thought process that led to the answer helps the students realize that they know how to use the clues in the text and will demonstrate the process to those students who have not yet developed the skill.

- Continue until the lesson is completed, giving each group one point for each correct answer (you may choose not to use points).

Day 6
TOOLS TO DEVELOP VOCABULARY:
Semantic Features Analysis

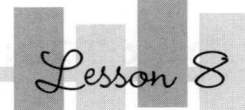

Lesson 8

▼ **Prepare for activity**

This lesson will be more effective if you make the Semantic Features Analysis matrix into a transparency and complete the lesson as a whole class using an overhead projector.

▼ **Introduce the concept**

Say: *Today we will examine the characteristics of word meanings to determine what properties they share and what properties they don't share. This will help develop your ability to analyze vocabulary.*

▼ **Introduce the activity**

Say: *We will complete a chart to study the ways in which animals from the fables are alike and how they are different.*

▼ **Complete the matrix**

1. Say: *Who can tell me the name of an animal that was in any one of the fables?*
   - List the animals in the right-hand column on the transparency: hen, wolf, baboon, gibbon, dog, ostrich, rhinoceros, pig, hippopotamus

2. Say: *Describe the animals. What are some of the animal's features?*
   - List the features across the top of the transparency. Possible features include: mammal, reptile, amphibian, insect, bird, crustacean; carnivore, herbivore, omnivore; swims, runs, flies; beak, snout, furry, feathers, tail, mane; two legs, four legs, and so forth.

3. Say: *Now, let's think about each animal to see what features they have or don't have.*
   - Fill in the matrix with a plus (+) or minus (−) to indicate the presence or absence of each feature.

▼ **Review the matrix**

Say: *Let's look at the chart to see which features the animals share or don't share. What do you see?*

Help students discover that no two animals have exactly the same pattern of pluses and minuses—none are identical. Even the animals that are most alike will reveal their differences if enough features are added. This is true for any category of words you might examine.

▼ Assign homework

Give students the crossword puzzle; review the instructions and the due date.

Day 7
WORD WIZARD REVIEW

Lesson 8

▼ **Review the crossword puzzle homework**

1. Ask students for answers.

2. Direct students to correct their own answers if needed.

3. The crossword puzzle answer key for Lessons 6–10 can be found in the Teacher Answer Keys for Lesson 6.

▼ **Prepare for activity**

Instruct students to divide into their Word Wizard groups, taking the sentences they have collected throughout the 2 weeks.

▼ **Review Word Wizard**

- Allow students a few minutes to share sentences within their group and tell where they heard or read the word.

- Ask each group to share a few sentences with the class.

     Hint: The more enthusiasm you demonstrate and motivation you provide for this activity, the more the students will participate. Once the students are "hooked," it is most rewarding to observe their enthusiasm and to know that they have incorporated the vocabulary activities into other areas of their lives. You may want to bring in a few examples of your own for extra motivation.

- Allow students to post their sentences on the Word Wizard Wall.

You may choose to give the teams points to encourage participation.

▼ **Vocabulary assessment**

Part 1: Instruct the students to circle the word that corresponds to the definition on the Vocabulary Assessment worksheet.

Part 2: Instruct students to write sentences that demonstrate their knowledge of the word's meaning on the Vocabulary Assessment Sentences worksheet.

Hint: You may need to provide examples of sentences that demonstrate knowledge of the meaning. For example, if the vocabulary word were **ring,** then the sentence "I have a ring" does not demonstrate knowledge of the meaning. **Nose, car, friend, house,** or any number of other words could be substituted for **ring** in the sentence. The sentence "I wear a ring on my finger" demonstrates knowledge of the meaning.

Teacher answer keys

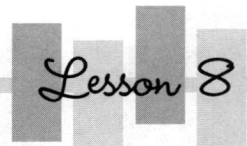

Lesson 8

VOCABULARY REVIEW HOMEWORK

- Read the definitions.
- Find the word in the box that matches the definition.
- Write the correct word next to the definition.

portion	dab	regret	gaze
satisfy	gloom	forlorn	budge
enormous	appetite	morsel	tug

1. **gloom** : a dark and depressing atmosphere

2. **forlorn** : sad or lonely

3. **portion** : a serving of food

4. **appetite** : desire for food

5. **gaze** : to look at something steadily

6. **dab** : to touch a surface gently with something soft

7. **satisfy** : to please someone by giving them enough

8. **enormous** : having great size, number, or degree

9. **morsel** : a small piece of food

10. **regret** : to be sad or sorry about something

11. **tug** : to pull hard

12. **budge** : to start or cause to move

RELATED WORDS WORKSHEET

1. Hot is to cold as tiny is to __**enormous**__ .
   antonyms

2. House is to rooms as meal is to __**portions**__ .
   a house contains rooms, and a meal contains portions

3. Water is to desert as light is to __**gloom**__ .
   there is very little water in a desert
   there is very little light in a place filled with gloom

4. Pleased is to happy as lonely is to __**forlorn**__ .
   pleased is a characteristic of happy
   lonely is a characteristic of forlorn

5. Throw is to toss as stare is to __**gaze**__ .
   throw is a strong toss
   stare is a strong gaze

6. Jog is to run as yank is to __**tug**__ .
   synonyms

7. Rough is to shove as gentle is to __**dab**__ .
   rough is a characteristic of shove
   gentle is a characteristic of dab

8. Boulder is to pebble as heap is to __**morsel**__ .
   antonyms

9. Shoe is to boot as hunger is to __**appetite**__ .
   synonyms

10. Successes are to pride as mistakes are to __**regret**__ .
    successes cause pride
    mistakes cause regret

11. Dull is to bore as plenty is to __**satisfy**__ .
    something dull causes a person to be bored
    plenty of something causes a person to be satisfied

MYSTERY WORDS WORKSHEET

- Pick a definition from the box that might go with the bold word.
- Write the number for the definition in the space beside the word.
- Check the definition you chose using the steps listed on the Hints for Solving Mystery Words sheet in your Word Book.

---

1. Very dangerous
2. Separate off
3. Something that happens without a clear reason
4. Travel, especially on foot
5. Closeness; nearness
6. Kept from doing something; frustrated
7. A big number; plenty

GRASSLANDS

In the grasslands of Africa, millions of animals **peregrinate** __4__ over 500 miles each year in search of food. Their path seems **haphazard** __3__ to the observer, but the animals clearly know where they are going to find food.

There is a **plethora** __7__ of wildlife in Tanzania. Many different animals move about in large herds. There is a reason for their **propinquity** __5__. Animals stay together in herds for protection.

One **pernicious** __1__ animal that hunts other animals for food is the lion. The deadly lions run around the herd, trying to **disengage** __2__ single animals from the rest of the herd. Sometimes they succeed but they usually do not, and the **thwarted** __6__ lions go home hungry.

USING WORDS IN CONTEXT WORKSHEET

appetite	budge	enormously	forlornly	gloomy
morsel	portions	regretted	Tug	

1. My cousin Joe is always hungry, and he always eats all of his food. He has a good __**appetite**__ .

2. At dinner, Joe ate all of the rice on his plate, and then he asked for a second helping. He finished that and then asked for another serving. He ate three __**portions**__ of rice in all.

3. The dog sat by the dinner table, hoping that someone would drop a tasty little __**morsel**__ of food.

4. Hercules is very strong. He's tremendously strong. He's __**enormously**__ strong.

5. The huge tree that fell on the road was so enormously heavy that even Hercules was not strong enough to __**budge**__ it.

6. On Field Day, two teams pulled a rope in a game called __**Tug**__ O' War.

7. In the fable, the hippopotamus __**regretted**__ that he ate too much.

8. Sometimes the weather can affect my feelings. On sunny days, I feel happy and cheerful. On cloudy days, I feel sad and __**gloomy**__ .

9. When no one came to pick up the little boy after his first day of kindergarten, he cried and waited __**forlornly**__ in the school office.

appetite	budge	forlorn	gloomy	morsels
portions	satisfied	regrets	tug	

10. My mom says if we eat too many snacks after school, then we won't be hungry for dinner. "Don't spoil your __**appetite**__."

11. The abandoned house had broken windows and torn curtains; no one was caring for it. On this cloudy day it looked __**forlorn**__ and __**gloomy**__.

12. My uncle can't get a good job because he doesn't have a high school diploma. He says that he __**regrets**__ that he dropped out of school.

13. The little pieces of chocolate that are used to make chocolate chip cookies are sometimes called chocolate __**morsels**__.

14. A small strong boat that pulls big ships into harbor is called a __**tug**__ boat.

15. I asked that boy to move out of my way, but he wouldn't __**budge**__.

16. We don't go to the Rio restaurant any more because the __**portions**__ are too small, and we're still hungry when the meal is finished.

17. At the Rio restaurant, the servings are so tiny that you can eat a whole meal and still not feel __**satisfied**__.

Lesson 8

VOCABULARY ASSESSMENT WORKSHEET

- Circle the word that matches the definition.

1. Sad or lonely

    gaze   (forlorn)   portion   enormous

2. To be sad or sorry about something

    budge   appetite   (regret)   gloom

3. To please someone by giving them enough

    (satisfy)   tug   morsel   portion

4. To look at something steadily

    budge   (gaze)   portion   dab

5. To start or cause to move

    gaze   appetite   (budge)   portion

6. Desire for food

    morsel   satisfy   (appetite)   tug

7. A dark and depressing atmosphere

    (gloom)   portion   enormous   regret

8. To pull hard

    dab   morsel   forlorn   (tug)

9. To touch a surface gently with something soft

    regret   (dab)   gaze   budge

10. A serving of food

    tug   satisfy   (portion)   enormous

11. A small piece of food

    (morsel)   appetite   tug   forlorn

12. Having great size, number, or degree

    satisfy   regret   (enormous)   gaze

Reproducible materials

satisfy

portions

enormously

appetite

morsel

dabbed

Lesson 8

forlornly

budge

tugged

Vocabulary Improvement Program for English Language Learners and Their Classmates, 4th Grade, by Teresa Lively, Diane August, María Carlo, and Catherine Snow © 2003 Paul H. Brookes Publishing Co., Inc. All rights reserved.

regret

gloom

gazed

VOCABULARY REVIEW HOMEWORK

• Read the definitions.
• Find the word in the box that matches the definition.
• Write the correct word next to the definition.

portion	dab	regret	gaze
satisfy	gloom	forlorn	budge
enormous	appetite	morsel	tug

1. _____: a dark and depressing atmosphere

2. _____: sad or lonely

3. _____: a serving of food

4. _____: desire for food

5. _____: to look at something steadily

6. _____: to touch a surface gently with something soft

7. _____: to please someone by giving them enough

8. _____: having great size, number, or degree

9. _____: a small piece of food

10. _____: to be sad or sorry about something

11. _____: to pull hard

12. _____: to start or cause to move

RELATED WORDS WORKSHEET

1. Hot is to cold   **as**   tiny is to _____

2. House is to room   **as**   meal is to _____

3. Water is to desert   **as**   light is to _____

4. Pleased is to happy   **as**   lonely is to _____

5. Throw is to toss   **as**   stare is to _____

6. Jog is to run   **as**   yank is to _____

7. Rough is to shove   **as**   gentle is to _____

8. Boulder is to pebble   **as**   heap is to _____

9. Shoe is to boot   **as**   hunger is to _____

10. Successes are to pride   **as**   mistakes are to _____

11. Dull is to bore   **as**   plenty is to _____

Vocabulary Improvement Program for English Language Learners and Their Classmates, 4th Grade, by Teresa Lively, Diane August, María Carlo, and Catherine Snow © 2003 Paul H. Brookes Publishing Co., Inc. All rights reserved.

WORD WIZARD LIST

• Each time you hear or read one of these words used in a sentence at home, at school, on television, or on the radio, write the sentence on an index card or sticky note.

appetite: desire for food

budge: to start or cause to move

dabbed (dab): to touch a surface gently with something soft

enormously (enormous): having great size, number, or degree

forlornly (forlorn): sad or lonely

gazed (gaze): to look at something steadily

gloom: a dark and depressing atmosphere

morsel: a small piece of food

portions (portion): a serving of food

regret: to be sad or sorry about something

satisfy: to please somebody by giving them enough

tugged (tug): to pull hard

MYSTERY WORDS WORKSHEET

- Pick a definition from the box that might go with the bold word.
- Write the number for the definition in the space beside the word.
- Check the definition you chose using the steps listed on the Hints for Solving Mystery Words sheet in your Word Book.

---

1. Very dangerous
2. Separate off
3. Something that happens without a clear reason
4. Travel, especially on foot
5. Closeness; nearness
6. Kept from doing something; frustrated
7. A big number; plenty

GRASSLANDS

In the grasslands of Africa, millions of animals **peregrinate** ____ over 500 miles each year in search of food. Their path seems **haphazard** ____ to the observer, but the animals clearly know where they are going to find food.

There is a **plethora** ____ of wildlife in Tanzania. Many different animals move about in large herds. There is a reason for their **propinquity** ____. Animals stay together in herds for protection.

One **pernicious** ____ animal that hunts other animals for food is the lion. The deadly lions run around the herd, trying to **disengage** ____ single animals from the rest of the herd. Sometimes they succeed but they usually do not, and the **thwarted** ____ lions go home hungry.

USING WORDS IN CONTEXT WORKSHEET

appetite	budge	enormously	forlornly	gloomy
morsel	portions	regretted	Tug	

1. My cousin Joe is always hungry, and he always eats all of his food. He has a good
_____.

2. At dinner, Joe ate all of the rice on his plate, and then he asked for a second helping. He finished that and then asked for another serving. He ate three _____ of rice in all.

3. The dog sat by the dinner table, hoping that someone would drop a tasty little _____ of food.

4. Hercules is very strong. He's tremendously strong. He's _____ strong.

5. The huge tree that fell on the road was so enormously heavy that even Hercules was not strong enough to _____ it.

6. On Field Day, two teams pulled a rope in a game called _____ O' War.

7. In the fable, the hippopotamus _____ that he ate too much.

8. Sometimes the weather can affect my feelings. On sunny days, I feel happy and cheerful. On cloudy days, I feel sad and _____.

9. When no one came to pick up the little boy after his first day of kindergarten, he cried and waited _____ in the school office.

USING WORDS IN CONTEXT WORKSHEET (*continued*)

appetite	budge	forlorn	gloomy	morsels
portions	satisfied	regrets	tug	

10. My mom says if we eat too many snacks after school, then we won't be hungry for dinner. "Don't spoil your _____."

11. The abandoned house had broken windows and torn curtains; no one was caring for it. On this cloudy day it looked _____ and _____.

12. My uncle can't get a good job because he doesn't have a high school diploma. He says that he _____ that he dropped out of school.

13. The little pieces of chocolate that are used to make chocolate chip cookies are sometimes called chocolate _____.

14. A small strong boat that pulls big ships into harbor is called a _____ boat.

15. I asked that boy to move out of my way, but he wouldn't _____.

16. We don't go to the Rio restaurant any more because the _____ are too small, and we're still hungry when the meal is finished.

17. At the Rio restaurant, the servings are so tiny that you can eat a whole meal and still not feel _____.

SEMANTIC FEATURES ANALYSIS

Name: _____

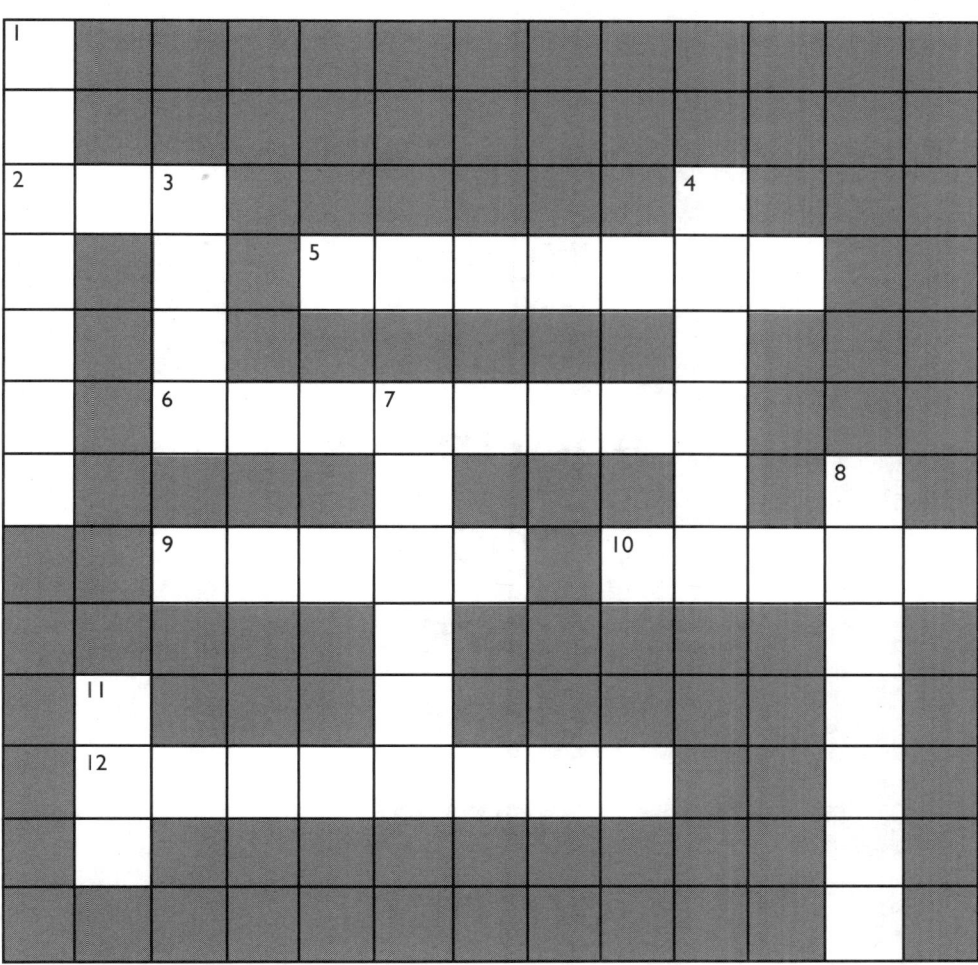

ACROSS

2. To pull hard
5. A serving of food
6. Having great size, number, or degree
9. To start or cause to move
10. A dark and depressing atmosphere
12. Desire for food

DOWN

1. To please someone by giving them enough
3. To look at something steadily
4. A small piece of food
7. To be sad or sorry about something
8. Sad or lonely
11. To touch a surface gently with something soft

appetite

budge

dab

enormous

forlorn

gaze

gloom

morsel

portion

regret

satisfy

tug

VOCABULARY ASSESSMENT WORKSHEET

• Circle the word that matches the definition.

1. Sad or lonely

   gaze   forlorn   portion   enormous

2. To be sad or sorry about something

   budge   appetite   regret   gloom

3. To please someone by giving them enough

   satisfy   tug   morsel   portion

4. To look at something steadily

   budge   gaze   portion   dab

5. To start or cause to move

   gaze   appetite   budge   portion

6. Desire for food

   morsel   satisfy   appetite   tug

7. A dark and depressing atmosphere

   gloom   portion   enormous   regret

8. To pull hard

   dab   morsel   forlorn   tug

9. To touch a surface gently with something soft

   regret   dab   gaze   budge

10. A serving of food

    tug   satisfy   portion   enormous

11. A small piece of food

    morsel   appetite   tug   forlorn

12. Having great size, number, or degree

    satisfy   regret   enormous   gaze

Name: _____

VOCABULARY ASSESSMENT
SENTENCES WORKSHEET

• Write a sentence with each of these four vocabulary words to show that you know what the word means.

dab   regret   morsel   gaze

1. _____

_____

2. _____

_____

3. _____

_____

4. _____

_____

Lesson 9

The Mouse at the Seashore

▼ OVERVIEW OF ACTIVITIES

Day 1	Day 2	Day 3	Day 4
TEXT INTRODUCTION • Predict storyline • Read fable • Discuss fable	**VOCABULARY INTRODUCTION** • Extract definitions • Review cognates • Assign homework	**EXPAND MEANING** • Review homework • Word Substitution • Assign homework	**TOOLS TO DEVELOP VOCABULARY** • Multiple Meanings

Day 5	Day 6	Day 7	Day 8
USING WORDS IN CONTEXT • Contexting activity	**TOOLS TO DEVELOP VOCABULARY** • Word Roots • Assign homework	**WORD WIZARD REVIEW** • Review homework • Word Wizard review	**ASSESSMENT**

▼ WORD LIST

The word in bold is the base word, followed by its definition. If the word has more than one meaning, then we provide only the definition used in the text. *Please review the definitions prior to instruction.*

1. **alarm:** to frighten
2. **bloody:** full of blood or covered with blood
3. **bruise:** to injure soft tissue or bone without breaking the skin
4. **content:** satisfied; happy
5. **dawn:** the beginning of the day; sunrise
6. **decide:** to make up one's mind about something
7. **firm:** definite and not easily changed

8. **narrow:** barely enough; almost not enough
9. **overwhelm:** to have a very strong effect
10. **roll:** to move forward by turning over and over
11. **several:** more than two but not many
12. **terror:** something that causes great fear

335

IDIOMATIC EXPRESSIONS

- **high time:** the proper time for something that has been delayed too long
- **ran for his life:** run very quickly to escape danger
- **change my mind:** form a new opinion

OTHER WORDS WORTH DEFINING

- **seashore:** sandy or rocky land next to the sea
- **sunset:** time when the sun sinks below the horizon

▼ **Prepare for activity**

Post Classroom Word List.

Materials: Student Word Books, *Fables*

▼ **Predict storyline**

Show students the illustration for "The Mouse at the Seashore" in the color insert or turn to page 41 of *Fables.*.

Say: *Today we are going to read the fable "The Mouse at the Seashore." What do you think this fable will be about when you look at the illustration and hear the title?*

Encourage a student discussion.

▼ **Ask the students to listen as you read the fable aloud**

▼ **Discuss the fable and moral; relate it to the students' lives**

- *Who are the main characters in this fable?*
- *What did Mouse want to do?*
- *What did his parents think about the trip?*
- *Have you ever wanted to do something your parents thought was dangerous?*
- *Do you think your parents were right?*
- *What happened to Mouse on the way to the seashore?*
- *What was it like after Mouse arrived at the seashore?*

▼ **Reread the moral**

- *What do you think the moral means?*
- *Mouse was lucky and arrived safely at the seashore. Do you think it is always a good idea to disregard your parents' advice? Why or why not?*

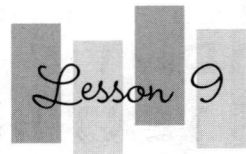

The Mouse
at the Seashore

A Mouse told his mother and father that he was going on a trip to the seashore.

"We are very **alarmed**!" they cried. "The world is full of **terrors.** You must not go!"

"I have made my **decision**," said the Mouse **firmly.** "I have never seen the ocean, and it is high time that I did. Nothing can make me change my mind."

"Then we cannot stop you," said Mother and Father Mouse, "but be careful!"

The next day, in the first light of **dawn,** the Mouse began his journey. Even before the morning had ended, the Mouse came to know trouble and fear.

A Cat jumped out from behind a tree.

"I will eat you for lunch," he said.

It was a **narrow** escape for the Mouse. He ran for his life, but he left a part of his tail in the mouth of the Cat.

By afternoon the Mouse had been attacked by birds and dogs. He had lost his way **several** times. He was **bruised** and **bloodied.** He was tired and frightened.

At evening the Mouse slowly climbed the last hill and saw the seashore spreading out before him. He watched the waves **rolling** onto the beach, one after another. All the colors of the sunset filled the sky.

"How beautiful!" cried the Mouse. "I wish that Mother and Father were here to see this with me."

The moon and the stars began to appear over the ocean. The Mouse sat silently on the top of the hill. He was **overwhelmed** by a feeling of deep peace and **contentment.**

All the miles of a hard road are worth a moment of true happiness.

Day 2
VOCABULARY INTRODUCTION

 *Lesson 9*

▼ Review the sections titled "Idiomatic Expressions" and "Other Words Worth Defining"

▼ Read posted target words to students, or ask students to read them

- Before you reread the fable, say: *Follow along in your Student Word Book as I read the fable again. Circle the target word when I read it. If you think you know what the word means* **without reading the definition,** *then raise your hand and I will call on you.* After students have suggested meanings, say: *Let's check the definition to see how close you were.*

   Note: The target words appear in the same order in the fable as on the word list. To help students find the words more easily, point out each target word on the list before looking for it in the text.

- There are no target words for which meaning can be inferred this week.

▼ Assign Vocabulary Review homework

Instruct students to write the correct vocabulary word in the space beside the definition.

▼ Cognates

If the students are bilingual, then you may wish to review the cognates from the fable.

English word	Spanish word
alarmed	alarmado
terrors	terrores
decision	decisión
ocean	océano
escape	escape
attacked	atacó
colors	colores
silently	silenciosamente

TARGET WORD DEFINITIONS

- The base word is bold and is the word defined.
- If there is more than one meaning, then the bold definition is the one used in the fable.
- The Spanish translation is provided for the meaning used in the fable.

1. alarmed (**alarm**)
   a) a device with a bell, buzzer, or siren that warns people of danger
   b) to frighten
   c) the sounding mechanism of an alarm clock
   - alarma; sobresalto

2. bloodied (**bloody**)
   a) full of blood or covered with blood
   b) violent or showing blood
   - sangriento; manchado con sangre

3. bruised (**bruise**)
   a) to injure soft tissue or bone without breaking the skin
   b) to hurt, especially feelings
   - cardenal; mancha amoratada, negruzca o amarillenta de la piel

4. contentment (**content**)
   satisfied; happy
   - contento; satisfecho; feliz

5. **dawn**
   a) the beginning of the day; sunrise
   b) the start of something new
   c) to begin to be understood
   - amanecer, alba; primera luz del día antes de salir el sol

6. decision (**decide**)
   a) to make up one's mind about something
   b) to settle something
   - decisión; determinación o resolución que se toma o se da en una cosa dudosa

7. firmly (**firm**)
   a) strong and solid (firm mattress)
   b) definite and not easily changed
   c) strong (a firm voice)
   d) a business or company
   - firme; definitivo e inalterable

8. **narrow**
   a) not broad or wide
   b) limited in size; small (narrow group of friends)
   c) lacking flexibility; rigid
   d) barely enough; almost not enough
   - estrecho; rígido, austero, exacto

9. overwhelmed (**overwhelm**)
   a) to defeat or overcome completely
   b) to have a very strong effect
   - abrumar, inundar; agobiar con algún grande peso

10. rolling (**roll**)
    a) to move forward by turning over and over
    b) to make something into the shape of a ball or tube
    c) something that is in the shape of a tube
    d) to flatten something by pushing a rounded object over it
    e) a small round piece of baked bread
    f) a list of names
    g) to move in a side-to-side or up-and-down way (ship rolls)
    h) to make a deep, loud sound (drum roll)
    i) to start (let's get rolling)
    - rodar, revolcar; mover hacia adelante dando vueltas

11. **several**
    more than two but not many
    - varios; más que dos pero no muchos

12. terrors (**terror**)
    something that causes great fear
    - temor; que causa miedo

EXPAND MEANING:
Word Substitution

▼ **Review Vocabulary Review homework**

1. Ask students for answers.

2. Direct students to correct their own answers if needed.

▼ **Prepare for activity**

Materials: Word Substitution worksheet

You might choose to have students work together in heterogeneous language groups to create new sentences that replace the underlined word with a synonymous word or phrase.

▼ **Introduce the concept**

Say: *In today's activity, you will figure out how to substitute your own words for a vocabulary word in a sentence. This will encourage you to think deeply about what each word means.*

▼ **Introduce the activity**

Say: *Now we are going to read sentences that use a vocabulary word. I want you to think about what the bold vocabulary word means. Then, figure out how to* **replace** *the bold word with another word or phrase that means about the same thing. I will call on you to read the sentence again, substituting the new word or phrase for the vocabulary word. You may use your Student Word Book.*

> *For example: When you see ducks walk, they* **waddle.**
>
> *When you see ducks walk, they* **take short steps and move from side to side.**

Read each sentence on the Word Substitution worksheet.

Encourage all students to respond.

▼ **Review the activity**

Say: *Was it hard to figure out a way to replace the word? Do you think it helped you understand the word better by thinking about it, even if you weren't called on?*

▼ **Word Wizard**

Motivate students to find sentences with this week's vocabulary. Say: *You are all going to continue being word wizards and even build your skills with this week's vocabulary words! Just like last week, I want you to demonstrate your wizardry in the following way: Each time you hear or read one of this week's words used at home, at school, or even on television, I want you to write the sentence on an index card (or sticky note). Write down where you heard or read it.*

Give students the Word Wizard List.

TOOLS TO DEVELOP
VOCABULARY: Multiple Meanings

▼ **Prepare for activity**

Divide students into mixed language pairs.

Materials: Multiple Meanings worksheet

▼ **Review the concept: Multiple Meanings**

Say: *Who remembers what multiple meanings are? That's right, they are more than one meaning for one word. Who can give me an example?*

Encourage multiple examples.

▼ **Introduce the activity**

Give each pair of students a Multiple Meanings worksheet.

Say: *Each of the bold words on this page has more than one meaning. Your job is to talk with your partner and decide what the word means in each sentence and then write the meaning in the space provided. You may use your Student Word Book to help with the definitions.*

Allow the students to work together until they have completed the worksheet.

▼ **Review the activity**

Say: *Who can tell me what* **firm** *means in this sentence? How did you know that was the definition for* **firm** *in this sentence? What clues in the sentence helped you?*

Emphasize the context that helped the student identify the correct definition.

Continue until all words have been defined.

USING WORDS IN CONTEXT

Using Words in Context is designed to develop students' ability to decipher the meaning of a word by using clues in the surrounding text.

▼ Prepare for activity

Place students in heterogeneous language groups, ideally four to five students.

Materials: Using Words in Context worksheet

If this activity is challenging for your students, then you may choose to complete it as a whole-group activity. It is helpful to make the worksheet into a transparency so that you can point out the context clues.

▼ Introduce the activity

Say: *Today's activity will help you practice using the target words in sentences. Your job is to figure out which word fits in the blank using the clues that are in the sentence. After you figure out the right word, think about **how** you figured it out; what were the clues in the rest of the sentence that helped you. When everyone in the group knows the correct word and **why it fits,** raise your hands. I'll call on one of the first groups ready. You will get a point if you get the correct answer (you may choose not to use points). Remember, everyone in your group must know the answer and why it is correct.*

Read the first sentence aloud to the class to illustrate the process.

▼ Review the activity

- Ask one student at a table for the correct answer **and to explain how he or she figured it out**—which clues in the contexts helped. Explaining the thought process that led to the answer helps the students realize that they know how to use the clues in the text and will demonstrate the process to those students who have not yet developed the skill.

- Continue until the lesson is completed, giving each group one point for each correct answer (you may choose not to use points).

TOOLS TO DEVELOP VOCABULARY: Word Roots

▼ **Prepare for activity**

Place students in mixed language groups of four students.

Materials: Root Words and Find the Roots worksheets

▼ **Review the concept: Word Roots**

Say: *Today we are going to study the roots of a few words. Who remembers what a word root is? That's right, it is the base part of a word; the part from which the word originally came. By studying* **a few** *roots, you will be able to figure out* **a lot of** *words because many words come from the same root.*

▼ **Introduce the activity**

Say: *I am going to give each group a worksheet with some words on it. Your job is to:*

1. *Read all of the words and look for the parts that are the same in the different words; these are the roots. Clue: there are four different roots.*

2. *Figure out what the root is in each of these words and then circle it.*

3. *Write one root at the top of each box on the worksheet.*

4. *Write the words in the box below their root.*

5. *Read each list of words and study them with the other people in your group.*

6. *Discuss what the root might mean.*

▼ **Review the activity**

1. Ask students to name the roots they found and read the words that share each root.

2. Call on respondents from the different groups to suggest possible meanings for each root. Ask them to explain their suggestions.

   Say: *Good thinking! Let's see how close you were.*

3. Read the explanation from Definitions of the Roots, and discuss.

▼ **Assign homework**

Give students the crossword puzzle; review the instructions and the due date.

If you notice that students are simply matching the number of spaces with the number of letters in a word, remind them that this activity will not give them practice with the words and definitions if it becomes a counting exercise. Counting is useful to check their answers.

DEFINITIONS OF THE ROOTS

Word root: graph   *The root "graph" comes from a Greek word meaning "write."*

bio**graphy:** the *written* history of a person's life

calli**graphy:** elegant hand*writing*

para**graph:** a subdivision of a *written* work

auto**graph:** a person's hand*written* signature

cardio**graph:** a machine that shows the movements of the heart in *written* form

Word root: manu   *The root "manu" comes from a Latin word meaning "hand." (What is the cognate?)*

manual: operated or done by *hand* rather than automatically

manipulate: to treat or work with the *hands*

manicure: a treatment for the care of the *hands* and nails

manufacture: to make from raw materials by *hand* or by machine

manuscript: original *hand*written pages of a book, poem, and so forth.

Word root: mot   *The root word "mot" comes from a Greek word meaning "to move."*

motivate: to provide with a reason to act or *move*

motion: *movement*

motor: something that causes *movement*

motive: something that causes a person to act or *move*

Word root: ped or **pod**   *The root "ped" comes from a Latin word meaning "foot." "Pod" is a similar Greek root.*

pedal: a lever or bar that is pushed with the *foot*

pedestal: the support or *foot* of a statue or column

pedestrian: someone who travels on *foot*

tri**pod:** a three-*footed* stand

podiatrist: someone who cares for the human *foot*

Day 7
WORD WIZARD REVIEW

▼ **Review the crossword puzzle homework**

1. Ask students for answers.

2. Direct students to correct their own answers if needed.

3. The crossword puzzle answer key for Lessons 6–10 can be found in the Teacher Answer Keys for Lesson 6.

▼ **Prepare for activity**

Instruct students to divide into their Word Wizard groups, taking the sentences they have collected throughout the 2 weeks.

▼ **Review Word Wizard**

• Allow students a few minutes to share sentences within their group and tell where they heard or read the word.

• Ask each group to share a few sentences with the class.

   Hint: The more enthusiasm you demonstrate and motivation you provide for this activity, the more the students will participate. Once the students are "hooked," it is most rewarding to observe their enthusiasm and to know that they have incorporated the vocabulary activities into other areas of their lives. You may want to bring in a few examples of your own for extra motivation.

• Allow students to post their sentences on the Word Wizard Wall.

You may choose to give the teams points to encourage participation.

▼ **Vocabulary assessment**

Part 1: Instruct the students to circle the word that corresponds to the definition on the Vocabulary Assessment worksheet.

Part 2: Instruct students to write sentences that demonstrate their knowledge of the word's meaning on the Vocabulary Assessment Sentences worksheet.

Hint: You may need to provide examples of sentences that demonstrate knowledge of the meaning. For example, if the vocabulary word were **ring,** then the sentence "I have a ring" does not demonstrate knowledge of the meaning. **Nose, car, friend, house,** or any number of other words could be substituted for **ring** in the sentence. The sentence "I wear a ring on my finger" demonstrates knowledge of the meaning.

Teacher answer keys

VOCABULARY REVIEW HOMEWORK

- Read the definitions.
- Find the word in the box that matches the definition.
- Write the correct word next to the definition.

several	decide	content	bruise
overwhelm	bloody	dawn	roll
narrow	firm	alarm	terror

1. __**firm**__ : definite and not easily changed

2. __**several**__ : more than two but not many

3. __**bloody**__ : full of blood or covered with blood

4. __**overwhelm**__ : to have a very strong effect

5. __**content**__ : satisfied; happy

6. __**narrow**__ : barely enough; almost not enough

7. __**alarm**__ : to frighten

8. __**decide**__ : to make up one's mind about something

9. __**roll**__ : to move forward by turning over and over

10. __**dawn**__ : the beginning of the day; sunrise

11. __**terror**__ : something that causes great fear

12. __**bruise**__ : to injure soft tissue or bone without breaking the skin

Lesson 9

MULTIPLE MEANINGS WORKSHEET

- Read the sentences below.
- Each group of sentences has one word in common, which is in bold.
- Using your Student Word Book, discuss how the meaning is different in each sentence.
- Write what the correct definition below the sentence.

---

1. I'm a **firm** believer in telling the truth
   definite and not easily changed

2. My mom works for a law **firm**.
   a business or company

3. I liked her **firm** handshake.
   strong and solid

---

4. Let's get the game **rolling** or we won't have time to finish before dark.
   to start

5. The lifeboat **rolled** in the waves.
   to move in a side-to-side or up-and-down way

6. My grandpa can **roll** the pie crust into a perfect circle.
   to flatten something by pushing a rounded object over it

7. **Rolls** are my favorite part of dinner.
   a small round piece of baked bread

---

8. The sky is usually beautiful at **dawn**.
   the beginning of the day; sunrise

9. When I spelled every word correctly on the test, it **dawned** on me that studying helps.
   to begin to be understood

10. The **dawn** of the age of airplanes was an exciting time.
    the start of something new

---

11. When my mom wouldn't let me go to the concert, I thought she was **narrow**-minded.
    lacking flexibility; rigid

12. My soccer team won the game but it was a **narrow** margin.
    limited in size; small

13. The path through the woods was so **narrow** in places that I could barely pass through.
    not broad or wide

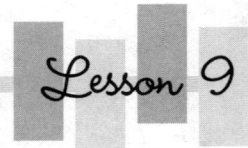

USING WORDS IN CONTEXT WORKSHEET

alarmed	bloodied	bruised	content	dawn
firmly	narrow	overwhelmed	Terror	

1. Tom's dad was **worried** when he did not arrive home from school by 3:00 p.m. He became __alarmed__ when Tom was still not home by 6 p.m.

2. When Tom finally came home, his dad could see that his son was **hurt.** His face was __bruised__ and __bloodied__ .

3. I like to read the *Goosebumps* series by R.L. Stine because the books are so **scary**. My favorite one is __Terror__ *Tower.*

4. I love watching the **sunrise** at the lake. We wake up when its still dark outside and drive to the lake before __dawn__ to go fishing.

5. My grandmother says she feels __content__ when all of her children and grandchildren are around her.

6. A lot of model cars and airplanes come with stickers. The directions say to press the stickers __firmly__ onto the plastic so that they will stay on.

7. The wide truck couldn't go down our street because the street is too __narrow__ .

8. My uncle cries all the time since my aunt died. He doesn't talk to anyone or go anywhere. He is __overwhelmed__ by sadness.

bloody	bruises	contentment	dawned	firm
narrowly	terrified	terror	overwhelmed	

9. You must not be mean if you want your puppy to obey you. But, you must give him orders in a **strong** and **firm** voice.

10. There was **almost** an accident. When the truck turned the corner it **narrowly** missed hitting the bicycle.

11. The bicyclist was **terrified** when he saw the truck coming toward him.

12. The truck didn't hit the bike, but the cyclist fell off his bike anyway. For weeks, the cyclist had black and blue **bruises** all over his body.

13. When he fell, he hit his head on the pavement and got a **bloody** nose.

14. General Santa Ana's Mexican army of **5,000 soldiers** **overwhelmed** the 188 Texans who were defending the Alamo.

15. After the baby finished his bottle, he lay in his mother's arms making sweet little noises of **contentment**.

16. In the story, *The Ransom of Red Chief*, the kidnappers have to pay a child's parents to take him back because the child is such a **terror**.

17. Luckily, graduation day **dawned** bright and sunny.

VOCABULARY ASSESSMENT WORKSHEET

• Circle the word that matches the definition.

1. To make up one's mind about something

    content   (decide)   overwhelm   firmly

2. To move forward by turning over and over

    terror   bloody   (roll)   several

3. Satisfied; happy

    decision   (content)   bruise   dawn

4. To have a very strong effect

    (overwhelm)   roll   narrow   alarm

5. Something that causes great fear

    content   firmly   dawn   (terror)

6. Full of blood or covered with blood

    overwhelm   several   (bloody)   bruise

7. Barely enough; almost not enough

    (narrow)   decision   several   roll

8. Definite and not easily changed

    alarm   decision   (firmly)   several

9. To injure soft tissue or bone without breaking the skin

    content   (bruise)   terror   dawn

10. More than two but not many

    overwhelm   narrow   roll   (several)

11. The beginning of the day; sunrise

    bruise   (dawn)   firmly   content

12. To frighten

    narrow   bloody   several   (alarm)

Reproducible materials

decision

terrors

alarmed

narrow

dawn

firmly

Vocabulary Improvement Program for English Language Learners and Their Classmates, 4th Grade, by Teresa Lively, Diane August, María Carlo, and Catherine Snow © 2003 Paul H. Brookes Publishing Co., Inc. All rights reserved.

bloodied

bruised

several

contentment

overwhelmed

rolling

Name: _____

VOCABULARY REVIEW HOMEWORK

- Read the definitions.
- Find the word in the box that matches the definition.
- Write the correct word next to the definition.

several	decide	content	bruise
overwhelm	bloody	dawn	roll
narrow	firm	alarm	terror

1. _____: definite and not easily changed

2. _____: more than two but not many

3. _____: full of blood or covered with blood

4. _____: to have a very strong effect

5. _____: satisfied; happy

6. _____: barely enough; almost not enough

7. _____: to frighten

8. _____: to make up one's mind about something

9. _____: to move forward by turning over and over

10. _____: the beginning of the day; sunrise

11. _____: something that causes great fear

12. _____: to injure soft tissue or bone without breaking the skin

WORD SUBSTITUTION WORKSHEET

1. It would **alarm** my mother to find out that we forgot to lock the door.

2. I looked at the enormous, growling dog with **terror**.

3. When given the choice, I **decided** that I would rather go to school than to work.

4. My sister made a **firm** decision that she would finish college.

5. My mom sometimes wakes up before **dawn** to go to work.

6. My friend **narrowly** avoided detention when she broke a school rule.

7. We have **several** more tickets to the play.

8. Jessica had a **bruise** from where the door had hit her leg.

9. I would not want to see anyone **bloodied**!

10. Have you ever **rolled** down a hill?

11. My family laughs all the time since we won the lotto; we are **overwhelmed** with joy.

12. However, we know that money is not all it takes to make us feel **content**.

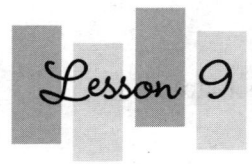

WORD WIZARD LIST

- Each time you hear or read one of these words used in a sentence at home, at school, on television, or on the radio, write the sentence on an index card or sticky note.

alarmed (alarm): to frighten

bloodied (bloody): full of blood or covered with blood

bruised (bruise): to injure soft tissue or bone without breaking the skin

contentment (content): satisfied; happy

dawn: the beginning of the day; sunrise

decision (decide): to make up one's mind about something

firmly (firm): definite and not easily changed

narrow: barely enough; almost not enough

overwhelmed (overwhelm): to have a very strong effect

rolling (roll): to move forward by turning over and over

several: more than two but not many

terrors (terror): something that causes great fear

MULTIPLE MEANINGS WORKSHEET

- Read the sentences below.
- Each group of sentences has one word in common, which is in bold.
- Using your Student Word Book, discuss how the meaning is different in each sentence.
- Write the correct definition below the sentence.

---

1. I'm a **firm** believer in telling the truth.

2. My mom works for a law **firm.**

3. I liked her **firm** handshake.

---

4. Let's get the game **rolling** or we won't have time to finish before dark.

5. The lifeboat **rolled** in the waves.

6. My grandpa can **roll** the pie crust into a perfect circle.

7. **Rolls** are my favorite part of dinner.

---

8. The sky is usually beautiful at **dawn.**

9. When I spelled every word correctly on the test, it **dawned** on me that studying helps.

10. The **dawn** of the age of airplanes was an exciting time.

---

11. When my mom wouldn't let me go to the concert, I thought she was **narrow**-minded.

12. My soccer team won the game but it was a **narrow** margin.

13. The path through the woods was so **narrow** in places that I could barely pass through.

Name: _____

USING WORDS IN CONTEXT WORKSHEET

alarmed	bloodied	bruised	content	dawn
firmly	narrow	overwhelmed	Terror	

1. Tom's dad was **worried** when he did not arrive home from school by 3:00 p.m. He became _____ when Tom was still not home by 6 p.m.

2. When Tom finally came home, his dad could see that his son was **hurt**. His face was _____ and _____.

3. I like to read the *Goosebumps* series by R.L. Stine because the books are so **scary**. My favorite one is _____ *Tower*.

4. I love watching the **sunrise** at the lake. We wake up when its still dark outside and drive to the lake before _____ to go fishing.

5. My grandmother says she feels _____ when all of her children and grandchildren are around her.

6. A lot of model cars and airplanes come with stickers. The directions say to press the stickers _____ onto the plastic so that they will stay on.

7. The wide truck couldn't go down our street because the street is too _____.

8. My uncle cries all the time since my aunt died. He doesn't talk to anyone or go anywhere. He is _____ by sadness.

USING WORDS IN CONTEXT WORKSHEET *(continued)*

bloody	bruises	contentment	dawned	firm
narrowly	terrified	terror	overwhelmed	

9. You must not be mean if you want your puppy to obey you. But, you must give him orders in a **strong** and _____ voice.

10. There was **almost** an accident. When the truck turned the corner it _____ missed hitting the bicycle.

11. The bicyclist was _____ when he saw the truck coming toward him.

12. The truck didn't hit the bike, but the cyclist fell off his bike anyway. For weeks, the cyclist had black and blue _____ all over his body.

13. When he fell, he hit his head on the pavement and got a _____ nose.

14. General Santa Ana's Mexican army of **5,000 soldiers** _____ the 188 Texans who were defending the Alamo.

15. After the baby finished his bottle, he lay in his mother's arms making sweet little noises of _____.

16. In the story, *The Ransom of Red Chief,* the kidnappers have to pay a child's parents to take him back because the child is such a _____.

17. Luckily, graduation day _____ bright and sunny.

FIND THE ROOTS WORKSHEET

• Find the word roots and circle them.

biography motor

manuscript manufacture

pedal autograph

pedestrian motive

paragraph manual

motion calligraphy

tripod manicure

podiatrist pedestal

cardiograph manipulate

motivate

Name: _____

ROOT WORDS WORKSHEET

- Write one word root at the top of each list.
- Write the words that you circled on the Find the Roots worksheet in the list for the matching root.
- Study the words and discuss what the root might mean. Be sure that everyone in your group knows what the root means.

Root: _____

_____   _____
_____   _____
_____   _____
_____   _____

Root: _____

_____   _____
_____   _____
_____   _____
_____   _____

Root: _____

_____   _____
_____   _____
_____   _____
_____   _____

Root: _____

_____   _____
_____   _____
_____   _____
_____   _____

Name: _____

ACROSS

2. Satisfied; happy
5. Very great fear
6. To move forward by turning over and over
9. To have a very strong effect
11. The beginning of the day; sunrise
12. To injure soft tissue or bone without breaking the skin

DOWN

1. More than two but not many
3. Barely enough; almost not enough
4. Full of blood or covered with blood
7. To make up one's mind about something
8. To frighten
10. Definite and not easily changed

Lesson 9

alarm

bloody

bruise

content

dawn

decide

firm

narrow

overwhelm

roll

several

terror

Vocabulary Improvement Program for English Language Learners and Their Classmates, 4th Grade, by Teresa Lively, Diane August, María Carlo, and Catherine Snow © 2003 Paul H. Brookes Publishing Co., Inc. All rights reserved.

VOCABULARY ASSESSMENT WORKSHEET

• Circle the word that matches the definition.

1. To make up one's mind about something

    content   decide   overwhelm   firmly

2. To move forward by turning over and over

    terror   bloody   roll   several

3. Satisfied; happy

    decision   content   bruise   dawn

4. To have a very strong effect

    overwhelm   roll   narrow   alarm

5. Something that causes great fear

    content   firmly   dawn   terror

6. Full of blood or covered with blood

    overwhelm   several   bloody   bruise

7. Barely enough; almost not enough

    narrow   decision   several   roll

8. Definite and not easily changed

    alarm   decision   firmly   several

9. To injure soft tissue or bone without breaking the skin

    content   bruise   terror   dawn

10. More than two but not many

    overwhelm   narrow   roll   several

11. The beginning of the day; sunrise

    bruise   dawn   firmly   content

12. To frighten

    narrow   bloody   several   alarm

Name: _____

VOCABULARY ASSESSMENT
SENTENCES WORKSHEET

• Write a sentence with each of the four vocabulary words to show that you know what the word means.

several   overwhelm   content   decide

1. _____

_____

2. _____

_____

3. _____

_____

4. _____

_____

Review Week

▼ OVERVIEW OF ACTIVITIES

Review Day 1
REVIEW SENTENCES • Assign homework

Review Day 2
WORD BEE

Review Day 3
CHARADES • Assign homework

Review Day 4
ANTONYMS/ SYNONYMS • Review homework

Review Day 5
POSTTEST

▼ **Introduce review week**

Say: *This week we will play several games to help us review **all** of the vocabulary words that we studied during the past four lessons. That may sound like a lot of work, but I think we will have a lot of fun!*

If you review the words and definitions from the past four lessons, then you will find this week's activities more fun.

It will help the students with the week's activities if they study the words and definitions as homework on the first day.

Post the Classroom Word Lists from the past four lessons for the students to use as a reference throughout the week.

REVIEW SENTENCES

▼ **Prepare the activity**

Separate students into heterogeneous language pairs.

    Materials: Word Cards (Please cut words apart to make cards.)
    Give 12 cards to each pair of students.

▼ **Introduce the activity**

Say: *To begin the review, I will give each pair of students a set of Word Cards. Your job is to make sentences with the words. You may add three words that are not on the cards to help you make complete sentences. You may make the sentences silly if you choose. After you make a sentence with the cards, write it on a sheet of paper so that you can share it with the class later. Let's see how many sentences you can write!*

▼ **Review the activity**

Allow the students to read their sentences to the class.

▼ **Assign homework**

Review target words and their definitions from the past four lessons.

Review Day 2
WORD BEE

▼ Prepare for activity

1. Cut apart the Word Bee Cards.
2. Display word lists from Lessons 6–9.
3. Divide students into heterogeneous language groups of four to five students.
4. Provide paper and pencils to each team.

▼ Introduce the activity: Word Bee

Say:

1. *The objective of this game is for team members to work together to give a good definition for each vocabulary word.*
2. *Each team will be given a card with a vocabulary word and will have 2 minutes to work together to write a definition for the word.*
3. *You may not use your Student Word Books. I want to see what you remember.*
4. *When you have finished writing the definition, one team member will present the definition to the class.*
5. *The remainder of the class will judge the accuracy of the definition.*
   - *If you think the definition is right, then put your thumbs up.*
   - *If you think the definition is wrong, then put your thumbs down, and another team can try to define the word.*

You may choose to give points to the teams.

   If a team is unable to give an accurate definition, then please give the correct definition.

▼ Begin play

1. Give each team one Word Bee Card (all teams will work on their definitions simultaneously).
2. Play continues between the teams until all cards have been used and all definitions presented.

Review Day 2: WORD BEE

Word	Definition
appetite	desire for food
bloody	full of blood or covered with blood
completely	in every way
envy	the wish to have what someone else has
gloom	a dark and depressing atmosphere
morsel	a small piece of food
regret	to be sad or sorry about something
salesperson	a man or woman who sells goods or services
sprout	to emerge and develop rapidly
tempt	to try to convince someone to do something wrong
terror	something that causes great fear
willpower	the strength to control one's actions

Review Day 3
CHARADES

▼ Prepare for activity

1. Display Classroom Word Lists from Lessons 6–9.
2. Cut apart the Charades Cards.
3. Students may use their Student Word Books to review word meanings.
4. Divide the class into heterogeneous language teams of six to eight students each.

▼ Introduce the concept: Charades

Say: *Has anyone ever played Charades? Who can tell us what the object of Charades is?*

That's right, Charades is a game in which students act out a word **without talking** *while the other students on their own team try to guess what word they are acting out.*

▼ Introduce the activity

1. Divide the Charades Cards evenly between the teams.
2. Two teams will compete while the others observe.
3. The students on Team A choose a word and give it to three students on Team B.
4. The students on Team B act out the word for their team **without talking.**
5. Team B has three chances to guess the correct word. If they fail, then Team A tells them the word and defines it.
6. Team B then selects a word for Team C to act out. After Team C has its turn, they select the word for Team D to act out. The last team picks a word for team A.

Play continues until time or words run out.

▼ Assign homework

Instruct students to complete the crossword puzzle; review the instructions and the due date.

ANTONYMS/SYNONYMS

▼ **Review the crossword puzzle homework**

1. Ask students for answers.

2. Direct students to correct their own answers if needed.

3. The crossword puzzle answer key for Lessons 6–10 can be found in the Teacher Answer Keys for Lesson 6.

▼ **Expanding meaning: Antonyms/synonyms**

Students will identify a target word when given either its synonym or antonym. This will help students to develop their understanding of synonyms and antonyms as well as reinforce the meanings of the vocabulary words.

▼ **Introduce the concept: Antonyms/Synonyms**

1. Say: *I am going to say a word or phrase that will help you think of one of the target words, kind of like a clue. Your job is to think about which target word goes with the clue. The clues I give you will be either synonyms or antonyms.*

   Does anyone remember what synonyms are? That's right, **synonyms** *are words that have the same meanings, such as* **furious** *and* **angry.**

   Does anyone remember what antonyms are? That's right, **antonyms** *are words that have opposite meanings, such as* **hot** *and* **cold.**

   Who can give me an example of a pair of antonyms? Who can give me an example of a pair of synonyms? Elicit several examples from students before proceeding with the lesson.

2. Say: *What target word do you think of when I say* _____ *? Provide an associated word. Please explain why you think the target word goes with the clue. Is it a synonym or an antonym?*

Give the associated words one at a time. Accept any plausible answer that the student can justify.

Associated word	Vocabulary word	Synonym/antonym
fearful; cowardly	courage	antonym
decorated; fancy	adorned	synonym
fulfill	satisfy	synonym
unhappiness; sadness	contentment	antonym
some; various	several	synonym
evening; sunset	dawn	antonym
gently; easily	firmly	antonym
unhappy; alone	forlorn	synonym
support; urge; encourage	discourage	antonym
voyage; trip	journey	synonym
comply; agree	resist	antonym
belittle; insult	flatter	antonym

Direct students to think of antonyms, synonyms, or words otherwise associated for the vocabulary words.

Review Day 5
POSTTEST FOR LESSONS 6–9

▼ **Prepare for activity**

- Separate students so that they will work individually.
- Hand out the extra copy of the assessment forms that you made when you gave the pretest.

▼ **Introduce the activity**

Say: *In this lesson, you will complete three worksheets to see which of the target words you have learned. You have completed activities like these before. I will show you examples of each of the three different activities before you begin.*

1. Write the following example on the board.

fun	big	happy

I am _____ when the sun is shining.

Say: *The first worksheet has a box at the top with words in it. Sentences below the box have a line in them to show that a word is missing. First, you will read a sentence. Then, you will look in the box for a word that makes sense if you write it in the space.*

*Who can read the sentence on the board? Good, now what word makes the most sense if we put it in the space? That's right, so I am going to write **happy** in the space.*

Note: Be sure that students know they are to **use each word only one time.**

2. Again, write the example on the board.

A toy that spins

sled	top	puzzle	kite

Say: *The second worksheet has definitions and four words from which to choose. Who can raise their hand to read the definition on the board? Good, now who can read the four words below the definition? Which word goes with the definition? That's right, so now I will draw a circle around the word **top**.*

3. Say: *For the last worksheet, you are going to work with words that have more than one meaning. For example, let's think about the word top again. Who can think of one meaning of top? You can tell me either a definition or a sentence.*

Write responses on the board, eliciting examples of both definitions and meaningful sentences for the word *top*. For example:

1. María stood on *top* of the table.

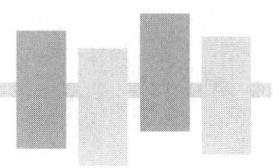

2. A *top* is a toy that spins around quickly.

3. José was the *top* student in his class.

4. Jenny wore a new *top*.

5. I save bottle *tops*.

Say: *In this activity, you will see four words that have more than one meaning. Think about the different meanings of each word. Write one sentence for each of the meanings that you know, or write the definition if that is easier for you. Write as many meanings as you can.*

• Distribute the activity.

• Leave the examples on the board as a reference for the students.

• Monitor the students as they work to be certain they understand the activity.

Reproducible materials

Please cut words apart.

adorned	flattery
salesperson	sprouted
completely	spun
glamorous	glowing
admiration	twinkle
envy	contained
absolutely	heartburn
frowning	halfway
stared	journey
resist	willpower

WORD CARDS

likely	budge	narrow
discourage	forlornly	several
temptation	gazed	bruised
enormously	gloom	roll
portions	regret	overwhelm
satisfy	alarmed	contentment
appetite	terrors	allure
morsel	decision	bloodied
dab	firmly	
tug	dawn	

WORD BEE CARDS

Please cut words apart.

salesperson	appetite
completely	morsel
envy	gloom
sprout	regret
willpower	terror
tempt	bloody

CHARADES CARDS

Please cut words apart.

glamorous   dab

frown   tug

stare   alarm

spin   narrow

heartburn   bruise

halfway   roll

enormous

Name: _____

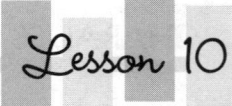

Lesson 10

ACROSS

5. Certainly
9. To shine with quick flashes of light
10. Give off a steady, low light
11. To think of, or look at, with pleasure and respect
12. To have a very strong effect

DOWN

1. To attract
2. Probable
3. To look at something steadily
4. To have inside; hold
6. A serving of food
7. To start or cause something to move
8. To make up one's mind about something

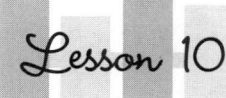

absolutely

admire

allure

budge

contain

decide

gaze

glow

likely

overwhelm

portion

twinkle

References

Anderson, J.C., & Nagy, W.E. (1992). The vocabulary conundrum. *American Educator,* 14–16, 44–48.

Beck, I., McKeown, M.G., & Omanson, R.C. (1987). In M.G. McKeown & M.E. Curtis (Eds.), *The nature of vocabulary acquisition* (pp. 147–163). Mahwah, NJ: Lawrence Erlbaum Associates.

Lobel, A. (1980). *Fables.* New York: HarperCollins.

Terban, M. (1996). *Scholastic dictionary of idioms.* New York: Scholastic.

Student word book

4th Grade

Name: _____

The Hen and
the Apple Tree

One October day, a Hen looked out her window. She saw an apple tree growing in her backyard.

"Now that is odd," said the Hen. "I am certain that there was no tree standing in that spot yesterday."

"There are some of us that grow fast," said the tree.

The Hen looked at the bottom of the tree.

"I have never seen a tree," she said, "that has ten furry toes."

"There are some of us that do," said the tree. "Hen, come outside and enjoy the cool shade of my leafy branches."

The Hen looked at the top of the tree.

"I have never seen a tree," she said, "that has two long, pointed ears."

"There are some of us that have," said the tree. "Hen, come outside and eat one of my delicious apples."

"Come to think of it," said the Hen, "I have never heard a tree speak from a mouth that is full of sharp teeth."

"There are some of us that can," said the tree. "Hen, come outside and rest your back against the bark of my trunk."

"I have heard," said the Hen, "that some of you trees lose all of your leaves at this time of the year."

"Oh, yes," said the tree, "there are some of us that will." The tree began to quiver and shake. All of its leaves quickly dropped off.

The Hen was not surprised to see a large Wolf in the place where an apple tree had been standing just a moment before. She locked her shutters and slammed her window closed.

The Wolf knew he had been outsmarted. He stormed away in a hungry rage.

It is always difficult to pose as something that one is not.

TARGET WORD DEFINITIONS

Lesson 1

- The base word is bold and is the word defined.
- If there is more than one meaning, then the bold definition is the one used in the fable.
- The Spanish translation is provided for the meaning used in the fable.

1. **bark**
   a) short, loud sound that an animal makes
   b) the hard covering on the outside of a tree
   c) to shout at someone gruffly
   • corteza; parte exterior y dura de un árbol

2. **certain**
   a) proved beyond all doubt to be true
   b) particular
   • saber; tener certeza: conocimiento seguro y claro de alguna cosa

3. **delicious**
   very pleasing to taste or smell
   • delicioso; placentero al olfato o paladar

4. furry (**fur**)
   the soft, thick, hairy coat of an animal
   • peludo; con mucho pelo

5. leafy (**leaf**)
   a) the flat and usually green parts of a plant or tree that grow out from a stem, twig, or branch
   b) removable parts of a table top
   c) to turn over pages
   • frondoso; abundante en hojas y ramas

6. **odd**
   a) strange or unusual
   b) not matching
   c) a number that cannot be divided evenly by two
   • extraño; raro o singular

7. outsmartec (**outsmart**)
   to defeat by being clever
   • ser más listo; engañar

8. quickly (**quick**)
   a) rapid; fast
   b) fast in understanding or thinking
   • rápidamente; con ímpetu, rapidez o celeridad

9. **quiver**
   a) to shake or move with a slight tremble; to vibrate
   b) a case for carrying arrows
   • estremecerse; temblar repentinamente

10. **rage**
    a) wild, uncontrollable anger
    b) to be violent without control
    c) a very popular fashion
    • rabia; ira, enojo, cólera

11. **shade**
    a) area sheltered from light
    b) something that provides shelter from light
    c) to shelter from light
    d) the degree of darkness of a color
    e) to make part of a drawing darker than the rest
    f) a small amount or difference
    • sombra; área protegida de la luz

12. **trunk**
    a) the main stem of a tree
    b) a large case used for storage or for carrying clothes on a long journey
    c) the long nose of an elephant
    d) enclosed part of a car where luggage and a spare tire can be stored
    • tronco; tallo fuerte y macizo de los árboles y arbustos

Vocabulary Improvement Program for English Language Learners and Their Classmates, 4th Grade, by Teresa Lively, Diane August, María Carlo, and Catherine Snow © 2003 Paul H. Brookes Publishing Co., Inc. All rights reserved.

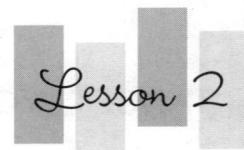

The Baboon's Umbrella

The Baboon was taking his daily walk in the jungle. He met his friend, the Gibbon, on the path.

"My good friend," said the Gibbon, "how strange to find you holding an open umbrella over your head on such a sunshiny day as this."

"Yes," said the Baboon. "I am most annoyed. I cannot close this disagreeable umbrella. It is stuck. I would not think of walking without my umbrella in case it should rain. But, as you see, I am not able to enjoy the sunshine underneath this dark shadow. It is a sad predicament."

"There is a simple solution," said the Gibbon, "You need only to cut some holes in your umbrella. Then the sun will shine on you."

"What a good idea!" cried the Baboon. "I do thank you."

The Baboon ran home. With his scissors, he cut large holes in the top of his umbrella. When the Baboon returned to his walk, the warm sunshine came down through the holes.

"How delightful," said the Baboon.

However, the sun disappeared behind some clouds. There were a few drops of rain. Then it began to pour. The rain fell through all of the holes in the umbrella. In just a short time, the unhappy Baboon was soaked to the skin.

Advice from friends is like the weather. Some of it is good; some of it is bad.

TARGET WORD DEFINITIONS

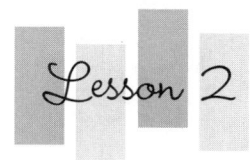

Lesson 2

- The base word is bold and is the word defined.
- If there is more than one meaning, then the bold definition is the one used in the fable.
- The Spanish translation is provided for the meaning used in the fable.

1. **advice**
   a suggestion about what someone should do
   - consejo; sugerencia, parecer, o dictamen que se da o toma con respecto a algo

2. annoyed (**annoy**)
   to make someone lose patience or feel angry
   - enfadado; irritado, enojado, disgustado

3. **baboon**
   a large monkey that lives in the jungle
   - mandril; mono de gran tamaño que vive en la jungla (selva)

4. **delightful**
   giving great pleasure
   - que deleita; que produce placer

5. **disagreeable**
   a) describing something or someone that causes discomfort
   b) uncooperative; bad tempered
   - desagradable; de mal genio

6. **gibbon**
   a small ape with long, slender arms and no tail
   - mono pequeño de brazos largos y delgados, sin rabo

7. **jungle**
   land in warm, tropical areas near the equator covered with trees, vines, and bushes
   - jungla; terreno de vegetación muy espesa (selva)

8. **predicament**
   an awkward or difficult situation
   - apuro o predicamento; aprieto, conflicto, dificultad

9. **scissors**
   a sharp tool with two blades used for cutting paper or fabric
   - tijeras; instrumento compuesto de dos cuchillos de un sólo filo que se usa para cortar

10. **solution**
    a) the answer to a problem
    b) a liquid mixture
    - solución; respuesta a una duda o dificultad

11. **stuck**
    fixed in a particular position
    - atorado; atascado

12. **underneath**
    under or below
    - debajo

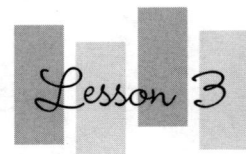

The Poor Old Dog

There was an old Dog who was very poor. The only coat he had to wear was mostly holes held together by ragged threads. He could feel the pebbles on the pavement through the thin soles of his tattered shoes. He slept in the park because he had no home.

The Dog spent most of his time searching in garbage cans. He found bits of string and buttons. These he sold for pennies to passersby.

The Dog always walked with his nose close to the curb, looking for things to sell. That is how he came to find the gold ring that was lying in the gutter.

"My luck has changed," cried the Dog, "for I am sure that this is a magic ring!"

The Dog rubbed the ring and said, "I wish for a new coat. I wish for new shoes. I wish for a house to live in. I wish these things would come true right now!"

But nothing happened. The Dog felt the wind through the holes in his coat. He felt the pebbles under his thin shoes. That night he slept in his usual bench in the park.

Several days later, the Dog saw a note on a lamppost. The note said "Lost: gold ring. Large reward. Mr. Terrier. Ten Wealthy Lane."

The old Dog hurried to Wealthy Lane. Mr. Terrier was overjoyed to have his ring returned. He thanked the Dog profusely and gave him a bulging purse full of coins.

The Dog bought a warm fur coat. He bought a pair of good shoes with thick soles.

There was a large amount of money left over. The Dog used the rest of it as a down payment on a cozy little house. He moved right in and never had to sleep in the park again.

Wishes, on their way to coming true, will not be rushed.

TARGET WORD DEFINITIONS

Lesson 3

- The base word is bold and is the word defined.
- If there is more than one meaning, then the bold definition is the one used in the fable.
- The Spanish translation is provided for the meaning used in the fable.

1. bulging (**bulge**)
   to swell or curve outward
   - protuberante; que sobresale

2. **cozy**
   comfortable or snug
   - cómodo

3. **curb**
   a) **a raised border along the edge of a paved street**
   b) to control or hold something back
   - orilla de la acera

4. **gutter**
   a channel or length of tubing through which rain is drained away from a road or from the roof of a building
   - cuneta; zanja en cada uno de los lados de un camino o carretera que canaliza el agua de la lluvia

5. **overjoyed**
   extremely happy
   - lleno de alegría; contento

6. passersby (**passerby**)
   someone who happens to be going past
   - transeúnte; alguien que transita o pasa por un lugar

7. **pavement**
   a hard material, such as concrete or asphalt, that is used to cover roads or sidewalks
   - pavimento; piso artificial de concreto o asfalto que cubre aceras o carreteras

8. profusely (**profuse**)
   plentiful or more than enough
   - abundantemente; generosamente; en gran cantidad

9. **ragged**
   old, torn, and worn out
   - harapiento, andrajoso; viejo y muy usado

10. **reward**
    something that is received for doing something good or useful
    - recompensa, se otorga para premiar un favor, virtud o mérito

11. **tattered**
    old and torn
    - andrajoso; viejo y roto

12. **wealthy**
    having a large amount of money or property
    - adinerado, rico; que posee gran cantidad de dinero o propiedades

The Ostrich
in Love

On Sunday the ostrich saw a young lady walking in the park. He fell in love with her at once. He followed behind her at a distance, putting his feet in the very places she had stepped.

On Monday the Ostrich gathered violets as a gift to his beloved. He was too shy to give them to her. He left them at her door and ran away, but there was a great joy in his heart.

On Tuesday the Ostrich composed a song for his beloved. He sang it over and over. He thought it was the most beautiful music he had ever heard.

On Wednesday the Ostrich watched his beloved dining in a restaurant. He forgot to order supper for himself. He was too happy to be hungry.

On Thursday the Ostrich wrote a poem to his beloved. It was the first poem he had ever written, but he did not have the courage to read it to her.

On Friday the Ostrich bought a new suit of clothes. He fluffed his feathers, feeling fine and handsome. He hoped that his beloved might notice.

On Saturday the Ostrich dreamed that he was waltzing with his beloved in a great ballroom. He held her tightly as they whirled around and around to the music. He awoke feeling wonderfully alive.

On Sunday the Ostrich returned to the park. When he saw the young lady walking there, his heart fluttered wildly, but he said to himself, "Alas, it seems that I am much too shy for love. Yet, surely this has been a week well spent."

Love can be its own reward.

TARGET WORD DEFINITIONS

Lesson 4

- The base word is bold and is the word defined.
- If there is more than one meaning, then the bold definition is the one used in the fable.
- The Spanish translation is provided for the meaning used in the fable.

1. **beloved**

   someone who is greatly loved

   - amado; alguien querido

2. composed (**compose**)

   a) **to write music or poetry**

   b) to make calm and quiet

   c) to be formed from (composed of)

   - componer; hacer versos o producir obras musicales

3. **courage**

   bravery or fearlessness

   - valor, valentía; sin miedo

4. fluffed (**fluff**)

   a) light down or fuzz, as on a young bird or dandelion

   b) **to make something appear larger by shaking or brushing**

   c) something that's not very important

   - sacudir

5. fluttered (**flutter**)

   to move quickly and lightly

   - revolotear; venir por el aire dando vueltas

6. gathered (**gather**)

   a) **to collect or pick things**

   b) to come together in a group

   c) to understand from something said or done

   d) to gain little by little

   - recoger; juntar o congregar cosas

7. **handsome**

   a) **attractive in appearance**

   b) large or generous

   - guapo; bien parecido

8. **shy**

   a) **uncomfortable or nervous around people or with strangers**

   b) lacking or falling short

   c) to draw back suddenly, as from fear or caution

   - tímido; temeroso de otras personas o extraños

9. **surely**

   a) with confidence; unhesitatingly

   b) **certainly; without a doubt**

   - seguramente; con certeza

10. waltzing (**waltz**)

    to dance a smooth, gliding ballroom dance

    - vals; baile de origen alemán que ejecutan las parejas con movimiento giratorio y de traslaciún

11. whirled (**whirl**)

    to move around quickly in a circle

    - arremolinar; moverse rápidamente y en círculos

12. wildly (**wild**)

    a) natural and not tamed by humans

    b) **not controlled; unruly**

    c) overcome with an emotion such as grief, anger, or happiness

    d) crazy, fantastic, or reckless

    - salvaje; sin control

Vocabulary Improvement Program for English Language Learners and Their Classmates, 4th Grade, by Teresa Lively, Diane August, María Carlo, and Catherine Snow © 2003 Paul H. Brookes Publishing Co., Inc. All rights reserved.

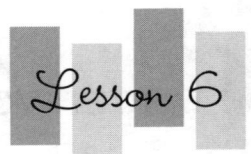

Madame Rhinoceros
and Her Dress

Madame Rhinoceros saw a dress in the window of a shop. It was covered with polka dots and flowers. It was adorned with ribbons and lace. She admired it for a moment and then entered the shop.

"That dress in the window," said Madame Rhinoceros to a salesperson, "I would like to try it on."

Madame Rhinoceros put on the dress. She looked at herself in the mirror. "I do not think this dress is at all attractive on me," she said.

"But Madame," said the salesperson, "you are completely wrong. This dress makes you look glamorous and alluring."

"If only I were sure," said Madame Rhinoceros.

"Ah, Madame," said the salesperson, "everyone who sees you wearing this dress will be filled with admiration and envy."

"Do you really think so?" asked Madame Rhinoceros, turning around and around in front of the mirror.

"Absolutely," said the salesperson. "You have my word."

"Very well," said Madame Rhinoceros, "I will buy the dress, and I will wear it now."

Madame Rhinoceros left the shop. As she walked up the avenue, she saw that people were smiling and laughing at her.

"Admiration," thought Madame Rhinoceros.

She saw some people who were shaking their heads and frowning.

"Envy," thought Madame Rhinoceros.

She continued up the avenue. Everyone who saw her stopped and stared. Madame Rhinoceros felt more glamorous and alluring every step.

Nothing is harder to resist than a bit of flattery.

TARGET WORD DEFINITIONS

- The base word is bold and is the word defined.
- If there is more than one meaning, then the bold definition is the one used in the fable.
- The Spanish translation is provided for the meaning used in the fable.

1. **absolutely**
   certainly
   - absolutamente; de manera segura

2. admiration (**admire**)
   to think of or look at with pleasure and respect
   - admiración; contemplar o considerar con estima o agrado

3. adorned (**adorn**)
   to make more beautiful or interesting by decorating
   - adornar; engalanar con adornos que dan mejor parecer a personas o cosas

4. alluring (**allure**)
   to attract
   - fascinar; atraer irresistiblemente

5. completely (**complete**)
   a) having all necessary or normal parts
   b) to finish something
   c) total; in every way
   - completo; acabado; perfecto

6. **envy**
   the wish to have what someone else has
   - envidia; deseo de algo que no se posee

7. flattery (**flatter**)
   a) to praise too much and often insincerely, especially in order to get a favor
   b) to make a person look better or more beautiful
   - halagar; adular o decir a uno insinceramente cosas que le agraden

8. frowning (**frown**)
   to wrinkle the forehead when one is unhappy
   - fruncir el entrecejo

9. glamorous (**glamour**)
   attractive and exciting quality of something special
   - encantador; que hace muy viva y grata impresión en el alma o los sentidos

10. **resist**
    a) to refuse to accept; to oppose
    b) to fight back
    c) to stop oneself from doing something that one would like to do
    - resistir; rechazar; contrariar; contradecir

11. **salesperson**
    a man or woman who sells goods or services
    - vendedor o vendedora; que vende bienes o servicios

12. stared (**stare**)
    to look directly at someone or something for a long time without moving the eyes
    - mirar fijamente

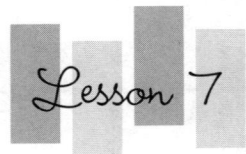

The Pig at the Candy Store

All night long, the sleeping Pig dreamed of candy. He sprouted wings of spun sugar. He flew through marshmallow clouds to a glowing marzipan moon. The stars that twinkled in the sky were chocolate kisses wrapped in shiny foil.

The Pig woke up with his mouth watering.

"Candy," he cried. "I must have some this minute!"

The Pig ran to the candy dish. It was empty. The box of chocolate creams in the cupboard contained nothing but paper wrappers.

"I will go to the candy store," said the Pig, as he put on his clothes and rushed out of his house.

"On second thought," said the Pig, "I must remember that candy is bad for me. It makes me fatter than I already am. It gives me gas and heartburn."

Then the Pig remembered his sweet dreams. He decided that since he was halfway to the candy store, he might as well finish the journey.

"Just a few peppermints will not hurt me," he said.

As the Pig came near the store, his mouth began to water again. "Maybe I will buy a small bag of gumdrops as well."

But the candy store was closed. A sign on the door said "On Vacation."

The Pig went back home.

"What wonderful willpower I have!" he cried happily. "I did not eat a single piece of candy!"

That night the Pig had a vegetable salad for supper. He drank a glass of cold, fresh milk. He felt thin and had neither gas nor heartburn.

A locked door is very likely to discourage temptation.

TARGET WORD DEFINITIONS

- The base word is bold and is the word defined.
- If there is more than one meaning, then the bold definition is the one used in the fable.
- The Spanish translation is provided for the meaning used in the fable.

1. contained (**contain**):
   a) to have inside; hold
   b) to include or be a part of
   c) to hold or keep within limits; restrain
   - contener; tener dentro de si, sugetar

2. **discourage:**
   a) to take away someone's courage or confidence
   b) persuade someone not to do something
   - desalentar; quitar el ánimo, acobardar

3. glowing (**glow**):
   a) give off a steady, low light
   b) to show a bright, warm, or healthy color
   c) to show a warm feeling
   - candente; que emana luz

4. **halfway:**
   a) half the distance from one place to another
   b) not thorough or complete
   - a medio camino

5. **heartburn:**
   an unpleasant burning in the chest caused by acid acting on food in the stomach
   - acidez; exceso de ácido en el estómago

6. **journey:**
   a long trip
   - jornada; viaje

7. **likely:**
   probable
   - probable; hay buenas razones para creer que suceder

8. sprouted (**sprout**):
   a) to begin to grow; give off shoots or buds (as in plants)
   b) to emerge (come out) and develop rapidly
   - germinar; brotar y comenzar a crecer

9. spun (**spin**):
   a) to make thread by twisting fine fibers together
   b) to make a web or cocoon from a liquid that hardens into thread
   c) to rotate or whirl around
   d) to tell or relate
   - hilar; reducir a hilo el lino, lana, seda, algodón, etc.

10. temptation (**tempt**):
    a) to try to convince someone to do something wrong
    b) to appeal strongly to
    - tentación; que induce o persuade a una cosa mala

11. twinkled (**twinkle**):
    to shine with quick flashes of light
    - centellear o titular; que despide rayos de luz de intensidad o coloración variables

12. **willpower:**
    the strength to control one's actions
    - fuerza de voluntad

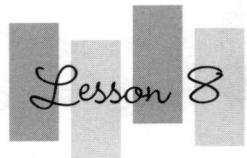

The Hippopotamus at Dinner

The Hippopotamus went into a restaurant. He sat at his favorite table.

"Waiter!" called the Hippopotamus. "I will have the bean soup, the Brussels sprouts, and the mashed potatoes. Please hurry, I am enormously hungry tonight!"

In a short while, the waiter returned with the order. The Hippopotamus glared down at his plate.

"Waiter," he said, "do you call this a meal? These portions are much too small. They would not satisfy a bird. I want a *bathtub* of bean soup, a *bucket* of Brussels sprouts, and a *mountain* of mashed potatoes. I tell you I have an APPETITE!"

The waiter went back into the kitchen. He returned carrying enough bean soup to fill a bathtub, enough Brussels sprouts to fill a bucket, and a mountain of mashed potatoes. In no time, the Hippopotamus had eaten every last morsel.

"Delicious!" said the Hippopotamus, as he dabbed his mouth with a napkin and prepared to leave.

To his surprise, he could not move. His stomach, which had grown considerably larger, was caught between the table and the chair. He pulled and tugged, but it was no use. He could not budge.

The hour grew late. The other customers in the restaurant finished their dinners and left. The cooks took off their aprons and put away their pots. The waiters cleared the dishes and turned out the lights. They all went home.

The Hippopotamus remained there, sitting forlornly at the table.

"Perhaps I should not have eaten quite so many Brussels sprouts," he said, as he gazed into the gloom of the darkened restaurant. Occasionally, he burped.

Too much of anything often leaves one with a feeling of regret.

TARGET WORD DEFINITIONS

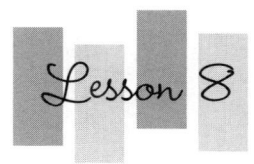

Lesson 8

- The base word is bold and is the word defined.
- If there is more than one meaning, then the bold definition is the one used in the fable.
- The Spanish translation is provided for the meaning used in the fable.

1. **appetite**
   a) **desire for food**
   b) great enjoyment of something
   - apetito; deseo de alimento

2. **budge**
   to start or cause to move
   - moverse

3. dabbed (**dab**)
   to touch a surface gently with something soft
   - tocar suavemente

4. enormously (**enormous**)
   having great size, number, or degree
   - enorme; de gran tamaño o cantidad

5. forlornly (**forlorn**)
   sad or lonely
   - abandonado o desamparado; solo

6. gazed (**gaze**)
   to look at something steadily
   - contemplar; fijar la vista

7. **gloom**
   a) a sense of hopelessness
   b) **a dark and depressing atmosphere**
   - tenebrosidad; ambiente depresivo

8. **morsel**
   a small piece of food
   - bocado de comida

9. portions (**portion**)
   a) a part or piece of something
   b) a share of something that is divided among two or more people
   c) a serving of food
   - porción; pedazo

10. **regret**
    to be sad or sorry about something
    - remordimiento; sentir; tener pena

11. **satisfy**
    a) **to please someone by giving them enough**
    b) to convince or to free from doubt
    - satisfacer; agradar; saciar un apetito

12. tugged (**tug**)
    a) **to pull hard**
    b) a small, powerful boat that tows or pushes ships and barges
    - tirón; halar con fuerza

Vocabulary Improvement Program for English Language Learners and Their Classmates, 4th Grade, by Teresa Lively, Diane August, María Carlo, and Catherine Snow © 2003 Paul H. Brookes Publishing Co., Inc. All rights reserved.

The Mouse
at the Seashore

A Mouse told his mother and father that he was going on a trip to the seashore.

"We are very alarmed!" they cried. "The world is full of terrors. You must not go!"

"I have made my decision," said the Mouse firmly. "I have never seen the ocean, and it is high time that I did. Nothing can make me change my mind."

"Then we cannot stop you," said Mother and Father Mouse, "but be careful!"

The next day, in the first light of dawn, the Mouse began his journey. Even before the morning had ended, the Mouse came to know trouble and fear.

A Cat jumped out from behind a tree.

"I will eat you for lunch," he said.

It was a narrow escape for the Mouse. He ran for his life, but he left a part of his tail in the mouth of the Cat.

By afternoon the Mouse had been attacked by birds and dogs. He had lost his way several times. He was bruised and bloodied. He was tired and frightened.

At evening the Mouse slowly climbed the last hill and saw the seashore spreading out before him. He watched the waves rolling onto the beach, one after another. All the colors of the sunset filled the sky.

"How beautiful!" cried the Mouse. "I wish that Mother and Father were here to see this with me."

The moon and the stars began to appear over the ocean. The Mouse sat silently on the top of the hill. He was overwhelmed by a feeling of deep peace and contentment.

All the miles of a hard road are worth a moment of true happiness.

TARGET WORD DEFINITIONS

- The base word is bold and is the word defined.
- If there is more than one meaning, then the bold definition is the one used in the fable.
- The Spanish translation is provided for the meaning used in the fable.

1. alarmed (**alarm**)
   a) a device with a bell, buzzer, or siren that warns people of danger
   b) to frighten
   c) the sounding mechanism of an alarm clock
   - alarma; sobresalto

2. bloodied (**bloody**)
   a) full of blood or covered with blood
   b) violent or showing blood
   - sangriento; manchado con sangre

3. bruised (**bruise**)
   a) to injure soft tissue or bone without breaking the skin
   b) to hurt, especially feelings
   - cardenal; mancha amoratada, negruzca o amarillenta de la piel

4. contentment (**content**)
   satisfied; happy
   - contento; satisfecho; feliz

5. **dawn**
   a) the beginning of the day; sunrise
   b) the start of something new
   c) to begin to be understood
   - amanecer, alba; primera luz del día antes de salir el sol

6. decision (**decide**)
   a) to make up one's mind about something
   b) to settle something
   - decisión; determinación o resolución que se toma o se da en una cosa dudosa

7. firmly (**firm**)
   a) strong and solid (firm mattress)
   b) definite and not easily changed
   c) strong (a firm voice)
   d) a business or company
   - firme; definitivo e inalterable

8. **narrow**
   a) not broad or wide
   b) limited in size; small (narrow group of friends)
   c) lacking flexibility; rigid
   d) barely enough; almost not enough
   - estrecho; rígido, austero, exacto

9. overwhelmed (**overwhelm**)
   a) to defeat or overcome completely
   b) to have a very strong effect
   - abrumar, inundar; agobiar con algún grande peso

10. rolling (**roll**)
    a) to move forward by turning over and over
    b) to make something into the shape of a ball or tube
    c) something that is in the shape of a tube
    d) to flatten something by pushing a rounded object over it
    e) a small round piece of baked bread
    f) a list of names
    g) to move in a side-to-side or up-and-down way (ship rolls)
    h) to make a deep, loud sound (drum roll)
    i) to start (let's get rolling)
    - rodar, revolcar; mover hacia adelante dando vueltas

11. **several**
    more than two but not many
    - varios; más que dos pero no muchos

12. terrors (**terror**)
    something that causes great fear
    - temor; que causa miedo

Hints for Solving Mystery Words

1. Sound out the word.

2. Look for word parts you recognize.

3. Reread the paragraph.

4. Discuss with the group and decide on a meaning.

5. Substitute the meaning for the underlined word in the sentence.

6. Does it make sense?

7. If not, try again.

Vocabulary Improvement Program for English Language Learners and Their Classmates, 4th Grade, by Teresa Lively, Diane August, María Carlo, and Catherine Snow © 2003 Paul H. Brookes Publishing Co., Inc. All rights reserved.